SEVENTEENTH-CENTURY AMERICA

PUBLISHED FOR THE
Institute of Early American History and Culture
AT WILLIAMSBURG, VIRGINIA

Seventeenth-Century America

America

ESSAYS IN COLONIAL HISTORY

EDITED BY

James Morton Smith

The Norton Library
W·W·NORTON & COMPANY·INC·
NEW YORK

First published in the Norton Library 1972
by arrangement with the University of North Carolina Press

Books That Live

The Norton imprint on a book means that in the publisher's
estimation it is a book not for a single season but for the years.
W. W. Norton & Company, Inc.

Library of Congress Cataloging in Publication Data

Smith, James Morton, ed.
    Seventeenth-century America.

    (The Norton library)
    Based upon original papers presented at a symposium sponsored
by the Institute of Early American History and Culture at Williamsburg, Va., in 1957.
    1. U. S.—Social life and customs—Colonial period—Addresses,
essays, lectures. 2. U. S.—History—Colonial period—Addresses,
essays, lectures. 3. U. S.—Church history—Colonial period—
Addresses, essays, lectures. I. Institute of Early American History and
Culture, Williamsburg, Va. II. Title.
[E162.S66 1972]   917.3'03'2   78-39145
ISBN 0-393-00629-8

SBN 393 00629 8

PREFACE

SEVENTEENTH-CENTURY America began in 1607 at Jamestown, the child of two continents. In 1957 the 350th anniversary of the Jamestown settlement was celebrated with appropriate commemorative events. As a scholarly contribution to that celebration, the Institute of Early American History and Culture planned and sponsored a symposium on seventeenth-century colonial history not only to commemorate the beginnings of America but more particularly to examine some of the more important manifestations of the American colonial experience.

Sixteen scholars were invited to participate in a series of working conferences from April 7 to 12, 1957. Nine of them prepared papers on what they knew best and what interested them most about the seventeenth century. These essays were circulated in advance of the Symposium so that the daily conferences could be devoted to discussions of two or more papers on such topics as people and classes, church and state, the role of the Indian, and seventeenth-century history. The essays in this volume are based upon the original papers, which have been considerably revised in the light of the Symposium discussions.

In addition to the essayists, the participants in the conferences were Wesley Frank Craven, Edmund S. Morgan, John E. Pomfret, Max Savelle, Alan Simpson, Raymond P. Stearns, and Frederick B. Tolles. The Symposium was planned by the staff of the Institute—Lester J. Cappon, Lawrence W. Towner, Wilcomb E. Washburn, Michael G. Hall, and J. M. Smith—in consultation with the Institute's Council and the Symposium participants. It was supported by subventions from the Virginia 350th Anniversary Commission, the federal Jamestown-Williamsburg-Yorktown Celebration Commission, the College of William and Mary, and Colonial Williamsburg, Inc.

I wish to thank the authors of the essays and the other symposium members for their cooperation from planning to publication. To Frederick A. Hetzel, assistant editor of publications at the Institute, I want to express my gratitude for his thoughtful suggestions and his careful editorial assistance in preparing this volume for the press.

JAMES MORTON SMITH

Williamsburg, Va.
December 20, 1958

CONTENTS

CONTENTS

PART FOUR: CHURCH AND STATE

PART FIVE: HISTORY AND HISTORIANS

INTRODUCTION

And thou shalt say unto him, The Lord God of the
Hebrews hath sent me unto thee, saying, Let my people go,
that they may serve me in the wilderness.—Exodus 7:16.

"IN THE BEGINNING," wrote John Locke, "all the world was America."
At the beginning of the seventeenth century, all America was a vast
expanse of the unknown and the unexpected. To this strange and wonder-
ful New World came the vanguard of the most massive migration of
people in the history of the world. By the end of the century, English
colonists had spread in a straggling line up and down the coast from the
precarious beginning in Virginia to successive settlements at Plymouth and
Massachusetts Bay, Narragansett Bay and the Connecticut Valley,
Chesapeake Bay in Maryland, and the wildernesses of the Carolinas and
Pennsylvania.

The purpose of this book is to examine some of the more important
aspects of seventeenth-century colonial activity. The essays do not pretend
to cover the whole field. Although based on a rather logical plan, their
arrangement was not rigidly constructed at the time of the Symposium,
nor is it now. Some of the topics overlap; others are not confined strictly
to the seventeenth century. Some of the authors have gone back to the
sixteenth century or earlier for their purposes and others have moved
forward to the twentieth, one reaching into outer space to make his point.
Nor have the authors felt compelled to formulate among themselves a

coherent and mutually acceptable point of view on the events and meaning of the seventeenth century.

And yet there is a unity to these essays which transcends the divergent tendencies of early America. Two fundamental factors shaped the lives of the settlers, the influences of the environment of the New World and the aspirations, motives, and pressures impelling people to leave the Old. As Lewis Mumford has observed, the settlement of America had its origins in the unsettlement of Europe. The first immigrants brought with them a hierarchical sense of order but it was perhaps inevitable that they should have quickly discovered that their former ways of living had not prepared them for life in the wilderness. Adapting their traditional English institutions to meet new demands, they transformed what they transplanted.

The unexpected perspectives of the New World led to new ways of looking at politics, religion, knowledge, and indeed, as Oscar Handlin points out, at the whole social order. Handlin's essay, unlike the others at the Symposium, was delivered as a public lecture and was designed as a retrospective view of the seventeenth century to gain perspective on the road the Americans have since traveled. He suggests that much of the peculiarity of subsequent American development can be accounted for in terms of the seventeenth-century colonial experience. As the twig is bent, he seems to say, so grows the tree.

Of particular importance in bending the twig were the Indians. Their presence throughout the colonial period created a unique historical situation, but historians have too often failed to assess the significance of their role in shaping seventeenth-century society. In their essays on Indian-white contacts, Wilcomb E. Washburn discusses the white man's theories justifying the uprooting of the Indians and Nancy O. Lurie analyzes the red man's cultural adjustment to the intruders in his midst. Just as Theodore Roosevelt took the Panama Canal Zone and let Congress debate, the colonists took the land and let the philosophers and theologians debate; and while the debate went on, the process of white settlement and Indian accommodation did also. But ever since the age of discovery, if not before, conquerors have felt the necessity of justifying their actions before the conscience of society, and the English settlers were no exception. During the early years at Jamestown, the Reverend Robert Gray asked "by what right or warrant we can enter into the land of these Savages, take away their rightfull inheritance . . . , and plant ourselves in their places, being unwronged or unprovoked by them." It was a question of immense moral and legal complexity, and Washburn seeks only to give an impressionistic sketch of the problems raised by the displacing of the

Indian by white settlement. Whether the Europeans based their justification on papal grant or royal charter, discovery or occupancy, conquest or conversion of the heathen, he points out they were more often concerned with countering the claims of rival powers than in examining the rights of the Indians.

Underlying all their arguments was the fundamental factor of force. As a Supreme Court justice has written recently, the "tribes of this continent were deprived of their ancestral ranges by force." And there is no doubt that the English were unbeatable when prepared and alerted. In the Cherokee cases in the nineteenth century, however, John Marshall based his decision not on conquest but on justification by discovery. Legally, that is where the matter still rests. But as D. H. Lawrence once observed, even though the Indian will never again possess the broadlands of America, "his ghost will." Since 1946 his ghost has, for in that year the federal government passed the Indian Claims Commission Act, which allows Indians to bring suits on behalf of their ancestors who signed treaties, in peace and war, giving away the broadlands of America. Washburn stresses the importance of this legislation, not only because it seems to have opened the door to the righting of an ancient wrong, but because it also has recognized that law, however belatedly, "must sometimes concede to morality if justice is not to become a synonym for injustice."

The expansion of one people into the territory occupied by another has occurred often in history, but only in the past quarter of a century have anthropologists made detailed studies of the impact of white settlement on Indian culture. During the seventeenth century, Nancy Lurie shows, the Virginia Indians preferred resistance rather than accommodation to cultural change.[1] They do not appear to have been unduly impressed by the alleged superiority of white culture; there seemed little to emulate and much to reject. They were primarily concerned with obtaining new material goods, especially armaments and metal work, but there was no serious effort to bridge the cultural gap. Indeed, they seemed to prefer cultural annihilation to assimilation, for on three occasions—in 1622, 1644, and 1676—they engaged in large-scale warfare with the colonists.

After the massacre of 1622, the cultural gap widened as the English regrouped on the peninsula between the James and York rivers. When the settlers edged beyond this area of concentrated population, the Indians again launched an attack rather than adapt to a foreign culture. Defeated again in 1646, they agreed to a line reserving certain areas to them and

1. Mrs. Lurie's essay is based on the second half of her longer Symposium paper and stresses specific ethnohistorical circumstances of seventeenth-century Virginia. The theoretical portions, covering a wider geographic area and a greater time span, will be published in the *American Anthropologist.*

others to the whites. Bacon's Rebellion thirty years later marked the final defeat of the Virginia Indians, whose primary technique of cultural adjustment continued to be refusal to adjust. As a result, Mrs. Lurie concludes, their culture "simply disintegrated under the strain of continued pressure."

Perhaps George Santayana was not far wrong when he wrote that "the incidental destruction of the primitive or of barbaric cultures was not the dominant aim, but rather the need of space for the body and for the spirit as it is for flora and fauna in the jungle." Certainly the need of space for the body and for the spirit spurred an ever increasing number of seventeenth-century Englishmen to emigrate to the seaboard settlements. Historians have long been interested in the social status of the early colonists and Mildred Campbell, like other scholars, traces the origins of American settlers to the social strata which they occupied before sailing for the New World. But she is not equally concerned with all levels of the social structure. Those at the top—the nobility—were seldom settlers. Those from the next level—"men of quality"—played an important role in colonial society; passenger lists ordinarily distinguished these "gentlemen" from "the others." In terms of numbers, however, it was "the others" who peopled the colonies. Who were "the others"? Many, perhaps most, came as indentured servants, but there has been very little information on them. It is this important segment of colonial population which Miss Campbell discusses. Analyzing two sets of seventeenth-century records— a Bristol list for 1654-61 and a London list for 1683-84—she concludes that the overwhelming majority of indentured emigrants were from the middling, not the laboring, class. Most were farmers or skilled workers, not landless laborers. It was not the totally depressed but the partially dispossessed who aspired to a status they fell short of in English society.

No matter what their Old World origins, the first generation of colonists brought with them fixed ideas about an orderly social structure. Although they identified social authority with political power, the lines of class, status, and power were fluid on the wilderness frontier, and the development of provincial society altered the social foundations of political power. In his examination of politics and social structure in seventeenth-century Virginia, Bernard Bailyn probes the social origins of early American politics, tracing the differentiation from the European model and the evolution of a characteristically colonial pattern. Social and political leadership, formerly closely identified, increasingly split apart. After the massacre of 1622 and the collapse of the Virginia Company, the traditional ruling class was replaced by resident planters whose eminence was founded not on inherited status but on landed wealth and colonial accomplishments.

Colonial experience seemed to push in the direction of decentralized power as the planters stressed local home rule. The conflict between imperial and local tendencies came to a head with the ousting of Governor Harvey, whose insistence on the prerogatives of the royal governor threatened the local autonomy of the emerging planter group. While England's attention was diverted by the Puritan Revolution, civil war, and the Cromwellian interlude, Virginia leaders who controlled the county institutions molded the Assembly into a viable instrument of colonial self-government. Morever, the second generation immigrants of the 1640's, building upon the foundations laid by the first settlers, infused new life into the local landed gentry.

But the Restoration introduced a new element of social differentiation among the county leaders. Mercantile measures created a patronage which the royal governor used to build up a privileged group; the Council, appointed by the governor, became increasingly identified with royal officialdom and external authority. As the new role of the Council became clear, the county magistrates turned to burgess representation, eventually separating from the Council. After Bacon's Rebellion, the distinction between central and local authority increased. Governor Berkeley, who had resided in the colony for thirty-five years, was succeeded by a series of governors who were strangers to local society, and the external element in Virginia politics led to further differentiation between social and political leadership. Social leadership became identified with administrative officialdom—governor and Council, focused at Williamsburg but reaching ultimately to London; political leadership was decentralized and remained rooted in the counties. "The highest public authority," Bailyn concludes, "was no longer merely one expression of a general social authority." Social and political leadership were no longer identical.

Just as state and society became differentiated in the New World, so did the church in America differ in structure and operation from the mother church. The Anglican Church was transplanted in Virginia "as neere as may be," but with one big difference: there was no ecclesiastical hierarchy in Virginia. Disagreement in England as to the direction the church should take prevented the implementation of any plan for colonial development, and the episcopal organization was never completed. Instead, the Anglican Church in Virginia evolved a congregationalism not unlike the Puritan Church in New England. When Bishop Compton became concerned late in the seventeenth century, the Virginia Church had already developed its distinctive characteristics, particularly the power of the self-governing parish vestry.

William H. Seiler's discussion of the vestry, the most important administrative unit in ecclesiastical affairs, shows that, in church as in state, power devolved to counties and parishes. Local self-government in church affairs paralleled self-government in political affairs; beyond diocesan control, the vestry became virtually autonomous. The absence of ruling bishops and the scarcity of ministers increased lay authority throughout the seventeenth century; indeed, the laity's freedom of action became the distinguishing mark of the Anglican Church in the colonies. In time the vestries came to choose their ministers, their churchwardens, and their fellow vestrymen. In addition to church affairs, secular responsibilities, such as the administration of poor relief, occupied much of the attention of the vestries.

Like the Virginians, the Puritans of New England devoted much of their energies to local government—providing for the poor, policing morals, and taking disciplinary action to maintain community standards of behavior. Emil Oberholzer's essay is a study of the Puritan experiment in applied theology, the application of religion in everyday life to social problems. As the ministers of Boston pointed out in 1680, it was not doctrine so much as "what concerns Worship and Discipline, that caused our Fathers to come into this wilderness." Oberholzer concentrates on the problem of the Christian who falls below the standards expected and on the application of ecclesiastical discipline to the offender. Because of the Puritans' aversion to ecclesiastical tribunals, each congregation functioned as a court when necessary, following informal procedures that were usually quasi-judicial. Oberholzer studies these church trial records not only to indicate the nature of the Puritan social enterprise but also to illuminate certain aspects of seventeenth-century jurisprudence in New England. He disagrees with Roscoe Pound's view that the Puritans were consistent opponents of equity, pointing out many aspects of equity which they incorporated into their judicial and religious practices. If we cut through the argument about common law and equity, however, we can see that the community builders in the "city upon a hill" were adapting ancient legal institutions of Old England to the needs of the residents of New England.

In the Old World, as in seventeenth-century America, religious and political institutions were being altered, but in England and Europe theory and practice moved toward the same goal, a centralized state deriving all authority from a single source. Philip Haffenden observes that the mercantilist principles of Restoration economic policy were designed to create a self-sufficient imperial system through centralized control of the colonies and suggests that the political role of religion needs to be studied within this imperial framework. In England crown and church pursued a policy of control of religious practice and observance, but the colonies were allowed a considerable latitude of worship. Was toleration consciously used as an instrument of colonial policy, or did Restoration administrators view the overseas development of the Anglican Church with greater favor than historians usually concede? Haffenden argues that imperial politicians after 1660 were not dedicated to religious toleration in the colonies as an integral part of a farsighted imperial policy. Domestic upheaval and the reversal of royal policy under James better explain the failure of the Anglican Church to become a more active instrument in Restoration colonial policy than does the traditional view that religious toleration was preferable to Anglican domination in the colonies.

Perhaps the contrast between imperial and colonial points of view was most sharply etched in the historical writings of the seventeenth century. Richard S. Dunn summarizes the work of the colonial chroniclers, whose increasing pride of place reflected a self-conscious identification with their new land, and of the English historians, whose growing sense of England's dominion over the colonies reflected an emerging awareness that they held a large empire. The English authors viewed the settlements as offshoots of the economic and cultural life of the mother country rather than as separate colonies with lives of their own. Although Dunn carefully contrasts the New England writers with the Virginians, he also delineates the colonial observers' evolving sense of distinction from the mother country; the ties of transplanted traditionalism were loosened by the growing loyalty to localism. As a matter of fact, Beverley's *History and Present State of Virginia* was inspired by the mistakes which he found in Oldmixon's *British Empire in America,* which he read in manuscript five years before publication. The titles alone indicate the difference between the English colonists' sense of loyalty to locality and the imperial consciousness of Englishmen at home. At the end of the seventeenth century, Dunn concludes, "the transatlantic difference in outlook was steadily widening, while the regional colonial difference was not."

In one way or another, then, nearly all of these essays, implicitly or explicitly, point up the transformation of the English colonist into the colonial Englishman with strong local loyalties. The diverse tendencies of primitive America had profoundly altered colonial society during the seventeenth century. By 1700 it was becoming increasingly clear that the emerging civilization of the English colonies was something more than a transatlantic projection of England.

PART ONE

Historical Perspective

Plantations are amongst ancient, primitive, and heroical works.

FRANCIS BACON

I.

THE SIGNIFICANCE OF THE
SEVENTEENTH CENTURY

Oscar Handlin
HARVARD UNIVERSITY

THE HISTORIAN IS TRAINED to see the past in its own terms. He studies the seventeenth century as the product of that which had gone before it, and he attempts to reconstruct the culture and society of the American colonies as those might have seemed to the men who lived in them.

This is the necessary perspective for an understanding of the period. An impressive body of recent studies has shown that the settlements along the coast of North America were elements of imperial systems that had their counterparts in many other regions of the world. We have learned that the institutional life of the colonies can only be understood against a background that reaches back to the medieval past. The labor system, the forms of government, even the modes of thought of the seventeenth century extended patterns that had long before been developing in Europe. To see in them the forerunners or prototypes of what would emerge in the eighteenth or nineteenth century is grievously to misinterpret them.

But our purpose in celebrating the 350th anniversary of the settlement of the Jamestown colony must be somewhat different. The seventeenth century should have general meaning, for we—and the historians along with the rest of us—live, after all, in the twentieth century; and we expect somehow that the experiences of the men who began to come off the ships at Jamestown have also a meaning for us in the twentieth century. A commemorative occasion is a time for retrospection—for looking backward from the present to take account of the way we have come. It has its picturesque and interesting aspects, of course. But its true value arises from the opportunity it offers us to acquire perspective on the present and the future. From that point of view, it is our obligation to look back to the seventeenth century for what it can reveal of the antecedents of our own culture.

In that respect the seventeenth century was immensely significant. In the decades after the settlement at Jamestown, three generations of Americans—the first Americans—began to shape the social order, the way of life, and an interpretation of their own experience that would influence much of subsequent American history. Pick up the story where you will—in the eighteenth or nineteenth century or in our own times—and invariably in these matters the threads lead back to the seventeenth century. It will be worth while to discuss each of these developments briefly.

The colonists who settled at Jamestown and elsewhere along the coast after 1607 brought with them fixed conceptions of what a social order should be like. Their whole effort thereafter was devoted to re-creating the forms they had known at home. Yet in practice their experience persistently led them away from the patterns they judged desirable. The American social order that finally emerged was abnormal. That is, it not only diverged from the experience of the European society from which the newcomers emigrated, but it was also contrary to their own expectations of what a social order should be.

The settlers were loyal to the governments from which they emigrated, and they were conservative in their attitudes toward existing institutions. Repeatedly they explained that their emigration was not intended to disrupt but rather to preserve and improve the society they left. Nevertheless they were constantly moving off on tangents through the force of circumstance and the pressure of the environment. A number of examples will clarify this point.

The forms of colonial government developed slowly and erratically. The first settlers transplanted two forms commonplace in the practice of Europeans in this period. The chartered commercial companies, as in Virginia and Plymouth, carried across to their plantations institutions that went back to the medieval boroughs. The proprietary colonies rested on old feudal precedents. Both efforts at imitation quickly proved unstable, however, and the colonies of either sort passed through a period of rapid change.

The problem of changing political forms was, of course, also troubling Europe in the seventeenth century. But in the Old World this era witnessed the emergence of the centralized bureaucratic state. Theory and practice moved in the same direction, toward the derivation of all authority from a single source, such as the Crown, however defined.

The colonies accepted the theory. Their most prominent men were surprisingly legalistic and had no inclination to dispute the authority under which their government functioned. But practice took another direction. Power tended to devolve to its local sources. Whether that involved the town, as in New England, or the local powers sitting in the vestry, as in Virginia, the characteristic political organization was decentralized. Whatever acknowledgment might be given to the authority of the Crown, political institutions were decisively shaped by the necessity of defining connections to local power. Significantly, the most stable colonies of this period were Connecticut and Rhode Island, where the organization of local government in the towns preceded and remained basic to the organization of central political institutions.

The dispersal of power to local sources was, however, characteristic of other, nonpolitical institutions also. The churches developed a *de facto* congregational form, despite the fact that their communicants theoretically held to a belief in centralized authority. Apart from the Plymouth Separatists, there was no disposition to challenge the traditional hierarchical and centralized structure of the church. Yet, the New England Puritans, once here, found themselves closer to the Separatists than to the Church of England of which they had expected to remain adherents. Most strikingly, the members of the Church of England throughout the colonies continued to acknowledge that a bishop was essential to the full practice of their religious duties. Yet in practice, delays, obstructions, and evasions prevented the emergence of an episcopate before the Revolution. Religious functions too seemed to devolve to their local sources.

These developments were related to the structure of the population, which was also anomalous in the sense that it ran contrary to the expectations of those who planted the colonies. The founders expected that their societies would consist of functionaries and peasants. The companies anticipated plantations populated by servants, that is, by soldiers and clerks, who would carry forth the business of trade and defense. The proprietors looked forward to a population of native or imported peasants who would reconstruct some sort of manorial system in the New World. This was evident, even toward the end of the seventeenth century, in the plans of the Carolina proprietors.

Instead, surprisingly, all the colonies developed a society of yeomen and artisans—not by plan, and often, it seemed, simply through the want of an alternative. Yet the consequences were radical. There developed in the mainland colonies of the seventeenth century a wide variety of social types, a microcosm of the Old World as it were, ranging from slaves and servants at the bottom through yeoman farmers and artisans, to a gentry at the top. Within this variety of types there were both the recognition of actual stratification and a high degree of mobility. The fact that a servant was different from a yeoman and yet that a servant could become a yeoman led to the definition of a new concept of freedom and to the development of distinctive social institutions.

In the structure of the population, therefore, as in the evolution of governmental and other institutions, the seventeenth-century colonies followed an abnormal path, one which was different from the experience of Europeans at home or in other parts of the world and one which was contrary to their own expectations. The causes of this abnormality were complex. In part it was due to the extensive quality of the land to which these settlers came. They had pitched upon the edge of an almost empty continent; and the existence of open space to which men could withdraw remained a constant condition of their life. That in itself was an element tending toward looseness of social structure.

Furthermore, they encountered no going society with fixed institutions of its own. The Indians who inhabited the region had a culture, of course. But they were so few in number and so little prepared to resist as to have relatively little effect upon the whites. The Europeans of the same period in India or even in Africa were significantly influenced by the institutions they encountered there; those in America, hardly at all. Indeed the American colonists were often disappointed in their natives. The continued inclination to refer to the Indian kings, queens, and nobility reflected an eagerness to discover in the red men a fixity of forms that did not exist. Its absence was a further source of instability.

But most important, the institutional looseness of the seventeenth century was related to the way of life that developed in the colonies. The American seventeenth-century social order was disorderly by the expectations of normal men. But the settlers were not normal men. The terms of American existence compelled frequent and serious deviations from the norms of behavior accepted by the men who peopled the colonies. Every aspect of their existence combined to produce disorder.

The century was occupied by a succession of waves of immigration, so that the experience of transplantation was not limited to one group or to one moment, but was repeated again and again. And that experience caused enormous shocks in the personal and social relationships of those involved in it. The circumstances of the crossing at once threw these men and women into disorder. It takes an effort of the imagination to conceive of the conditions of life on the three ships which came to Jamestown in 1607. These vessels of 100, 40, and 20 tons, respectively, were laden with the gear and the supplies and provisions for the voyage and also with all that the plantations would at first require. Yet, there was also room on these tiny craft for 140 people. The settlers were almost five months in transit, at the mercy of the winds and weather and of the unknown sea. Later voyages involved larger ships—but not much larger; and the time spent in crossing shrank, although not dependably. But accommodations were never commodious and the experience was never pleasant. Few immigrants recovered quickly from the difficulties of crowded and uncomfortable weeks at sea in tiny ships that carried them to their strange destinations.

Many of those who made the crossing were people whose life was already in disorder. Often, they had already been displaced and compelled to move once; their stamina had already been tried. The residents of London who came to the colonies had, as likely as not, been born in the country and had drifted to the city. Others among the newcomers, like the Pilgrims, like the Finns who settled on the Delaware, like the German sectarians, were already uprooted and had already deviated from the settled life of stable societies.

Hard conditions of life compounded the disorder for a greater or lesser time in each of the colonies. Everywhere the settlers who survived could look back upon a starving time, a period when the margin between life and death narrowed perilously and when the very existence of the feeble societies hung by a thread. So, in retrospect, the Virginia burgesses looked back to the administration of Sir Thomas Smith and recalled:

The allowance in those tymes for a man was only eight ounces of meale and half a pinte of pease for a daye the one & the other mouldy, rotten, full of Cobwebs and Maggots loathsome to man and not fytt for beasts; which forced many to flee for reliefe to the Savage Enemy, who being taken againe were putt to sundry deaths as by hanginge, shootinge and breakinge upon the wheele; & others were forced by famine to filch for their bellies, of whom one for steelinge 2 or 3 pints of oatmeale had a bodkinge thrust through his tongue and was tyed with a chaine to a tree untill he starved. Yf a man through his sickness had not been able tow worke, he had no allowance at all, and so consequently perished. Many through these extremities, being weery of life digged holes in the earth and hidd themselues till they famished. . . . So lamentable was our scarsitie that we were constrained to eat Doggs, Catts, ratts, Snakes, Toad-Stooles, horsehides and wt nott; one man out of the mysery he endured, killinge his wiefe powdered her upp to eate here, for wch he was burned. Many besides fedd on the Corps of dead men, and one who had gotten unsatiable, out of custome to that foode could not be restrayned, until such tyme as he was executed for it, and indeed soe miserable was our estate that the happyest day that eyer some of them hoped to see, was when the Indyands had killed a mare they wishing whilst she was boyling that St *Tho*: *Smith* [the Governor] was uppon her backe in the kettle.

Later prosperity never dimmed the memory of the early difficulties; and there remained always areas where the trying experience of survival was being repeated. As settlement spread, there was always at its edge a brutal and disorderly struggle for existence.

Some of the harsh features of pioneer life disappeared with the development of settled communities. But others endured for a long time. A high death rate remained constant and throughout the century embittered the personal relationships of the colonists. In the first winter at Plymouth, one-half the Pilgrims died. Between 1606 and 1623 about five thousand immigrants came to Virginia. They had children and raised families. Yet at the end of that period there were only one thousand left.

Nor was this cruel mortality simply a condition of initial settlement. It remained characteristic of seventeenth-century life. Infant mortality was murderous; and although many children were born, the number of survivors was distressingly low. It was rare in this century that a husband and wife should live into old age together. The frequency of remarriages by widowers and widows showed how familiar a factor in life was death.

More generally, constant nagging difficulties intruded in the management of the details of home or farm or shop. Old habits did not apply to new circumstances; and it was hard for individuals to fulfill the personal, family, religious, or communal roles they were expected to play. This, perhaps, explains the harsh judgments that the colonists were always making of one another. The lack of stability or orderliness even in the home was particularly troublesome. In the tight quarters of the seventeenth-century houses, large families had to learn to live with one another, and also with the Negroes and other strange servants. Emotional strains were inevitable and weak community discipline sometimes led to violence, desertion, or criminality. The lack of permanence, the constant mobility that shifted individuals and families about through the continent exacerbated all these tensions. By contrast, the old homes of the Old World in retrospect came to embody orderliness. Often, in thinking of what they had left in Europe, the colonists expressed a poignant sense of separation from the source of stability and culture.

Finally, their life was rendered harsh by the apparent hostility of the elements. The wilderness itself created problems for men accustomed to open spaces. In the folk literature of Europe the forests were peopled by wild, inhuman creatures often hostile to man. In America even the climate and the changes of the seasons were unfamiliar. Most important, the denizens of the wilderness were a constant threat to the flimsy structure of civilization. The Indians grew more and more fearsome as the century advanced; and on the borders French and Spanish Papists were a continuing threat. In the face of all these dangers, there was no security in the settlements. The precariousness of existence was at the root of the disorder that overwhelmed them. Everywhere from the moment they boarded ship the first Americans found risks of the greatest order inseparable from the conduct of their lives.

The native-born, that is, the second and third, generations were more at home in the wilderness and, never having known Europe, were less pressed by the necessity of making comparisons with that which had been left across the ocean. They had sources of instability of their own, in their heightened rootlessness and mobility. But they were likely to accept the disorder and precariousness that troubled their immigrant parents or grandparents as a way of life and to adjust to its conditions.

The men subject to so many elements of abnormality and disorder necessarily interpreted their own experiences in a distinctive way. They were constantly driven to ask questions that other men had no need to raise. People whose families had lived generations without end in the same village had no cause to wonder why they were where they were or to speculate on the significance of having been placed where they were. But the immigrants whose conditions of life and whose institutions had been driven so far from every ordinary course necessarily had to seek answers to such questions.

The necessity was particularly urgent in the seventeenth century when men ascribed to every event a deep meaning. Nothing that occurred was taken as simply random. Everything was the product of the intent of some mover. A tree did not fall; it was felled. If a monstrous child was born or a school of porpoises seen, that was a sign of something. In the same way, there was necessarily a significance to the painful shift of population that created colonial society. In an era in which men believed literally in signs, portents, curses, spells, and imprecations, to say nothing of witches, they had to seek a meaning to their own unusual experiences.

The first Americans continued the habit of explaining every occurrence in terms of a familiar dichotomy. On the one hand, they could see in some events good impulses, derived from God and reflecting a divine intent. But they also found abundant evidence of evil impulses or dark desires emanating from satanic intentions. The fearful men who lived with risk and disorder were constantly on the lookout for the means of identifying and interpreting what happened to them. As a simple matter of a guide to personal life, it was essential to know whether an incident was the product of divine or devilish interference.

The same confrontation of good and evil could be seen in the social world that surrounded the individual. There in the external wilderness, in the savagery of life without reliable guides, were the sources of corruption. Were not the Indians imps of Satan, and the Papists, creatures of the Devil, and was not therefore the whole American experience one which endangered man's salvation? On the other hand, was it not possible to identify that which lay across the ocean with that which was good and conducive to man's salvation? Europe, from the American perspective, was the source of morality, of law, of order, and of Christianity. But in that event, how was the colonist to explain his migration, away from order to disorder, away from law to savagery, away from Christianity to the spiritual perils of the New World?

The questions thus raised could be answered on both the personal and the social level; and the answer on the one offers an analogy to the answer on the other. The character of this response may be discerned in the poem that a grieving grandmother wrote in the 1660's to explain to herself the death of three grandchildren within four years. All were under the age of four. Surely these tender innocents had been stricken down through no fault, no evil deed, of their own. There was, however, a reason. Anne Bradstreet explained:

> By nature Trees do rot when they are grown.
> And Plumbs and Apples thoroughly ripe do fall,
> And corn and grass are in their season mown,
> And time brings down what is both strong and tall.
> But plants new set to be eradicate,
> And buds new blown, to have so short a date,
> Is by his hand alone that guides nature and fate.

An unnatural misfortune of this sort was thus in itself evidence of a particular divine concern. While the nature of God's intentions might be inscrutable to men and closed to fallible human understanding, the event itself nevertheless was a sure indication of some particular purpose. It could even supply a kind of assurance of divine interest and oversight.

It was also true that a way of life out of the usual course was evidence of some particular design. The whole character of the plantation of these settlements, by its very abnormality, indicated that there had been some special purpose to the coming to America. The fact that this whole area had been withheld from previous human habitation indicated that there was some special intention for its use. The fact that their institutions and their course of life did not follow any usual pattern was itself a sign that these settlements had an unusual destiny.

As the immigrants examined their own coming, they could see evidence of a larger will in their own careers. Their migration was largely the product of their own helplessness, of social forces over which they had no control—persecution by the Established Church, changes in agriculture and the unavailability of land, the disruption of the wool trade and the growth in the number of men without employment. But on the other hand, the migration was also the product of their own choice. Not all those who were persecuted or displaced or unemployed had come. Migration stemmed from a compulsion that forced the emigrant to leave and also the positive act of will by which he decided to go. The emigrant might thus be compared to a legate dispatched on a mission by a potentate, a legate who accepted the errand voluntarily. The fact, too, that not all those who went arrived reflected a process of survival and seemed to imply a kind of selection of some from among the rest.

In no other way could these people account for the experience but by the conclusion that somehow they had been chosen to depart from the ways of ordinary men and to become in their own lives extraordinary for some special purpose.

Among some of the colonists this intention was spelled out with considerable sophistication. New England Puritans thought of themselves as led by Divine Providence to a new Canaan where they were to create a new kind of society that would be a model for the whole world. Their city upon a hill would ultimately be emulated by all other men. It was a part of the scheme of divine redemption, occupying the stage at a critical turn in the cosmic drama that had begun with the Creation, that had been continued in the Reformation, and that would end in the Second Coming.

Elsewhere the explanation was less sophisticated, less explicit, and less literate. But there nonetheless emerged again and again expressions of conviction in a sense of mission—to convert the Indians or to civilize the wilderness. The newness of a New World reserved for some ultimate purpose and waiting for those who would bring it under cultivation or use it as the setting for their own experiments in salvation confirmed the successive groups of immigrants, in the seventeenth century and later, in the belief that there was a profound importance to their coming.

The second and third generations were different in this respect also. They were natives, not subject to the strains of the decisions that had burdened their parents or grandparents. Indeed, in the eyes of the immigrants, the second generation seemed a ruder, less cultivated, and wilder people. That accounts for the complaints about declension and about the loss of the sense of mission that began to be sounded in the last quarter of the century.

But the second generation had actually not lost the sense of mission so much as transformed it beyond the recognition of their predecessors. The very fact that they were a wilderness people, at home in the New World, gave them a sense of power. They could deal with the forest and the savage as their parents could not. Out of contact with the standards of the Old World, they developed their own, and their ability to do so generated confidence in their own capacity for achievement.

Therefore they too, although in a different form, were moved by a conviction of the grandeur of their destiny; and they could link that conviction to the potentialities of the land, which was not alien to them as it had been to their parents. Pride in their own power and in the future greatness of their homes created for them a picture of themselves as a people destined to conquer, an idea to be eloquently expressed just after the turn of the century by Robert Beverley.

In a variety of forms, the sense of mission has remained a continuing theme in American life. In the eighteenth century Jefferson's generation gave it secularized liberal expression. The nineteenth century imbued it with the spirit of liberal reform. And at the opening of the twentieth century, it was woven into the ideology of imperialism. So, too, social disorder, the acceptance of risk, and the precariousness of life that developed in the seventeenth century long remained characteristic of America. It was the significance of the seventeenth century to bring into being peculiarities of character and institutions, the influence of which was long thereafter felt in the history of the United States.

PART TWO

Colonists and Indians

Savages we call them, because their Manners differ from ours, which we think the Perfection of Civility: they think the same of theirs.

BENJAMIN FRANKLIN

II.

THE MORAL AND LEGAL JUSTIFICATIONS FOR DISPOSSESSING THE INDIANS

Wilcomb E. Washburn

SMITHSONIAN INSTITUTION

MANY STUDIES TELL US what the first explorers were trying to do. Many others tell us why they were trying to do it. But very few have attempted to describe the justice or injustice of the quest. Yet significant moral and legal problems were brought to the fore by the expansion of Europe into the various parts of the world. Kings, judges, soldiers, businessmen, priests, all considered the expansion in terms of right and wrong as well as in terms of personal and national advantage. Some were more explicit than others, but all had a point of view about the moral and legal right of the European to displace the American Indian in the newly·discovered lands.

The justifications which governments most frequently brought forward in the period of exploration and settlement—papal or royal grant, discovery, and possession—reflect the fact that the principal ethicolegal concern in the period was about the claims of rival European powers, not about the rights of the American Indian.[1] The bull of Alexander VI in 1493 which divided the world between Spain and Portugal, for example, was principally designed to prevent an unseemly and dangerous scramble among Christian nations for the spoils of the newly discovered areas. Those excluded from

---

1. The only principle on which the European nations were in agreement, writes Wheaton, was in "almost entirely disregarding the right of the native inhabitants of these regions." Henry Wheaton, *Elements of International Law* [1st edn., 1836], The Literal Reproduction of the Edition of 1866 by Richard Henry Dana, Jr., ed. by George Grafton Wilson [The Classics of International Law, No. 19] (Oxford, 1936), Pt. II, nos. 166, 202.

its benefits understandably disputed the papal pretensions. When the Spanish ambassador in England complained of Drake's piratical voyage around the world in 1577-80, he was told that "the queen does not acknowledge that her subjects and those of other nations may be excluded from the Indies on the claim that these have been donated to the king of Spain by the pope, whose authority to invest the Spanish king with the New World as with a fief she does not recognise." "The Spaniards," in Elizabeth's view, had "no claim to property there except that they have established a few settlements and named rivers and capes. . . . Prescription without possession is not valid."[2]

The English sovereigns, denying Rome's prerogatives, issued grants and charters of their own to the new-found lands. Because these concessions proved meaningful in terms of what happened later, modern writers have assumed that they expressed a carefully considered conception of the royal prerogative. It is more accurate to say, however, that because the colonizers were able to assert their paper rights against the Indians and against other Europeans, a literature to justify and explain the kingly attitude arose. Had the charters not proved effectual, there is little doubt that we would now have a literature, as we do in the case of the papal grants, showing that the English sovereigns were not really granting away other peoples' lands but only giving privileges of government conditional upon conversion of the Indians.

A guide to the intent and meaning of the royal grants of land in America is to be found in the previous practices of English sovereigns. In 1109 Henry I granted Gilbert de Clare "all the land of Cardigan, *if he could win it from the Welsh.*" One historian has applied the appropriate name "speculative" to this type of grant. It was a form of concession used frequently in later years against the Irish.[3] Similarly, in the letters patent of Henry VII authorizing John Cabot and his sons to seek out and discover "whatsoever isles, countreys, regions or provinces of the heathen and infidels . . . which before this time have bene unknowen to all Christians," the king granted the Cabots the right to "subdue, occupy and possesse all such townes, cities, castles and isles of them found, which they *can* subdue, occupy and possesse. . . ."[4] When Elizabeth I granted Raleigh

2. Edward P. Cheyney, "International Law under Queen Elizabeth," *Eng. Hist. Rev.*, 20 (1905), 660, quoting from Camden, *Annales* (1605 edn.), 309, about the reply to Spain, ca. 1580, either in the form of a paper drawn by the Privy Council and afterwards lost or suppressed, or in the form of the substance of a verbal statement made to the Spanish ambassador or some later commissioners.

3. Edmund Curtis, *A History of Medieval Ireland from 1086 to 1513* (London, [1938]), 38-39; the statement from Henry I is a direct quotation. My italics.

4. Letters patent to John Cabot, March 5, 1496, in Henry Steele Commager, ed., *Documents of American History* (New York, 1944), 5. My italics.

liberty to "discover, search, finde out, and view such remote, heathen and barbarous lands, countries and territories, not actually possessed of any Christian Prince, nor inhabited by Christian People," and the right to "have, holde, occupie, and enjoy" the same, it was with the assumption that Raleigh would succeed in conquering the regions; otherwise the grant was to be of no force.[5]

Most English arguments for title also made use of the Cabots' "discovery" in the Newfoundland area in 1497-98 to strengthen England's right to North America. This was the country's only argument of great priority, for she had slumbered during the hundred years following the Cabot voyages. As in the case of the king's charter, it is doubtful that the argument was accorded much weight even by the English themselves, except as a formal answer to the claims of prior discovery by other nations. Many Oriental regions, unknown in the same sense that many American regions were unknown in the period following Columbus' initial discovery, were "discovered" by Europeans in like fashion but rarely claimed as a result.

"Although many have stated that at the time of the European explorations of the fifteenth through seventeenth centuries discovery was a sufficient basis for a claim to sovereignty," writes William W. Bishop, "it is not clear whether the term 'discovery' meant more than the mere finding of the lands previously unknown to European civilization."[6] Three distinguished students of the question have also concluded that "throughout this lengthy period, no state appeared to regard mere discovery, in the sense of 'physical' discovery or simple 'visual apprehension,' as being in any way sufficient *per se* to establish a right of sovereignty over, or a valid title to, *terra nullius*. Furthermore, mere disembarkation upon any portion of such regions—or even extended penetration and exploration therein— was not regarded as sufficient itself to establish such a right or title."[7] The absurdity of gaining possession of a continent by sailing along its coast line was so obvious that some writers facetiously suggested that Europe would have to be conceded to any Indian prince who happened to send a ship to "discover" it.[8] By itself the assertion had little more effect in restraining

5. Charter to Sir Walter Raleigh, March 25, 1584, *ibid.*, 6.

6. William W. Bishop, Jr., *International Law: Cases and Materials* (New York, 1953), 272.

7. Arthur S. Keller, Oliver J. Lissitzyn, and Frederick J. Mann, *Creation of Rights of Sovereignty through Symbolic Acts, 1400-1800* (New York, 1938), 148.

8. "And to bring in the title of *First-discovery*, to me it seems as little reason, that the sailing of a Spanish Ship upon the coast of *India*, should intitle the King of Spain to that Countrey, as the sayling of an Indian or English Ship upon the coast of *Spain*, should intitle either the *Indians* or *English* unto the Dominion thereof. No question but the just right or title to those Countries appertains to the Natives

other countries from colonizing North America than had the Pope's bulls, which, as Sir Walter Raleigh pointed out, could not gore so well as they could bellow.[9]

It was natural, therefore, to reinforce citations of early discoveries with accounts of actual occupation of the land. Here again the question arose as to how much of the continent passed into the possession of those occupying a portion of it. Did a settlement on the tip of Cape Cod or the Florida peninsula give title to the entire North American continent?

The monarchs were most liberal. Since it cost them nothing to give all, they gave all, with grants usually extending to the South Sea. But with several kings making grants in North America, international conflicts were inevitable. Final settlement depended on the course of events and the power of the claimants. "Why shall they," asked the French, "being at 36 or 37 [degrees], advance to 45, rather than we being, as they admit, at 46, descend as far as 37? What right have they more than we? This is our answer to the English."[10] An early eighteenth-century English chronicler, on the other hand, expressed the English view of the extent of French sovereignty in America (which covered vast expanses on French maps) by asking: "Where then shall we find the Countries of *New-France* and *Louisiana,* unless it be within the reach of the great Guns of their Forts on the Rivers of *St. Lawrence* and *Mississippi.* . . ?"[11]

Unfortunately, international law was not able to resolve the dilemma. This inability is not to be wondered at, since international law has no central coercive power to establish its authority; enforcement must rest on the use of power by the individual sovereign states. Certain conventions, it is true, grew up in this period, but they developed principally because it was more expedient for the individual nations to compromise their exaggerated claims than to fight over them. One of the conventions which appeared at this time was an agreement not to consider acts of violence

themselves; who, if they shall willingly and freely invite the *English* to their protection, what title soever they have in them, no doubt but they may legally transferr it or communicate it to others." Thomas Gage, *The English-American his Travail by Sea and Land: Or a New Survey of the West-Indies, containing a Journall of Three thousand and Three hundred Miles within the main Land of America* (London, 1648), Epistle Dedicatory. J. Eric S. Thompson has edited a new edition of Gage's *Travels* (Norman, Okla., 1958).

9. "A Discourse of the Original and Fundamental Cause of Natural, Arbitrary, Necessary, and Unnatural War," in *The Works of Sir Walter Ralegh, Kt.* (Oxford, 1829), VIII, 277.

10. [Samuel de Champlain?], "Abstract of the Discoveries in New France," 1631, in E. B. O'Callaghan, ed., *Documents Relative to the Colonial History of the State of New York* (Albany, N. Y., 1855), IX, 2.

11. Thomas Salmon, *Modern History; or, the Present State of All Nations,* Vol. XXXI, Being the Fourth Volume of *America* (London, 1738), 557.

occurring beyond the papal line of demarcation in the Atlantic as breaking the peace in Europe. Neither Spain nor Portugal was willing at first to concede rights to others within the monopolies fixed by the line, but other European powers were unwilling to recognize that they might be barred. Hence, the area came to be excluded, at first by oral agreement and later by treaty arrangement, from the effect of European peace settlements. The phenomenon of "no peace beyond the line," as it was known, was not allowed to break the peace that might exist on the European side of the line. The special legal and moral character of acts committed in the area thus set aside suggests that the European monarchs realized that their territorial claims in the newly discovered areas had little basis in law or morality and could be increased, diminished, or surrendered, as expedient, without seriously threatening the vital interests of the mother country.[12]

Today we visualize English invasion of the North American continent as the establishment of a military beachhead. The assumption is general that the Indian was a hostile occupant of the territory which the English proposed to settle. Although this was true as soon as English intentions to conquer as well as to settle became evident, it is not an accurate description of the initial Indian attitude. Nothing is so frequently recorded in the earliest chronicles as the warmth of the reception accorded the first colonists.

The Indians believed in hospitality. The extent of their hospitality impressed the English; unfortunately, however, they were not impressed with the virtue of the Indians, but only with the power of their own God, who temporarily imbued the Indians with kindness. We read frequently such statements as "God caused the Indians to help us with fish at very cheap rates. . . ."[13] Perhaps such an attitude was natural to a people whose merit was based on salvation through a vicarious atonement. Since earthly success, as well as heavenly salvation, depended on God's will, not on man's effort, God was to be praised, not his terrestrial agents.

Another basis for English suspicion of Indian motives was the inherent fear of the unknown. Indians were strange creatures to the seventeenth-century Englishman, particularly since the sole basis of previous identification was in terms of heathen or infidel opponents of the True Faith. The Indians were expected to react hostilely. Their overt friendliness was often seen as proof of covert antagonism. Captain Christopher Newport, commanding the *Susan Constant*, *Godspeed*, and *Discovery*, reported after

12. See, for example, Arthur Percival Newton, *The Colonising Activities of the English Puritans* (New Haven, Conn., 1914), 96.
13. Roger Clap's "Memoirs" [London, 1731], in Alexander Young, ed., *Chronicles of the First Planters of the Colony of Massachusetts, from 1623 to 1636* (Boston, 1846), 350.

his trip up the James River in 1607 that the Indians "are naturally given to treachery, howbeit we could not finde it in o'r travell up the river, but rather a most kind and loving people."[14] William Symonds, editor of John Smith's *A Map of Virginia* (1612), expressed, with unconscious irony, the often-repeated complaint that the natives were "so malitious, that they seldome forget an injury. . . ."[15]

Nor was the tendency to see evil motives behind good deeds limited to the early colonists. Later writers have assumed that the Indians were secretly hostile to the colonists even when they granted them the most lavish hospitality or supplied food in their periods of want. Alexander Brown in 1898, for example, convinced himself that the Virginia Indians "were really the enemies of the English from the first. . . ." He explained the assistance given the settlers by the Indians in the fall of 1607 as follows:

All accounts agree that for some reason the Indians did daily relieve them for some weeks with corn and flesh. The supplies brought from England had been nearly exhausted; the colonists had been too sick to attend to their gardens properly, and this act of the Indians was regarded as a divine providence at that time. . . . What was the real motive for the kindly acts of the Indians may not be certainly known; but it probably boded the little colony a future harm.[16]

Relations, it is true, did not continue friendly for long; treachery was being plotted behind the outward benignity. But was it Indian treachery or white treachery? A detailed examination of the historical record would, I venture to suggest, show that the treachery was more frequently on the side of the white.[17]

The Virginia massacre of 1622, however, erased all previous accounts and provided the English with the "bloody shirt" needed to justify hostilities against the natives whenever convenient. Up until that time it was necessary to see malice in good will or to cite occasional Indian violence against small groups of settlers. Now the English could point to a full-scale war directed against all the settlements and carried out with terrible effects. Hundreds of English were slaughtered and the colony nearly wiped out. It would have been appropriate, of course, to determine whether the Indians were justified in attacking because of previous injuries

14. "Description of the Now-Discovered River and Country of Virginia," June 21, 1607, in *Va. Mag. of Hist. and Biog.*, 14 (1907), 377.

15. In Edward Arber and A. G. Bradley, eds., *Travels and Works of Captain John Smith* (Edinburgh, 1910), I, 65.

16. Alexander Brown, *The First Republic in America* (Boston, 1898), 41-42.

17. See the suggestions for such a study in Wilcomb E. Washburn, "A Moral History of Indian-White Relations: Needs and Opportunities for Study," *Ethnohistory*, 4 (1957), 47-61.

and because of the English refusal to respect their unqualified sovereignty in the area. The importance of such considerations was admitted by some,[18] but ignored or denied by most. Edward Waterhouse rejoiced that the massacre had occurred:

Our hands which before were tied with gentlenesse and faire usage, are now set at liberty by the treacherous violence of the Sausages [Savages]. . . . So that we, who hitherto have had possession of no more ground then their waste, and our purchase at a valuable consideration to their owne contentment, gained; may now by right of Warre, and law of Nations, invade the Country, and destroy them who sought to destroy us. . . . Now their cleared grounds in all their villages (which are situate in the fruitfullest places of the land) shall be inhabited by us, whereas heretofore the grubbing of woods was the greatest labour.[19]

The Virginia Company seized on the massacre to order a war against the Indians, dispossession of those near the settlements, and, as a gesture of mercy, the enslavement rather than slaughter of the younger people of both sexes.[20] The company's instructions were hardly necessary. The governor and council had already initiated a policy of exterminating the neighboring Indians. "Wee have anticipated your desire by setting uppon the Indyans in all places," they wrote proudly.[21] To aid in the project the natives were lulled into a sense of false security by the conclusion of a treaty, and the council in Virginia even went so far as to boast of this bit of treachery.[22] On one occasion poison was placed in the wine offered to the Indians on the conclusion of a peace treaty.[23] When chided by the company for their "false dealing," the council in Virginia replied that "wee hold nothinge injuste, that may tend to theire ruine, (except breach of faith). Stratagems were ever allowed against all enemies, but with these neither fayre Warr nor good quarter is ever to be held, nor is

18. George Thorpe to Sir Edwin Sandys, May 15, 1621, in Susan M. Kingsbury, ed., *The Records of the Virginia Company of London* (4 vols.; Washington, D. C., 1906-35), III, 446.

19. "A Declaration of the State of the Colony and . . . a Relation of the Barbarous Massacre . . ." (London, 1622), reprinted, *ibid.*, 556-57.

20. Treasurer and Council for Virginia to Governor and Council in Virginia, August 1, 1622, *ibid.*, 672; see also John Martin, "The Manner howe to bringe in the Indians into subjection without makinge an utter exterpation of them together with the reasons," December 15, 1622, *ibid.*, 704-7.

21. Council in Virginia to Virginia Company of London, January 20, 1622/23, *ibid.*, IV, 9.

22. See, for example, Council in Virginia to Virginia Company of London, April 3 and 4, 1623, *ibid.*, 99, 102.

23. Robert Bennett to Edward Bennett, June 9, 1623, *ibid.*, 221-22; also printed in *Amer. Hist. Rev.*, 27 (1922), 505-8.

there any other hope of theire subversione, who ever may informe you to the Contrarie."[24]

Next to treacherousness, "barbarism" was the most convenient accusation to hurl against the Indian in the seventeenth century. Yet, as John Daly Burk, the historian of Virginia, pointed out:

Notwithstanding the general charge of barbarism and treachery against the Indians of Virginia, and of cruelty and tyranny against Powhatan, with which the early historians abound, not a single fact is brought in support of this accusation; and in several instances, with an inconsistency for which it is difficult to account, the same writers speak with admiration of the exact order, which prevailed among all the tribes of which this empire was composed; and confess at the same time, that this order and security arose from the inviolable observance of customs, which time has consecrated as law and which were equally binding on the King and the people.[25]

Today the character of the American Indian is generally drawn in a derogatory manner. The views of the first explorers and missionaries, who frequently saw heroic qualities in the Indian and whose reports provided the basis for the earlier literary conception of the "noble savage," have long since been buried in the shifting sands of more recent intellectual movements. None of the studies of "the myth of the noble savage" considers the possibility that the early favorable observers of Indian character might not have been entirely deceived in their analysis. All such studies assume that any degree of nobility was a myth: so far have white arrogance and Indian abasement proceeded.[26]

Another common charge against the Indians, which became the basis of the most popular eighteenth- and nineteenth-century justification for dispossessing them, was that they were wandering hunters with no settled habitations. This mode of securing their livelihood, it was charged, was too wasteful in a world in which other countries faced (or thought they faced) problems of overpopulation.[27] The argument that hunters might justly be forced to alter their economy by a pastoral or agricultural people was voiced by many, humble and great, in the colonies and in England. John Locke was perhaps its most famous exponent, although, character-

24. Virginia Company of London to Governor and Council in Virginia, August 6, 1623, in Kingsbury, ed., *Records of the Virginia Company*, IV, 269-70; Council in Virginia to Virginia Company of London, January 30, 1623/24, *ibid.*, 451.

25. John Daly Burk, *The History of Virginia from its first Settlement to the Commencement of the Revolution* (Petersburg, Va., 1804-5), I, 308-9.

26. See Washburn, "A Moral History of Indian-White Relations," *Ethnohistory*, 4 (1957), 47-61.

27. England, in Elizabethan times, had a population of about two and a half to three million persons. J. B. Black, *The Reign of Elizabeth, 1558-1603* (Oxford, 1945), 195.

istically, he did not develop the argument logically or clearly.[28] The argument was later expressed most succinctly by Theodore Roosevelt, who wrote that "the settler and pioneer have at bottom had justice on their side; this great continent could not have been kept as nothing but a game preserve for squalid savages."[29]

Again, was not the European creating the myth he wished to use? Were the Indians in fact nomadic hunters? It was, of course, possible to find examples of nomadic hunting tribes in North America, and the Indians of the eastern coast, those referred to by the early theorists, depended upon hunting as an important part of their economy and an integral function of their social and religious life. But agriculture was also a conspicuously essential part of Indian subsistence, and we may regard with suspicion much of the literature of justification which overlooks this aspect of native life. The English knew well enough how important was Indian food: the early accounts are filled with references to the "Indian fields" along the rivers of Virginia, and little else but native produce sustained the whites in the early years of settlement. It was the Indians who taught the settlers techniques of agriculture, as the familiar story of Squanto and the Plymouth Colony relates, and the Virginia colonists also were instructed by the Indians on how to plant crops and how to retrieve food from the rivers and bays. The natives were hunters, but they were also, and probably more importantly, agriculturists and fishermen.[30]

The literature of justification similarly tends to overlook the fact that the Indians were, for the most part, town dwellers. The great body of contemporary graphic depictions in French, Spanish, and English sources of the sixteenth and seventeenth centuries shows substantial dwellings, palisaded villages, well-planned streets, garden plots, civic and religious centers. Indeed, throughout most of the seventeenth century in Virginia

28. John Locke, *An Essay Concerning the True Original, Extent and End of Civil Government* (1690), Chap. V, "Of Property." Immanuel Kant in *The Science of Right* (1796), Pt. I, Chap. II, sec. i, no. 15, writing as the representative of a nation which did not participate in the profitable overseas voyages, denounced the doctrine as impious and championed the right of the American Indian to hold his land in whatever way he pleased. Representatives of the expanding maritime nations, however, found no difficulty in justifying their nations' claims.

29. Theodore Roosevelt, *The Winning of the West* (New York, 1889-96), I, 90.

30. See, for example, Harold Underwood Faulkner, *American Economic History*, 5th edn. (New York, 1943), 58-60, and Roy Harvey Pearce, *The Savages of America: A Study of the Indian and the Idea of Civilization* (Baltimore, 1953), 66. An example of the inability to see the Indians as other than hunters is evident in Roger Burlingame's chapter "Mission in Virginia" in *The American Conscience* (New York, 1957). Burlingame quotes the passage of Edward Waterhouse (see p. 21) that "now their cleared lands [*sic*] . . . shall be inhabited by us" and immediately comments that "the policy hitherto observed of keeping hands off the Indian hunting would be ended . . ." (p. 68).

the only true town dwellers were the Indians; the English lived together compactly only during the fearful early years.

The literature of justification has never come to an easy and final solution. Men have thrashed over the morality of expansion without agreement, and the courts have interpreted the "law" involved without consistency. A few representative individual views and court decisions from the sixteenth to the twentieth century should make this clear.

Sir Thomas More, in his *Utopia* (1516), was one of the first Englishmen to express himself on the justice of expansion. When the Utopians, the inhabitants of More's ideal country, had fully populated their own cities they sent colonists to build "a town . . . in the next land, where the inhabitants have much waste and unoccupied ground." The native inhabitants are invited to dwell with the Utopians—under Utopian laws, of course, which are considered by the Utopians to be greatly superior. If the natives are foolish enough to resist this benevolence, they are driven off the land; if resistance continues, the Utopians have no choice but to make full-scale war against them. More's ideal people considered this the most just cause of war: "when any people holdeth a piece of ground void and vacant to no good or profitable use: keeping others from the use and possession of it, which, notwithstanding, by the law of nature, ought thereof to be nourished and relieved."[31]

Sir Walter Raleigh, a hundred years later, was considerably less positive than More. A people could deceive itself: for example, "a number can do a great wrong and call it right, and not one of that majority blush for it."[32] Raleigh noted sadly and cynically that wars over land ownership were likely to be inevitable because the "great charter whereby God bestowed the whole earth upon Adam and confirmed it unto the sons of Noah, being as brief in words, as large in effect, hath bred much quarrel of interpretation." English occupation of the Bermudas (first "discovered" by the Spanish) was clearly a moral action because the land had been uninhabited when the English landed. But what of inhabited areas? Here Raleigh pondered the question which must continue to be at the heart of all justifications for expansion in a world in which every individual human being is regarded as possessing roughly equivalent rights:

If the title of occupiers be good in land unpeopled, why should it be bad accounted in a country peopled over thinly? Should one family, or one thousand, hold possession of all the southern undiscovered continent, because they had seated themselves in Nova Guiana, or about the straits of

31. *Utopia*, Robinson trans. of 1551; new edn. by Rev. T. F. Didbin (London, 1808), Bk. II, Chap. V, 191-92.

32. "A Discourse of the Original and Fundamental Cause of Natural, Arbitrary, Necessary, and Unnatural War," in *Works of Sir Walter Ralegh, Kt.*, VIII, 291.

Magellan? Why might not then the like be done in Afric, in Europe, and in Asia? If these were most absurd to imagine, let then any man's wisdom determine, by lessening the territory, and increasing the number of inhabitants, what proportion is requisite to the peopling of a region in such a manner that the land shall neither be too narrow for those whom it feedeth, nor capable of a greater multitude? Until this can be concluded and agreed upon, one main and fundamental cause of the most grievous war that can be imagined is not like to be taken from the earth.[33]

Roger Williams, in the 1630's and 1640's, was one of the few Englishmen who dared to dismiss European claims to American soil as unjustified and illegal if the prior right of the Indian were not recognized. Full title was in the Indian, he asserted, from whom alone a valid title could be derived. The colonists should repent of receiving title by patent from a king who had no right to grant it. Williams, said John Cotton, held it "a National duty to renounce the Patent: which to have done would have subverted the fundamental State and Government of the Country."[34]

The distinction between the "Naturall Right" of the Indians to the land they occupied, now called "original Indian title," and the legal title of the English to sovereignty was thus brought into the open. The distinction has been a basic one throughout American history, but it had to be established as well as asserted. In the seventeenth century the rule was by no means established. It was never made explicit to the Indians, least of all to those who lived in actual independence beyond the frontiers of the various colonies. Nor was it established to the full understanding of those tribes which lived in closer association with the English until their defeat in such conflicts as King Philip's War in New England. The principle of English sovereignty based on the royal grants was, in sum, as "speculative" as the grants themselves and depended for its establishment on the course of events. Fortunately for the English, the fact proved equal to the assertion.

Roger Williams, despite his brave stand against the royal patent, was eventually forced to request a charter from the English parliamentary government in order to prevent the Rhode Island colony from being devoured by her neighboring English colonies.[35]

The question of Indian rights became more and more difficult for jurists and theorists as American settlement advanced and overran not only what European thinkers considered the natural rights of the Indians but those rights guaranteed by solemn treaty. This knowledge pained

33. *Ibid.*, 255.
34. Mass. Hist. Soc., *Proceedings, 1871-1873*, 12 (Boston, 1873), 348, 351.
35. Charles McLean Andrews, *The Colonial Period in American History* (New Haven, Conn., 1934-38), II, 4-5, 24-25.

Thomas Jefferson, who realized that the legal justification for European settlement in territory occupied by another race must necessarily rest on natural injustice.

"Whoever shall attempt to trace the claims of the European Nations to the Countrys in America from the principles of Justice, or reconcile the invasions made on the native Indians to the natural rights of mankind," wrote Jefferson, "will find that he is pursueing a Chimera, which exists only in his own imagination, against the evidence of indisputable facts."[36]

Although he regarded discovery as a fragile support for claims of just settlement, Jefferson, like John Marshall later, accepted its legality. "When America was first discovered by the Europeans," he wrote, "a general notion prevail'd, that the first discoverers of any particular part, had a right to take possession, in the name of that Kingdom or State of which they were Subjects; and that such discovery and formality of taking possession conferred a Title."[37]

As the eighteenth century passed into the nineteenth, the name of John Marshall came to dominate discussions of Indian rights. The great chief justice was in the strategic position of weighing the claims of a vigorous, rising nation and a faltering, declining race. On his decision hinged the title to the real estate of the nation, the independence of numerous Indian nations, the sanctity of treaty rights, and even the very existence of law and order. Marshall had to consider not only law but conscience and expediency as well. The "natural" rights of the Indians had to be seen in terms of the "speculative" rights of the earlier European monarchs, the "juridical" rights of their successor American states, and the "practical" economic demands of the millions who now populated the continent.

Marshall did not hesitate, and his decision has been the basis of all subsequent determinations of Indian right. In the case of *Johnson and Graham's Lessee* v. *McIntosh*, in 1823, Marshall declared that the Indians of the United States did not possess an unqualified sovereignty despite the centuries of relations conducted with them in terms of treaties and diplomatic agreements. Their right to "complete sovereignty, as independent nations" was diminished or denied, declared Marshall, by "the original fundamental principle that discovery gave exclusive title to those who made

36. "Vindication of Virginia's Claim Against the Proposed Colony of Vandalia" [ca. 1773-74], attributed to Jefferson by Julian P. Boyd *et al.*, eds., *The Papers of Thomas Jefferson* (Princeton, N. J., 1952), VI, Appendix III, 656.

37. *Ibid.* The "right of discovery" has been more realistically described, in the phrase of A. J. Leibling, as the principle of the "Pre-eminent Right of the First Trespasser." See his "A Reporter at Large: The Lake of the Ciu-ui Eaters— III," *The New Yorker* (January 15, 1955), 36.

it." "The history of America," the historian-chief justice concluded, "from its discovery to the present day, proves, we think, the universal recognition of these principles." Marshall declared further that the principle of discovery "was a right which all asserted for themselves, and to the assertion of which, by others, all assented." "However extravagant the pretension of converting the discovery of an inhabited country into conquest may appear," wrote Marshall in his decision, "if the principle has been asserted in the first instance, and afterwards sustained; if a country has been acquired and held under it; if the property of the great mass of the community originates in it, it becomes the law of the land and cannot be questioned."[38]

Marshall's decision encouraged the state of Georgia, beginning in 1824, to try to dispossess the Cherokee Indians living within its borders. Hitherto the Cherokee Nation had lived confident in the protection afforded by the many treaties concluded with the English and American governments before and after the Revolution. In all these agreements the Cherokee Nation had been treated as an independent political power possessing proprietary right and political authority in the land it occupied.

The Cherokees had, moreover, in the course of their contact with Europeans, adopted white customs of dress and white modes of cultivation. They had thus, in the words of James Madison, refuted the unfounded claim of the whites that they were nomadic savages, unqualified for formal ownership of land. Yet there was always an answer to Indian claims, and the Cherokees were now opposed on the "strange ground . . . that they had no right to alter their condition and become husbandmen."[39]

In 1828 the Cherokees held a convention to establish a permanent government and write a constitution for their nation. The state, anxious to prevent the creation of further obstacles to Indian removal, replied in 1829 with a series of laws invalidating all statutes and ordinances adopted by the Indians and authorizing the division of their lands. These laws were, of course, in violation of solemn treaties between the United States and the Cherokee Nation. President Jackson, whose frontier upbringing had left him with little sympathy for the Indians, was in complete accord with Georgia. When the Cherokees applied for federal protection against the efforts of Georgia to coerce them in violation of their treaty rights, Jackson replied that "the President of the United States has no power to protect them against the laws of Georgia."[40]

38. 8 Wheaton 574, 591.
39. Wirt to Madison, October 5, 1830, quoted in John P. Kennedy, *Memoirs of the Life of William Wirt, Attorney-General of the United States*, rev. edn. (Philadelphia, 1850-54), II, 262.
40. Quoted in Charles Warren, *The Supreme Court in United States History*, rev. edn. (Boston, 1937), I, 731.

Disappointed by this breach of faith, the Indians initiated legal action before the Supreme Court to prevent Georgia from carrying out its laws in violation of the Cherokee Nation's solemn treaty rights. Two distinguished lawyers agreed to represent the Cherokees: William Wirt, ex-Attorney General of the United States, and John Sergeant, former chief counsel for the Bank of the United States. Before taking the case, Wirt considered the moral and legal issues involved and read extensively on the controversy as it had been argued in Congress. "In making this examination," he said, "I was struck with the manifest determination, both of the President and the States, that the State laws should be extended over . . . [the Cherokees] *at every hazard*. This led me to reflect more seriously on the predicament in which I was about to place myself, and perhaps involve the Supreme Court of the United States."[41]

Chief Justice Marshall, though sympathetic to the plight of the Cherokees, had to consider the incalculable effects a decision in their favor might have on the authority of the Supreme Court: the President's probable refusal to enforce the orders of the court could destroy the authority so painstakingly built up by Marshall.[42] How much effect such considerations had on his decision is uncertain. At any rate, in the action brought by *The Cherokee Nation* v. *The State of Georgia* (1831), Marshall ruled that the Cherokee Nation, though a "State," was not a "foreign State" but a "domestic dependent nation," and that the court had no original jurisdiction of the cause.[43] Justice Smith Thompson dissented "in an opinion of immense power" in which Justice Joseph Story concurred.[44]

The decision on the right of the state of Georgia to impose its authority upon the Cherokees, though not met in this case, was faced in the case of *Samuel A. Worcester* v. *The State of Georgia* (1832). Here Georgia's right to force two missionaries with the Cherokees to obtain a license and take an oath of state allegiance was denied. Marshall, in his decision, held the Georgia statute unconstitutional on the ground that the jurisdiction of the federal government over the Cherokees was exclusive. Georgia, the court ruled, had no power to pass laws affecting the Cherokees or their territory.[45]

Having ruled the Cherokees dependent, Marshall now attempted to limit their dependence to the federal government and not to the state of

41. Wirt to Judge Dabney Carr, June 21, 1830, quoted in Kennedy, *Memoirs of Wirt*, II, 255.

42. Marshall to Judge Carr, n.d., quoted in Kennedy, *Memoirs of Wirt*, II, 258; Warren, *Supreme Court*, I, 751; Albert J. Beveridge, *The Life of John Marshall* (Boston, 1916-19), IV, 546.

43. 5 Peters 15-18; entire report, 1-80.

44. Beveridge, *Life of Marshall*, IV, 546.

45. 6 Peters 515-97.

Georgia. But even this ruling was dangerous under the conditions of power which existed. It failed to protect the Indians and it nearly toppled the court's authority. Just what President Jackson's precise feeling in the matter was we do not know; there seems little doubt, however, that he never intended to enforce the decision of the court against an unwilling Georgia. He wanted the Indians removed, by law or without law, in the name of whatever principle might be applied. And they were removed. The court's impotence threw Marshall into a deep gloom. "I yield slowly and reluctantly to the conviction that our constitution cannot last," he wrote to Justice Story on September 22, 1832.[46]

The success of the state of Georgia in defying the federal government encouraged the state of South Carolina to question the authority of the Supreme Court. But on this question Jackson reacted in a different manner. He rebuked South Carolina with the "Force Bill" and thereby bolstered the authority of the central government and the Supreme Court, even causing Georgia to pardon the missionaries upon the withdrawal of their suit. The crisis involving the court and the federal government passed; the only victim was the Cherokee Nation.

So great were the accumulated injuries suffered by the Indians, so difficult was redress under existing methods, and, most importantly, so sharply did the pricks of conscience begin to disturb the satiated conquerors, that Congress, in 1946, after nearly twenty years of consideration, passed the Indian Claims Commission Act to give belated justice to the Indians. Clause 5 of section 2 of the act provided for "claims based upon fair and honorable dealings that are not recognized by any existing rule of law or equity," an allowance which has introduced a new element into the battle over Indian justice.

The Justice Department has argued consistently that the act did not create any new causes of action, but merely provided a forum where Indian claimants could sue the United States only on those claims upon which the United States had already consented to be sued by non-Indians. It was a political and not a judicial function, it asserted, to recognize liability for claims without a legal or equitable basis under existing law.[47]

The view of the Justice Department, however, has not prevailed in the cases arising under the act of 1946. The Indians have acquired important justiciable rights under the statute as it has been interpreted by the Indian Claims Commission and by the Court of Claims. However,

46. Mass. Hist. Soc., *Proceedings, 1900-1901*, 2nd ser., 14 (Boston, 1901), 352.
47. *Otoe and Missouria Tribe of Indians* v. *United States*, 131 U.S. Court of Claims 598 (1955).

the Indian is still without constitutional support for his rights. In *Tee-Hit-Ton Indians* v. *The United States* (1954-55), a case not arising under the act of 1946, the Indians were held not entitled to compensation under the Fifth Amendment for the taking by the United States of lands long in their possession.[48] In upholding the decision of the Court of Claims, the Supreme Court, with Justice Reed delivering the opinion, noted that the Tee-Hit-Tons occupied the land, prior to the purchase of Alaska by the United States in 1867, by mere possession not specifically recognized as ownership by Congress or, in the commonly accepted phrase, by "original Indian title." "The line of cases adjudicating Indian rights on American soil," he asserted, "leads to the conclusion that Indian occupancy, not specifically recognized as ownership by action authorized by Congress, may be extinguished by the Government without compensation. Every American schoolboy knows that the savage tribes of this continent were deprived of their ancestral ranges by force and that, even when the Indian ceded millions of acres by treaty in return for blankets, food and trinkets, it was not a sale but the conquerors' will that deprived them of their land."[49]

The court took notice of certain decisions which had held for compensation under similar circumstances under the Fifth Amendment, but pointed out that they had been altered by later decisions, leaving "unimpaired the rule derived from *Johnson* v. *McIntosh* that the taking by the United States of unrecognized Indian title is not compensable under the Fifth Amendment." Not the least consideration that may have led to this conclusion was the estimate that, if the Fifth Amendment protection were allowed, it might cost the government nine billion dollars to pay for uncompensated aboriginal titles.[50]

Disclaiming any intention of upholding harshness as the most appropriate policy towards the Indians, Justice Reed asserted that the court spoke for the American people, who "have compassion for the descendants of those Indians who were deprived of their homes and hunting grounds by the drive of civilization. . . ." The court spoke approvingly of the "generous provision . . . willingly made to allow tribes to recover for wrongs, as a matter of grace, not of legal liability."[51] The Indian, thus, was to depend on the generosity and the grace of his despoilers. His rights

48. 128 Court of Claims 82.

49. 348 U.S. 289-90. The assumptions of the court as to the savagery of the Indians, their nomadic condition, and their subjection by conquest reflect popular beliefs more than they do historical facts. None of these assumptions can be made so lightly or so generally, particularly in the context of the seventeenth and eighteenth centuries.

50. 348 U.S. 283n, 284-85.

51. 348 U.S. 281-82.

were not to be afforded the protection of "constitutional principle" but satisfied by "gratuities for the termination of Indian occupancy."[52]

The status of Indian claims based on the "unrecognized title" of Indian occupancy, as opposed to "recognized title" deriving from treaties or acts of Congress, was temporarily thrown in doubt by this decision. However, by the *Otoe and Missouria* case (1955), the Court of Claims sustained the decision of the Indian Claims Commission, in an action brought under the Indian Claims Commission Act of 1946, holding the government liable to a claim based on aboriginal Indian title, and the Supreme Court refused to review the case. The Court of Claims was careful, however, to assert its essential agreement with the reasoning of the high court in the *Tee-Hit-Ton* case. It pointed out that Congress, by passing the Indian Claims Commission Act, had condescended, as a matter of grace, to allow the Indians to sue the United States on moral grounds and on the basis of "Indian title." The legal rights of the sovereign were not to be impaired, but sympathetic justice, not strict legality, was to be the guiding rule. Statutory, but not constitutional, liability, in other words, was to be admitted.[53]

Although cautiously interpreted by the courts, has not the Indian Claims Commission Act perhaps opened the door for broader and more fundamental moral claims? If the cost to honor, dignity, interest, or reason of recognizing the constitutional right of original Indian sovereignty in the New World should not seem too high to future generations, is it not possible that such a right will be conceded as justiciable as well as just?[54] The Indian Claims Commission Act has recognized that law must some-

52. 348 U.S. 294. It is noteworthy that three justices, including the chief justice, dissented from the opinion of the court.

53. For a full discussion of the question and references to further reading, see Nancy Oestreich Lurie, "The Indian Claims Commission Act," Amer. Acad. of Pol. and Soc. Sci., *Annals*, 311 (1957), 56-70.

54. For an important example of the growing tendency to concede constitutional protection to those previously excluded, see *U. S. A. ex rel. Gyula Paktorovics* v. *John L. Murff, District Director, Immigration and Naturalization Service for the District of New York* (U. S. Court of Appeals, Second Circuit), decided November 6, 1958 (Docket No. 24932). By a two-to-one majority the court reversed the decision of a lower tribunal and ruled that refugees from the 1956 Hungarian revolution who came to the United States without visas were nevertheless entitled to the full protection of the due process clause of the Fifth Amendment to the Constitution. The decision is another indication that "principles" have frequently, in the past, been applied step-by-step, first in behalf of members of the in-group and finally for the benefit of less privileged members of a society. The protection of American constitutional rights has been gradually extended outward from the descendants of the original European immigrants to those with darker skins, different customs, and antagonistic ideologies. It is not inconceivable that the canopy of protection will eventually extend to the American Indian himself.

times concede to morality if justice is not to be a synonym for injustice. Now that morality has a foot in the door, if only by the grace of the present lord of the manor, is it not possible that it will speak more persuasively than ever before? It has been hard for the Indian to accept the good faith of American "justice" based, as it has so often been, on a disregard of moral principle and an exaltation of the fluctuating pronouncements of the white man's law. The legal culture of the American Indian tends to regard the fine distinctions between law and morality so often made in the Western world as the product of a hypocritical mind. Perhaps in the future the Indian and white conceptions of law, justice, and morality will finally blend.

In the meantime the problem of the legality and morality of the expansion of one people into the territory of another will go on. Because the problem is unresolved in the mind of man, it cannot be lost in the mists of history. It is the problem of man attempting to restrain his ungovernable passions, man attempting to trust his "sovereign" reason, man attempting to better his economic condition. As we near the era of space travel we hear echoes of those who launched and justified the great age of oceanic discovery. "Space lawyers," noting the successful launching of Russian and American space satellites, advise us that by "international law" the first country able to land a man on the moon—or even to hit it—will be justified in claiming it, and in similar fashion all the other "islands and mainlands" of the celestial "ocean sea." Perhaps the creation of a circular crater resulting from a hydrogen bomb shot will be considered the "symbolic act" or "visible symbol" necessary to claim possession. Shades of Cabot's proprietary cruise down the coast of North America! The possession of worlds in outer space will not be determined fundamentally by priority of national grant, discovery, or occupancy any more than the ownership of the New World was determined by such considerations. Man thinking will continue to tell us what the law ought to be; man acting will tell us what the law is.

III.

INDIAN CULTURAL ADJUSTMENT TO EUROPEAN CIVILIZATION

Nancy Oestreich Lurie

UNIVERSITY OF MICHIGAN

In 1907, on the 300th anniversary of the beginning of English colonization in America, James Mooney made the brief observation that the Jamestown settlers "landed among a people who already knew and hated whites."
In effect, this remark summed up the accepted anthropological explanation
for the Indians' unpredictable behavior; it indicated why they alternated
elaborate expressions and actions of good will with apparent treachery.
Mooney implied that the Indians' attitudes and behavior were more than
justified by the demonstrated greed and aggressiveness of the whites.[1]

Little work was done in the succeeding years to explore the complete
significance of Mooney's remark or to probe more deeply into underlying
motivations for the Indians' actions. This neglect was inevitable, since
attention had to be devoted to a more fundamental problem. Before
achieving an understanding of Indian reaction to the effects of contact
with Europeans, it was necessary to establish a valid and cohesive picture
of aboriginal culture.[2] Thanks to the labors of such scholars as Mooney,

1. James Mooney, "The Powhatan Confederacy, Past and Present," *Amer.
Anthropologist*, 9 (1907), 129 and 120-52 *passim*. This Jamestown anniversary
issue featured articles dealing with the Virginia Indians.

2. It must be noted that while the concept of culture can be and often is treated
as an abstraction with an existence almost unto itself, this is no more than a semantic
devise. Human ideas and reasoning underlie culture and cultural change. Whenever
possible, I have devoted attention to the factors of human motivations which give
overt expression to observable cultural characteristics. The terms Indian culture
and European civilization merely indicate that comparisons are made of two cultures
having distinct origins and historical traditions, differing only in the local expressions
of certain universal aspects of culture.

Frank G. Speck, David I. Bushnell, John R. Swanton, Maurice A. Mook, and others, the fragmentary data relating to native life have been gathered into comprehensive and analytical accounts concerned with such problems as Indian demography, the cultural and linguistic identity of given tribes, tribal locations, and the prehistoric diffusion and changes in Indian cultures.

Likewise, in the past fifty years, general theoretical techniques of ethnological interpretation have been refined through field research in observable situations of culture contact. These acculturational studies, which are an invaluable aid in the interpretation of historical data, have investigated the reasons why some groups lose their cultural identity in a situation of culture contact while other groups continue to preserve ethnic integrity despite widespread alterations of purely native patterns.[3] With this backlog of necessary information and analysis, anthropologists have begun a more intensive consideration of the dynamics of culture contact in ethnohistorical terms.

Turning to Mooney's contention, there is evidence that the Virginia Indians had several opportunities to form opinions about Europeans both in terms of direct experience and of information communicated to them. Direct knowledge of Europeans may have occurred as early as the first quarter of the sixteenth century, when Giovanni de Verrazano and Estevan Gomez are believed to have made observations in the Chesapeake Bay region.[4] Of somewhat greater significance is the alleged founding of a Spanish Jesuit mission on the York River in 1570. According to this theory, the missionaries were killed by Indians under the leadership of a native known as Don Luis de Velasco, who had lived in Spain, where he was educated and converted to Christianity. The Spaniards had hoped that he would act as guide and model in the proselytizing of his people, but it appears that the effects of his early life negated his later training. In 1572 a punitive expedition under Pedro Menendez de Aviles attacked and defeated the Indians responsible for the destruction of the mission; in succeeding years Menendez made other forays into the region. A recent study insists that this area must have been along the Virginia coast.[5]

3. Two valuable publications dealing with the general topic of acculturation are: The Social Science Research Council Summer Seminar in Acculturation, 1953, "Acculturation, An Exploratory Formulation," *Amer. Anthropologist*, 56 (1954), 973-1005; and Verne F. Ray, ed., *Proceedings of the 1957 Annual Spring Meeting of the American Ethnological Society* (Seattle, 1957). The latter discusses cultural change and stability.

4. For a good brief account, see John Bartlett Brebner, *The Explorers of North America, 1492-1806*, reprint edn. (New York, 1955).

5. Clifford M. Lewis, S.J., and Albert J. Loomie, S.J., *The Spanish Jesuit Mission in Virginia, 1570-1572* (Chapel Hill, 1953), is an exhaustive study, but the Indian data are treated so summarily throughout that they neither help to substantiate the argument nor cast much light on the influence of the mission among the Indians, wherever it was established.

Whether or not the case for a sixteenth-century mission in Virginia has been proved is problematical. Many details are uncertain: the precise location of the mission on the York River, the tribal affiliations of Don Luis, the extent of his leadership, his age at the time he lived in Spain, and his possible genealogical affiliations with the ruling hierarchy of the Virginia Indians of the seventeenth century. However, historical investigation leaves no doubt of Spanish activity at this time, and these ventures must have occurred between St. Augustine and the Potomac River. The natives of Virginia, who borrowed cultural traits from neighboring tribes along the coast and further inland, could have received news of European explorations to the south and west by the same routes that carried purely native ideas. Generalized impressions of Europeans were doubtless prevalent in the Virginia area long before 1607.

The Spaniards came to America primarily as adventurers and fortune seekers. Although they attempted to found settlements their efforts usually met with failure. They plundered Indian villages but did not remain long in any one region; they were frequently routed by angry Indians or by their own inability to subsist in a strange terrain. After 1520, raids were conducted along the Gulf and southern Atlantic coast to obtain slaves for shipment to the West Indies. News of these incursions may have reached Virginia via the various coast tribes, and similarly Virginia natives may have heard of De Soto's hapless wanderings to the south and west. Even though the Spaniards later achieved success in colonization in Florida through the use of missionaries, the first hostile impressions had been made.

The French entered the scene to the south of Virginia in 1562. Because of lack of supplies and Spanish aggression, they failed in their attempts to establish a foothold in the region. However, the interests of France as well as of Britain were served by unknown numbers of piratical freebooters from the Caribbean area who touched along the coast of the Carolinas and intrigued with the Indians. Not until 1580 was Spain able to dislodge foreign intruders and punish recalcitrant Indians. Even then, Spanish dominion remained precarious, although the Spanish Franciscans continued to extend their missions up the coast. Finally, in 1597, a general uprising among the Carolina tribes destroyed these religious outposts and forced Spain again to concentrate most of her forces in Florida.

Thus, during much of the sixteenth century Europeans were active in regions immediately adjacent to Virginia and possibly in Virginia itself. Their activity was often associated with violence, and there was sufficient time for rumors concerning them to have reached the Virginia natives before any direct contacts were made. By the time the English attempted to found colonies on the east coast toward the close of the sixteenth century, they encountered difficulties which may have been more than the simple result of European inexperience in developing techniques for survival in the New World. Raleigh's enterprise, for example, may have been singularly ill-timed. A general unrest in Indian-white relationships marked the period from 1577 to 1597 in the Carolina region where Raleigh's followers chose to remain. Pemisipan, a Secotan chief who attempted to organize opposition to the British in 1585, could hardly have been blamed if he saw a curious similarity to accounts he may have heard concerning the Spanish when, for the trifling matter of the theft of a silver cup, the English burned the corn and destroyed the buildings at his village of Aquascogoc.[6]

The later events at Cape Henry, the first landfall of the Jamestown colonists, suggest that the immediate hostility expressed by the Indians was inspired by fear of reprisals for the fate of Raleigh's colony. The Indians who attacked the English belonged to the Chesapeake tribe, immediately adjacent to the tribes with whom Pemisipan conspired.[7] It is also possible, as Mooney implies, that by 1607 the Virginia Indians evaluated any sudden appearance of Europeans as evil and took immediate measures to repel them. However, this view oversimplifies several important factors. Long before any Europeans arrived at Jamestown, the Indians had been fighting over matters of principle important to them, such as possession of land and tribal leadership. If they were aware of the fate of other Indians at the hands of Europeans, there was no reason for them to assume that their fate would be similar; they were not necessarily allied with the beleaguered tribes, nor did they share a sense of racial kinship. Sharp cultural differences and even sharper linguistic differences separated the various Indian societies. While there was reason to fear and hate the Europeans as invaders who made indiscriminate war on all Indians, the fear was only that of being taken unawares and the hate could be modified if the tribes which had fallen victim thus far were strangers or even enemies. If the Indians of Virginia had any knowledge of Europeans, they must have been aware that the white men were fundamentally outnumbered, frequently unable to support themselves in an environment which the Indians found eminently satisfactory, and that European settlements were usually short lived. The appearance of the English was probably far less alarming than 350 years of hindsight indicate ought to have been the case.

6. Maurice A. Mook, "Algonkian Ethnohistory of the Carolina Sound," *Jour. of The Washington Academy of Sciences*, 34 (1944), 185-86, quotes and discusses the journal of 1585, usually attributed to Sir Richard Grenville, regarding this incident and also establishes the location of Aquascogoc in North Carolina.

7. [George Percy], "Observations gathered out of *A Discourse of the Plantation of the Southerne Colonie in Virginia by the English, 1606:* written by that Honorable Gentleman, Master George Percy," in Edward Arber, ed., *Captain John Smith . . . Works, 1608-1631* (Birmingham, Eng., 1884), xl-li.

This is demonstrated by the fact that the Virginia Indians under the leadership of Powhatan seem to have made their first adjustments to Europeans in terms of existing native conditions.[8] Primary among these conditions were Powhatan's efforts to gain firmer control over his subject tribes and to fight tribes traditionally at enmity with his followers. It was expedient to help the settlers stay alive, for they could be useful allies in his established plans; but at the same time he could not allow them to gain ascendancy. The situation was complicated by factionalism in Powhatan's ranks and lack of accord among the settlers. However, recognition of the fundamental aboriginal situation makes the early events at Jamestown understandable on a rational basis. It offers a logical foundation for subsequent developments in Indian-white relationships and Indian adjustments to European civilization as the result of something more than barbaric cupidity and a thirst for the white man's blood.

Certainly a wary sensitivity to any sign of hostility or treachery characterized the behavior of both whites and Indians at the outset of settlement at Jamestown. The Europeans were still seriously concerned about the probable fate of Raleigh's colony and they had already been attacked by the Indians at Cape Henry. The Indians, in turn, may well have possessed information concerning the alarmingly retributive temperament of Europeans, at least in terms of the incident at nearby Aquascogoc, if not through generalized opinions derived from the long history of intermittent European contact along the east coast.

Nevertheless, the party of Europeans that set out on exploration of the country about Jamestown encountered a welcome at the various Indian villages different from the greetings offered at Cape Henry. Except for one cold but not overtly hostile reception in the Weanoc country, the white men were feted, fed, and flattered. At the same time a suggestion of the uncertainty of the next years occurred before the exploring party had even returned to their headquarters—at Jamestown the remaining colonists were attacked by a party of local Indians.[9] Events of

8. There are many data to indicate that in culture contact situations, generally regular processes of cultural acceptance and rejection can be traced to the formulation of analogies between innovations and existing phenomena on the part of the recipient culture. See Melville J. Herskovits, *Man and His Works* (New York, 1950), 553-58, for a discussion of the processes of reinterpretation and syncretism; Ralph Linton, *The Study of Man* (New York, 1936), 317-18, and Homer G. Barnett, "Cultural Processes," *Amer. Anthropologist*, 42 (1940), 21-48, give similar but independent analyses of analogy formulation on the basis of form, function, meaning, and use or principle of given traits.

9. [Captain Gabriel Archer], "A Relayton of the Discovery &c. 21 May–22 June, 1607," in Arber, ed., *Works of John Smith*, li-lii. It is worth noting that news of the attack was apparently communicated to the Indians who were entertaining the exploring party, but that Powhatan had either been unable to prevent the attack or had not known of the plan until it was accomplished.

this nature as well as the general observations recorded during the first two years at Jamestown are particularly instructive in any attempt to understand Indian motivations and policy regarding the British.

The narratives are difficult to follow because of the variety of orthographies employed for Indian words. Certain features remain speculative because initial communication between whites and Indians was limited to the use of signs and the few native words that could be learned readily.[10] However, it is possible to see native culture in terms of regularities and consistencies which were not obvious to the colonists. Likewise, the apparent inconsistencies on the part of the natives, recounted by the settlers as innate savage treachery, indicate that the aboriginal culture was in a process of growth, elaboration, and internal change. These phases of culture, which included both extensive tendencies of intertribal confederation and divisive reactions expressed by individual tribes, were interrupted and redirected but not initiated by the arrival of Europeans in 1607.

From the viewpoint of the twentieth century, it is difficult to realize that the material differences between the Indians and the European colonists, who lived before the full development of the industrial revolution, were equalled if not outweighed by the similarities of culture. This was especially true in Virginia, where a local florescence of culture and a demonstrated ability to prevail over other tribes gave the Indians a sense of strength which blinded them to the enormity of the threat posed by the presence of Europeans. There was actually little in the Europeans' imported bag of tricks which the Indians could not syncretize with their own experience. Metal was not unknown to them: they used native copper, brought in from the West, for decorative purposes. Metal weapons and domestic utensils were simply new and effective forms of familiar objects to accomplish familiar tasks. Even guns were readily mastered after the noise, which evoked astonishment at first, was understood as necessary to their operation. Likewise, fabrics and articles of personal adornment were part of Indian technology. Many utilitarian objects such as nets, weirs, and gardening implements were very similar in both Indian and European culture. European ships were simply larger and different, as was fitting for a people interested in traveling greater distances by open water than the Indians had ever cared to do.

Expansive accounts of the size and permanence of the great European cities could easily have been likened by the natives to the impressive aboriginal developments in the lower Mississippi Valley; archeological evidence

10. Throughout the present study, spelling of Indian words, apart from direct quotations, has been regularized according to the pattern of Mook's publications.

suggests that knowledge of this cultural complex was widespread.[11]   Even
if these Indian models of nascent urbanization are discounted, the statements made by Europeans about their country and king may well have
sounded like the exaggerations of outnumbered strangers endeavoring to
buttress their weaknesses with talk of powerful but distant brothers.   This
explanation is admittedly conjectural, although we find ample documentation of the Indians' disinclination to admit any significant superiority in
white culture at a somewhat later period.   During the early nineteenth
century, when the industrial revolution was underway and the eastern
United States was heavily populated by whites, Indian visitors were brought
from the West in the hope that they would be cowed by the white man's
power and cease resistance to the forces of civilization.   The Indians remained singularly unimpressed.[12]   Furthermore, at the time Jamestown
was founded in the seventeenth century, the only knowledge Indians
possessed concerning Europeans indicated that Indians were well able to
oppose white settlement.   Raleigh's ill-fated colony was a clear reminder
of the Europeans' mortality.

Although the early accounts tend to take a patronizing view of the
Indians, the points on which the Europeans felt superior had little meaning
for the aborigines: literacy, different sexual mores, ideas of modesty, good
taste in dress and personal adornment, and Christian religious beliefs.   The
argument of technological superiority at that time was a weak one; despite
guns and large ships the Europeans could not wrest a living from a terrain
which, by Indian standards, supported an exceptionally large population.
Scientific knowledge of generally predictable group reactions thus suggests
that the degree of ethnocentrism was probably equal on both sides of the
contact between Indians and Europeans in Virginia.   Recognition of the
Indians' self-appraisal is necessary for a clear understanding of their basis
of motivation and consequent behavior in relation to Europeans.

Moreover, it was evident to the colonists that they were dealing with
a fairly complex society, exhibiting many characteristics of leadership,
social classes, occupational specialization, social control, and economic
concepts that were eminently comprehensible in European terms.   If the
exploring parties overstated the case when they translated *weroance* as

11. Paul Martin, George Quimby, and Donald Collier, *Indians Before Columbus*
(Chicago, 1947), offer useful illustrations of the far-flung continental diffusion of
cultural traits in prehistoric times, although dates assigned have been reassessed during
the last ten years.

12. See Katherine C. Turner, *Red Men Calling on the Great White Father*
(Norman, Okla., 1951), which presents a series of essays on such visits.   Although
the Indians considered their trips as entertaining educational experiences, their quoted
remarks in the main reveal opinions that the white man had an unnecessarily complex
and burdensome way of life at the expense of the finer one enjoyed by the Indians.

"king" and likened tribal territories to European kingdoms, they at least had a truer understanding of the nature of things than did the democratic Jefferson, who first designated the Virginia tribes as the "Powhatan Confederacy."[13] Since the term "Confederacy" is so firmly entrenched in the literature, it will be retained here as a matter of convenience; but, in reality, Powhatan was in the process of building something that approximated an empire. By 1607 it was not an accomplished fact, but the outlines were apparent and the process was sufficiently advanced to allow a geographical description of the extent of Powhatan's domain.

Powhatan's influence, if not his undisputed control, extended over some thirty Algonkian-speaking tribes along the entire length of the present Virginia coast, including the Accohannoc and Accomac of the Eastern Shore. The nucleus of this domain consisted of six tribes which were centrally located in the region drained by the James, Pamunkey, and Mattaponi rivers. These tribes were the Powhatan, Arrohattoc, Pamunkey, Youghtanund, Appomattoc, and Mattaponi, with Powhatan's own tribe, the Pamunkey, consistently referred to in the early narratives as the largest and most powerful.[14] The Confederacy was bounded to the north and south by other Algonkian tribes. Except on the basis of their declared political allegiance, the uniformity of language and culture in the region makes it difficult to differentiate between the tribes within the Confederacy and even between the Confederacy and neighboring Maryland and Carolina groups.

It is generally accepted that these Algonkian peoples moved into the lower coastal region from the north. According to their own account this had occurred about three hundred years before Jamestown was settled, although recent archeological investigations suggest a longer occupation.[15]

13. John Smith observed that "one as Emperour ruleth over many kings or governours." *A Map of Virginia with a Description of the Countrey* . . . and *The General Historie of Virginia*. . . , in Arber, ed., *Works of John Smith*, 79, 375. Mook, "Aboriginal Population of Tidewater Virginia," *Amer. Anthropologist*, 44 (1944), 197, attributes the first use of the term "Powhatan Confederacy" to Jefferson.

14. Mooney, "Powhatan Confederacy," *Amer. Anthropologist*, 9 (1907), 135-36, notes the possible inclusion of the Werowocomoco and Chiskiac in the nuclear group of tribes inherited by Powhatan. Mook, "Aboriginal Population," *ibid.*, 44 (1944), 194 ff., lists thirty tribes as the largest number in the Confederation at any one time.

15. The Indian informants of the seventeenth century may have referred merely to the period of development of the distinctive social and political characteristics of the region rather than to original occupation. Frank G. Speck, "The Ethnic Position of the Southeastern Algonkian," *Amer. Anthropologist*, 26 (1924), 194, substantially agrees with the Indian accounts. Professor James B. Griffin, University Museum, University of Michigan, stated in a personal communication that unpublished data regarding a site near Washington, D. C., indicate an Algonkian intrusion into the southern area long before 1300.

Once arrived, the Algonkians acquired numerous cultural traits from the Southeast culture area and developed many similarities to the interior Muskhogean-speaking groups. Some of these new elements were in turn transferred to the more northerly Algonkians, but they never existed there in the cohesive complexity found in the tidelands.[16]

Powhatan inherited the six central tribes as an already unified intertribal organization and extended his domain by conquest from the south bank of the Potomac to the Norfolk region. The Chesapeake Indians are included in the Confederacy, but this southernmost group was not fully under Powhatan's control at the time the settlers arrived. Their attack on the colonists at Cape Henry gave Powhatan the opportunity to gain favor with the English by swiftly avenging the hostile action. Although some historians have implied that Powhatan destroyed the entire tribe, it is far more likely that he simply killed the leaders and placed trusted kinsmen in these positions.[17]

Powhatan's method of fighting and his policy of expanding political control combined a reasoned plan of action with quick ferocity and a minimum of bloodshed. Indian warfare was generally limited to surprise attacks and sniping from cover. Constant replacements of fighting men kept the enemy occupied and wore down their resistance, while actual casualties were relatively limited in number. Accounts of Powhatan's conquests and the occurrences observed after 1607 point to a carefully devised method of establishing his control over a wide territory. Entire communities might be killed if they proved exceptionally obstinate in rendering homage and paying tribute, but in most cases Powhatan simply defeated groups of questionable loyalty and upon their surrender moved them to areas where he could keep better watch over them. Trusted members of the Confederacy were then sent to occupy the vacated regions, while Powhatan's relatives were distributed throughout the tribes in positions of leadership.[18] Mook's studies indicate that the degree of Powhatan's leadership decreased in almost direct proportion to the increase

16. Speck, "Southeastern Algonkian," *Amer. Anthropologist*, 26 (1924), 198, and 184-200 *passim*, sets forth this view of populational migration and cultural diffusion. Alfred L. Kroeber, *Cultural and Natural Areas of Native North America* (Berkeley, Calif., 1939), 94, disagrees with Speck as to the influence of southeastern Muskhogean peoples. Mook, "The Anthropological Position of the Indian Tribes of Tidewater Virginia," *Wm. and Mary College Qtly.*, 2nd ser., 23 (1943), 27-40, defends Speck's reconstruction with further evidence to substantiate the Muskhogean traits, and may be taken as the final word on the matter to date.

17. [Archer], "Relayton," Arber, ed., *Works of John Smith*, xliv; William Strachey, *The Historie of Travaile into Virginia Britannia*, Hakluyt Society edn. (London, 1849), 101, 105; Mooney, "Powhatan Confederacy," *Amer. Anthropologist*, 9 (1907), 130.

18. Mooney, "Powhatan Confederacy," *Amer. Anthropologist*, 9 (1907), 136.

in geographical distance between the Pamunkey and the location of a given tribe.[19] Throughout the entire region, however, the combination of ample sustenance, effective techniques of production, provident habits of food storage, and distribution of supplies through exchange offset shortcomings in the political framework connecting the tribes and helped to cement social ties and produce a commonality of culture.

Despite certain internal dissensions the Confederacy can be seen as a unified bloc, distinct from neighboring tribes. To the north were numerous small Algonkian-speaking tribes, either friendly or representing no serious danger to Powhatan. They tended to shade off in cultural characteristics toward the more northern Algonkian types to be found along the coast into New England. The best known of these tribes was the Nanticoke in eastern Maryland and Delaware. North of the Potomac lived the Conoy (Piscataway), Tocwough, Ozinie, and others, about whom little is recorded. At a later date the tribes in this region were known collectively as the "Doeg" Indians. Beyond the Conoy and up into the present state of Pennsylvania were the Susquehanna, in Captain John Smith's judgment a powerful and impressive group, distinguished from the Virginia tribes in both language and culture.[20] However, they seem to have felt closer ties of friendship with the Algonkians than they did with their Iroquoian linguistic affiliates to the north. The Nansemond and Chesapeake tribes formed the southern terminus of the Confederacy, and beyond them in the Carolina region were a number of linguistically and culturally similar tribes extending along the coast to the Neuse River. The Roanoke narratives and particularly the illustrations of John White provide somewhat fuller documentation for the southerly neighbors of the Confederacy than is available for the northern Algonkian groups.[21]

The western border, formed by the fall line and paralleling the coast, was characterized by greater cultural and linguistic differences than those observed to the north and south of the Confederacy; it also represented

19. Mook, "Virginia Ethnology from an Early Relation," *Wm. and Mary College Qtly.*, 2nd ser., 23 (1943), 115.

20. Mooney, "Powhatan Confederacy," *Amer. Anthropologist*, 9 (1907), 140, tentatively identifies the "Doeg" as the Nanticoke. A review of materials relating to Bacon's Rebellion as well as the accounts of the local tribes presented in Kroeber, *Cultural Areas*, 91, 93-94, suggests that "Doeg" was applied to the Nanticoke and other Algonkian groups north of the Potomac. For John Smith's discussion of the Susquehanna, see Arber, ed., *Works of John Smith*, 77, 367.

21. Reproductions of White's original works may be found in David I. Bushnell, "John White—The First English Artist to Visit America, 1585," *Va. Mag. of Hist. and Biog.*, 35 (1927), 419-30, and 36 (1928), 17-26, 124-34. Although less well known, these illustrations are preferable to DeBry's familiar engravings and the work of other copyists in representing the Carolina tribes to augment textual descriptions in the Roanoke accounts.

a definite danger area for Powhatan. Virtually all Indian occupation ended somewhat east of the falls, however, allowing a strip of land a mile to ten or twelve miles wide as a safe margin between the Powhatan tribes and their nearest neighbors, who were also their deadliest enemies, the tribes of the Virginia piedmont region. These peoples have long been designated as Siouan-speaking but a recent study casts doubt on this identification. It is now suggested that these groups spoke a highly divergent and extremely old dialect of the basic Algonkian language stock.[22] Except for linguistic distinctiveness little is known about these piedmont people. This is most unfortunate, since they appear to figure as a key to much of Powhatan's policy toward the English and helped to influence the course of Indian adjustment to European settlement.[23] A few of these tribes are known by name, but they are usually considered as having comprised two major confederacies, comparable in some measure to the groupings associated with Powhatan. These were the Manahoac on the upper Rappahannock and surrounding region, and the Monacan along the upper James and its tributary streams. Both were aggressive groups, and their incursions were a constant threat to the tidelands Indians. Powhatan's desire to subdue these westerly tribes as a matter of protection was underscored by another consideration: copper, highly prized by the Virginia Confederacy, came from the West, and the enemy tribes formed an obstacle to trade for that commodity.[24]

Thus, at the outset of colonization in 1607 Powhatan's policies can best be understood in relation to circumstances antedating the arrival of the Jamestown settlers. Powhatan saw the whites in his territory as potential allies and as a source of new and deadly weapons to be used in furthering his own plans for maintaining control over his Confederacy and protecting

22. Carl F. Miller, "Revaluation of the Eastern Siouan Problem with Particular Emphasis on the Virginia Branches—The Occaneechi, the Saponi, and the Tutelo," Bureau of American Ethnology, Smithsonian Institution Bulletin 164, *Anthropological Papers*, No. 52 (Washington, D. C., 1957), 115-211, discusses the origin of the conjecture that Siouan dialects were spoken in the piedmont area and indicates why such reasoning may be erroneous. However, the traditional view is far from abandoned; see William C. Sturtevant, "Siouan Languages in the East," *Amer. Anthropologist*, 60 (1958), 138-43, for a specific refutation of Miller's argument.

23. Ethnologists have long been aware of the significance of the so-called Siouans in Powhatan's actions, although the point is usually mentioned as a side issue in connection with village locations, population size, and tribal distributions. See Bushnell, "The Five Monacan Towns in Virginia," Smithsonian Institution, *Miscellaneous Collections*, 82 (1930), 1-38; "The Manahoac Tribes in Virginia," *ibid.*, 94 (1935), 1-56; John R. Swanton, "Early History of the Eastern Siouan Tribes," in *Essays in Anthropology Presented to A. L. Kroeber* (Berkeley, Calif., 1936), 371-81.

24. John Smith lists the locations and names of subsidiary tribes of the Monacan and Manahoac. Arber, ed., *Works of John Smith*, 71, 366-67.

the Confederacy as a whole against the threat posed by the alien tribes of the piedmont region. Likewise, existing concepts of intertribal trade in food-stuffs and other commodities were extended to include trade with the newly arrived whites. It is worth noting that European novelties, apart from weapons, were of far less interest to Powhatan than the fact that the British possessed copper, an object vested with traditional native values and heretofore obtained with great difficulty.[25]

In the initial stages of contact between the Indians and the whites, therefore, it is hardly surprising that Powhatan and his people felt at least equal to the English. The chieftain could appreciate the foreigners as allies in the familiar business of warfare and trade, but in general there seemed little to emulate in European culture and much to dislike about the white men. However, even in the most difficult phases of their early relationship, Powhatan did not indulge in a full-scale attack against the settlers. At that time he was still engaged in strengthening his Confederacy and perhaps he could not risk extensive Indian defection to the side of the whites. But there is an equal likelihood that Powhatan's primary motivation was the desire to control and use the whites for his own purposes rather than to annihilate them.

At the time Jamestown was founded, native civilization was enjoying a period of expansion, and Powhatan had ample reason for sometimes con-sidering the English as more an annoyance than a serious danger. The unusually rich natural environment and the security offered by the Con-federacy stimulated the growth of social institutions and cultural refine-ments. In addition, the Virginia Indians were exceptionally powerful and, by aboriginal standards, their population was large: the entire Confederacy numbered some 8,500 to 9,000 people, or a density of approximately one person to every square mile.[26] The Indians lived according to a well-ordered and impressively complex system of government. They dwelled in secure villages, had substantial houses and extensive gardens, and had a notable assemblage of artifacts for utilitarian, religious, and decorative purposes.

The Indians won the grudging respect of the colonists for their ad-vanced technology, but the Europeans were contemptuous of their seeming-ly hopeless commitment to superstition, while their ceremonialism appeared

25. "Their manner of trading is for copper, beads, and such like; for which they giue such commodities as they haue, as skins, fowle, fish, flesh, and their country corne." *Ibid.*, 74, 369. Smith reported that Powhatan requested him to abandon the settlement among the Paspehegh and move to his own country: "Hee promised to giue me Corne, Venison, or what I wanted to feede vs: Hatchets and Copper wee should make him, and none should disturb vs." *Ibid.*, 20.

26. Mook, "Aboriginal Population," *Amer. Anthropologist,* 44 (1944), 201, 208.

to the whites a ridiculous presumption of dignity.[27]   A typical bias of communication between Europeans and Indians is seen in Smith's account of the Quiyoughcohannock chief who begged the settlers to pray to the Christian God for rain because their own deities had not fulfilled the Indians' requests.   Smith asserted that the Indians appealed to the whites because they believed the Europeans' God superior to their own, just as the Europeans' guns were superior to bows and arrows.   Yet Smith notes with some wonder that the Quiyoughcohannock chief, despite his cordiality and interest in the Christian deity, could not be prevailed upon to "forsake his false Gods."[28]   Actually this chief of one of the lesser tribes of the Confederacy illustrated the common logic of polytheistic people who often have no objection to adding foreign deities to their pantheon if it seems to assure more efficient control of the natural universe.   The chief was not interested in changing his religious customs in emulation of the Europeans; he merely wished to improve his own culture by judicious borrowing—a gun at one time, a supernatural being at another.

Nor would the chief have dared respond to a new religion in its entirety, even if such an unlikely idea had occurred to him.   The whole structure of tribal life relied upon controlling the mysterious aspects of the world by a traditional body of beliefs which required the use of religious functionaries, temples, idols, and rituals.   These were awesome arrangements and not to be treated lightly, although improvement by minor innovations might be permitted.[29]

The geopolitical sophistication of the Virginia tribes is reflected in the secular hierarchy of leadership which extended in orderly and expanding fashion from the villages, through the separate tribes, up to Powhatan as head of the entire Confederacy.   A gauge of the complexity of government is the fact that the Confederacy shared with the Europeans such niceties of civilization as capital punishment.[30]   In small societies having a precarious economy, indemnities in goods or services are usually preferred to taking the life of a culprit even in crimes as serious as murder.   However, where the life of the offender or one of his kinsmen is exacted for the

27. [Archer], "Relayton," Arber, ed., *Works of John Smith*, 1, provides a characteristic response of the colonists in his description of Opechancanough, who "so set his Countenance stryving to be stately, as to our seeming he became a fool."

28. Arber, ed., *Works of John Smith*, 79, 374.

29. For a general account of religion derived from the basic sources, see Charles C. Willoughby, "The Virginia Indians of the Seventeenth Century," *Amer. Anthropologist*, 9 (1907), 61-63.   The most complete single account in the early narratives based on firsthand observation is included in Henry Spelman, "Relation of Virginea," 1613, in Arber, ed., *Works of John Smith*, cv-cvi.

30. Arber, ed., *Works of John Smith*, 81-82, 377-78; Spelman, "Relation," *ibid.*, cxi.

life of the victim, punishment is the concern of the particular families involved; the rest of the group merely signifies approval of the process as a means of restoring social equilibrium after an offense is committed. Powhatan's government, however, was much closer to that of the English than it was to many of the tribes of North America. Punishment was meted out by a designated executioner for an offense against the society as the society was symbolized in the person of the leader.

Nevertheless, despite its elaborate civil structure, the Confederacy exhibited a universal rule of any society: a complex theory of government does not necessarily assure complete success in application. Powhatan not only had unruly subjects to deal with, but entire tribes in his domain could not be trusted. Relations between whites and Indians therefore were always uncertain, largely because of political developments within the Confederacy. When the colonists were supported by Powhatan, they were in mortal danger from those dissatisfied tribes of the Confederacy which had the foresight to realize that the English might one day assist Powhatan to enforce his authority. When Powhatan and his closest associates turned upon the settlers, the less dependable tribes became friendly to the whites.

In view of this morass of political allegiances, it is little wonder that early accounts of the settlers are replete with material which seems to prove the innate treachery of the Indians. Yet the militant phases of Indian activity, as illustrated by the initial attack on Jamestown and Powhatan's vengeance on the offending Chesapeake tribe, must be seen as part of a larger policy involving alternative methods of settling inter-group differences. Although the settlers knew that dissatisfaction among Powhatan's followers offered a means of preventing a coordinated Indian attack, they also discovered that established mechanisms of diplomacy existed among the Indians that could be employed for their benefit. For example, the Jamestown settlement was located in the territory of the Paspehegh tribe, and relations with this tribe frequently became strained. The Powhatan forces represented by the leaders of the Pamunkey, Arrohattoc, Youghtanund, and Mattaponi offered to act as intermediaries in negotiating peace with the Paspehegh and other hostile tribes or, if necessary, to join forces with the settlers in an armed assault on mutual enemies.[31]

If the Europeans found it difficult to live among the Indians, the Europeans seemed equally unpredictable to the Indians. Early in his relationship with the English, Powhatan was promised five hundred men and supplies for a march on the Monacan and Manahoac; but instead of finding wholehearted support among his allies for this campaign, Powhatan discovered that the whites were helpless to support themselves in the New

31. [Archer], "Relayton," *ibid.*, lv.

World. As time wore on and they became increasingly desperate for food, the Europeans were less careful in the difficult business of trying to distinguish friends from enemies. They extorted supplies promiscuously, driving hard bargains by the expedient of burning villages and canoes.[32]

It is problematical whether, as Smith implies, Powhatan was actually unable to destroy the handful of English because he could not organize his tribes for a full-scale offensive or whether he was biding his time in the hope of eventually establishing a clear-cut power structure in which the colonists would be allowed to survive but remain subservient to his designs in native warfare. At any rate, after two years of English occupation at Jamestown, Powhatan moved from his traditional home on the Pamunkey River some fifteen miles from the Europeans and settled in a more remote village upstream on the Chickahominy River. Violence flared periodically during these early years: colonists were frequently killed and often captured. Sometimes, being far from united in their allegiance, they fled to the Indian villages, where they were usually well treated. Captives and runaways were exchanged as hostages when one side or the other found it convenient. However, if Powhatan was willing to take advantage of dissident feeling among the whites, he was no fool and he finally put to death two colonists who seemed to be traitors to both sides at the same time. The execution was much to Smith's satisfaction, for it saved him from performing the task and assured a far more brutal punishment than he would have been able to inflict upon the renegades.[33]

Throughout the period from 1607 to 1609, the chronicles include a complexity of half-told tales involving alliances and enmities and mutual suspicions, of Indians living among settlers and settlers living among Indians. Although this interaction was of an individual nature, the two groups learned something of each other; yet each side maintained its own values and traditions as a social entity. The Indians were primarily concerned with obtaining new material goods. By theft, trade, and the occupation of European artisans in their villages, they increased their supply of armaments and metal work. With the use of Indian guides and informants, the settlers became familiar with the geography of the region, and they also learned the secrets of exploiting their new environment

32. See Mooney, "Powhatan Confederacy," *Amer. Anthropologist*, 9 (1907), 136-39, for an exhaustive review of instances illustrating the ever harsher measures taken by the colonists in coercing the Indians. In his indignation, Mooney scarcely notes that the Indians took measures of revenge by killing whites so that the process of hostilities increased over a period of time, with each side intent on settling some score with the other side.

33. Smith admitted that Powhatan's move to the village of Orapaks was simply to get away from the settlers. Arber, ed., *Works of John Smith*, 20, 70-71, 366-67; for the execution, see *ibid.*, 487.

through techniques of native gardening. For the most part, however, conscious efforts to bridge the cultural gap were unavailing. There was one amusing attempt to syncretize concepts of Indian and European monarchy and thereby bring about closer communication, when Powhatan was treated to an elaborate "coronation." The chief *weroance* was only made more vain by the ceremonies; he was by no means transformed into a loyal subject of the English sovereign, as the white settlers had intended.[34]

An increasing number of settlers arrived in Virginia and, with the help of Indians who by this time had ample reason to let the whites perish, managed to weather the hazards of the "starving time." As the whites became more firmly established, competition between Europeans and Indians took on the familiar form of a struggle for land. Armed clashes occurred frequently, but there were no organized hostilities, and the Indians continued to trade with the English. A peace which was formally established in 1614 and lasted until 1622 is often attributed to a refinement of Powhatan's sensibilities because of the marriage of Pocahontas and John Rolfe. Although Pocahontas was indeed the favorite child of Powhatan, it is likely that the chieftain's interest in her marriage was not entirely paternal. This strengthening of the social bond between Indians and Europeans helped solidify Powhatan's power and prestige among the confederated tribes, as he was thus enduringly allied with the whites.

Continuation of harmony between Indians and whites for a period of eight years was doubtless rendered possible because enough land still remained in Virginia for both settlers and Indians to live according to their accustomed habits. The seriousness of the loss of Indian land along the James River was lessened by the existence of a strip of virtually unoccupied territory just east of the fall line which ran the length of the Confederacy's holdings. If properly armed and not disturbed by internal dissensions and skirmishes with the English, the Powhatan tribes could afford to settle at the doorstep of their piedmont neighbors and even hope to expand into enemy territory. Hostilities require weapons, and peaceful trade with the English meant easier access to arms which the Confederacy could turn against the Monacan and Manahoac. It is also possible that by this time Powhatan realized the vast strength of the English across the sea and was persuaded to keep the settlers as friends. Knowledge of Europe would have been available to the chieftain through such Indians as Machumps, described by William Strachey as having spent "somtym in England" as

34. *Ibid.*, 124-25, 434-35. Smith's disgust was aroused by the coronation because it not only made Powhatan conceited, but it threatened to disrupt the trade in copper. Powhatan had been willing to exchange huge amounts of corn for a pittance, and Smith feared he would be spoiled by the rich coronation gifts.

well as moving "to and fro amongst us as he dares and as Powhatan gives him leave."[35]

Whatever were Powhatan's reasons for accepting the peace, it appears that he utilized the lull in hostilities to unify the Confederacy and deal with his traditional enemies. We have no direct evidence of activities against the piedmont tribes, for there is little historical data regarding the western area at this time. However, by the time the fur trade became important in the West the Monacan and Manahoac had lost the power which had once inspired fear among the tribes of the Confederacy. In view of Powhatan's years of scheming and the probable closer proximity of the Confederacy to the piedmont region after 1614, it may be conjectured that the Virginia chieftain and his people took some part in the downfall of the Monacan and Manahoac.[36]

When Powhatan died in 1618, his brother Opechancanough succeeded him as leader of the Confederacy.[37] Opechancanough continued to observe Powhatan's policy of peace for four years, although relations between Indians and Europeans were again degenerating. The Indians' natural resources were threatened as the increasing tobacco crops encroached on land where berries had grown in abundance and game had once been hunted. In the face of European advance, the Indians became restive and complained of the settlers' activities; but these signs went unnoticed by the colonists.[38] Opechancanough was aware that the real danger to the Confederacy arose from neither internal dissensions nor traditional Indian enemies but from the inexorable growth of European society in Virginia. He was apparently able to convince all the member tribes of this fact, if they had not already drawn their own conclusions. The subsequent up-

35. Strachey, *Historie of Travaile into Virginia*, 54.

36. Throughout the accounts of 1607-8 there are references to aiding Powhatan in dealing with the piedmont Siouans and Powhatan's satisfaction in the promises. Arber, ed., *Works of John Smith*, 20, 70-71, 366-67; [Archer], "Relayton," *ibid.*, xlvii. As relations between Powhatan and the settlers became strained, Powhatan discouraged the settlers from going to the Monacan, fearing that the whites might ally themselves with his enemies. Smith quotes Powhatan: "As for the *Monacans*, I can revenge my own injuries." *Ibid.*, 124, and see 482-83. For the subsequent decline of the Monacan, see the journal of Batt's expedition reprinted from the British Museum manuscript in Bushnell, "Discoveries Beyond the Appalachian Mountains in September, 1671," *Amer. Anthropologist*, 9 (1907), 46-53.

37. Arber, ed., *Works of John Smith*, 451; Robert Beverley, *The History and Present State of Virginia*, ed. by Louis B. Wright (Chapel Hill, 1947), 61.

38. Edward D. Neill, *History of the Virginia Company of London* (Albany, N. Y., 1869), 317-19, cites references which suggest that the Indians expressed excessive protestations of kindness and friendship in order to lull the settlers' suspicions in 1622. Shortly after Powhatan's death, however, fear of the Indians was so intense that Captain Spelman was harshly dealt with on the belief that he was engaged in inciting the Indians to hostile acts.

rising of 1622 was a well-planned shock to the English; it was alarming not so much for the destruction wrought, since by that time the Europeans could sustain the loss of several hundred people, but for the fact that the Confederacy could now operate as a unified fighting organization. This was a solidarity which Powhatan either had been unable or was disinclined to achieve.

Doubtless Opechancanough expected reprisals, but he was totally unprepared for the unprecedented and utter devastation of his lands and the wholesale slaughter of his people. The tribes were scattered, some far beyond the traditional boundaries of their lands, and several of the smaller groups simply ceased to exist as definable entities. Gradually as the fury of revenge died down, the remnants of the Confederacy regrouped and began to return to their homelands. However, the settlers were no longer complacent about their Indian neighbors. In addition to campaigning against the natives, they erected a string of fortifications between Chesiac and Jamestown, and they tended to settle Virginia in the south rather than toward the north and west.[39] In effect, therefore, Opechancanough accomplished a limited objective; a line was established between Indians and Europeans, but the line was only temporary and the Indians paid a terrible price.

Moreover, the cultural gap widened during the ensuing years. Following the period of reprisals the Indians were left to make a living and manage their affairs as best they could. Many old grievances seemed to be forgotten, and the natives gave the appearance of accepting their defeat for all time. Opechancanough, who had eluded capture immediately after the attack of 1622, remained at large, but the Europeans attempted to win tribes away from his influence rather than hunt him down at the risk of inflaming his followers. Finally, white settlement once more began to spread beyond the safety of concentrated colonial population. Tensions were re-created on the frontier, and there were minor skirmishes; the Indians complained to the English, but they also continued their trading activities. Thus matters continued for more than twenty years until large-scale hostilities again broke out.[40]

The uprising of 1644 was surprisingly effective. It is generally known that in both the 1622 and the 1644 uprisings the percentage of Indians killed in relation to the total Indian population was far greater than the percentage of settlers killed in relation to the total white population. Yet

39. Mook, "Aboriginal Population," *Amer. Anthropologist*, 44 (1944), 204-5, discusses shifts in Indian tribal populations as a response to European movements after 1622.

40. Edward D. Neill, *Virginia Calororum: The Colony under the Rule of Charles the First and Second, A.D. 1625–A.D. 1685* (Albany, N. Y., 1886), 60-61.

with far fewer Indians to do the fighting, Opechancanough managed to kill at least as many Europeans in the second attack as he had in the first.[41] The uprising is another proof that the Indians' method of adjusting to changes wrought by the Europeans continued to be an attempt to prevail over or remove the source of anxiety—the settlers—rather than to adapt themselves to the foreign culture. Certainly the Indians never felt that their difficulties would be resolved by assimilation among the whites, a solution which the colonists at times hoped to effect through the adoption of Indian children, intermarriage, and Indian servitude.[42]

Hopeless though the uprising appears in retrospect, it was entirely logical within Opechancanough's own cultural frame of reasoning. It is impossible to determine whether the Indians were aware of the futility of their action, nor do we know enough about the psychology of these people to ascribe to them such a grim fatalism that they would prefer a quick and honorable death to the indignities of living in subjection to the whites. But there is something impressive about Opechancanough, an old and enfeebled man, being carried on a litter to the scene of battle. Whatever the outcome his days were numbered. His young warriors, however, knew of the horrible reprisals of 1622 and they understood the cost of being defeated by the white man. Yet they too were willing to risk an all-out attack.

There is little doubt that Opechancanough realized the danger inherent in rebellion. He was a shrewd strategist and a respected leader. It is entirely possible that he hoped for assistance from forces outside the Confederacy. Tension had existed between the whites of Virginia and Maryland for a number of years, and in one instance the Virginians had hoped to incite the Confederacy against their neighbors. Maryland had been settled only ten years before the second uprising, and although hostile incidents between whites and Indians had occurred, her Indian policy had been more just and humane than Virginia's. If Opechancanough did expect military assistance from whites for his uprising against whites, he had historical precedent to inspire him. Powhatan had exploited factionalism among the Jamestown settlers, and it may be that the tension between Virginia and Maryland suggested an extension of his policy to Opechancanough. Whatever the motivations behind Opechancanough's design for rebellion, the second uprising attested to the strength of the old

41. Mooney, "Powhatan Confederacy," *Amer. Anthropologist*, 9 (1907), 138-39, discusses reductions in Indian population. Opechancanough's secrecy inspires wonder, but the success of the attack is indicative of the degree of separation that marked the lives of the colonists and the Indians by 1644.

42. Neill, *Virginia Calororum*, 74.

Confederacy and indicated clearly the stubborn resistance of the Indians to cultural annihilation.

Although the usual revenge followed the attack of 1644, Virginia's Indian policy was beginning to change. The Powhatan tribes were too seriously reduced in numbers to benefit greatly by the progress, but their treatment at the hands of the colonists following the uprising marked a new development in Indian-white relations, one which eventually culminated in the modern reservation system. In 1646 a formal treaty was signed with the Powhatan Confederacy establishing a line between Indian and white lands and promising the Indians certain rights and protection in their holdings. While their movements were to be strictly regulated, the natives were guaranteed recognition for redress of wrongs before the law. There were two particularly important features of the treaty. First, the Indians were to act as scouts and allies against the possibility of outside tribes' invading the colony; this policy was in contrast to the earlier device of attempting to win the friendship of peripheral tribes to enforce order among the local Indians.[43] Second, and consistent with the growing importance of the fur trade in colonial economics, the Indians were to pay a tribute each year in beaver skins. During the following years various legislative acts were adopted to protect the Indians in their rights and establish mutual responsibilities with the tribes.[44]

As the treaty of 1646 symbolized the establishment of new policies in dealing with the Indians, so did the circumstances surrounding Bacon's Rebellion afford a glimpse of other future developments. Within the tangled events of the Rebellion was an indication of the later effects of the frontier on many Indian groups. The Rebellion reflected the heretofore traditional rivalry between Indians and whites; its outcome marked the final defeat of the Virginia Indians and the complete demise of some tribes. But in the records of Bacon's Rebellion appears a new element which was to have continuing influence in Indian adjustment to Europeans. By 1675 Indian-white relations were no longer highly localized. The English began to appreciate the need for greater unity among their scattered colonies —the struggle of European countries to establish sovereignty over all of

43. As early as 1609, the instructions given Thomas Gates as acting governor of the colony indicate the initial policy decided upon: "If you make friendship with any of thiese nations as you must doe, choose to do it with those that are farthest from you & enemies unto those amongst whom you dwell for you shall have least occasion to have differences with them, and by that means a surer league of amity." The entire text of Gates's instructions as they related to the Indians is quoted in Bushnell, "Virginia From Early Records," *Amer. Anthropologist*, 9 (1907), 35.

44. See Wesley Frank Craven, *The Southern Colonies in the Seventeenth Century, 1607-1689* (Baton Rouge, La., 1949), 361-66, for a discussion of changes in Virginia's Indian policy.

North America had begun—and they recognized the value of the Indians as allies rather than opponents in the design of empire.

The turmoil of international rivalry delayed the movement of settlement inland, and the development of the fur trade also promoted isolation of the West. The fur traders strongly opposed pioneer settlement, in order to protect the natural habitat of the beaver—and incidentally the status quo of the Indians who engaged in the actual business of hunting and trapping the animals. Thus circumstances combined to give the Indians of the inland tribes a vital delay. From the beginning of contact, the western natives had an opportunity to meet the white man on equal terms, and they came to accept the presence of Europeans as a permanent and in many ways a desirable phenomenon. They developed policies of negotiation, diplomacy, and warfare, and distinguished one European group from another as ally or enemy as seemed most expedient to their own interests. This was in sharp contrast to the coastal situation, where hostilities represented a more clear-cut contest between Indians and whites for supremacy.[45]

The events of Bacon's Rebellion in Virginia contributed to the final ruin of both the tidelands and the piedmont tribes, but the complications of alliances of interest groups illustrate the changing situation of the frontier as it affected the Indians. Initially the Rebellion involved the border settlers of Virginia and Maryland, and the Susquehanna, Seneca, and "Doeg" Indians. The Susquehanna had enjoyed friendly relations with the French as early as 1615, but, living on the Susquehanna River, they were too far removed from French outposts to benefit by the association.[46] To the north were their traditional enemies, the Seneca, a member tribe of the powerful league of the Iroquois. The Seneca, however, appeared as a threat to the colonists of Maryland, and the settlers in that area therefore allied themselves with the Susquehanna and supplied the tribe with arms. Later Maryland, an English colony, arranged a pact of peace with the Seneca in accordance with the general alliance of the Iroquois league with the English at that time. The Susquehanna, nominally allied with the French, were left without arms or nearby allies and were thus forced

45. These facts, central to the theoretical propositions underlying the initial research in the present study, doubtless contributed to continuing adaptability of the more inland tribes. It is possible to see striking destruction of coastal or peripheral tribes along both the Atlantic and the Pacific oceans in North America, while the groups somewhat inland have been able to preserve a greater degree of cultural integrity. The Plains area, however, represents a third zone in the effects of the frontier on Indian cultures; the absence of white allies and of a social symbiosis between whites and Indians based on the fur trade explains in large part the rapid cultural disorganization when the tide turned against the Indians.

46. Brebner, *Explorers*, 144-49, discusses the "Andastes" Indians, but they are easily identified by internal evidence as the Susquehanna.

by the new alliance to retreat from their homeland. In the face of armed action they took up residence north of the Potomac among the Algonkian-speaking tribes, although they were themselves of Iroquoian linguistic affiliation. Shifts of tribal residence and inter-Indian campaigns involved Iroquoian tribes of the Carolina region as well as certain so-called Siouan groups such as the Tutelo and Occaneechi, who were enemies of the Seneca.

Meanwhile white settlement had penetrated west and north to the extent that skirmishes between whites and the Indians occurred. The memories of the uprisings of 1622 and 1644 had not died easily among the English, and when protection furnished by Governor Berkeley seemed inadequate, an unofficial campaign against the natives was initiated by the border settlers of the once competitive Virginia and Maryland. Although the causes of Bacon's Rebellion were also deeply rooted in internal disputes among the colonists, its results were catastrophic for the Virginia Indians. Bacon's followers showed no disposition to distinguish Indians as friends or enemies; they made indiscriminate war on all natives. After Bacon's forces had decimated the Susquehanna and Algonkians, they turned upon the Occaneechi, who had long been allied with the English as middlemen in the fur trade between the coastal settlements and the tribes located farther inland. The final action was against the Pamunkey, peacefully residing on lands secured to them by the treaty of 1646.[47] The Pamunkey king had been killed some ten years after the treaty of 1646 while serving with the colonists against a presumed invasion of the colony by a group of strange Indians known as Richeharians.[48] Thus his people were considered doubly wronged, for they were not only at peace with the colonists, but they had made common cause with the English against Indian enemies.[49]

47. See Wilcomb E. Washburn, *The Governor and the Rebel, A History of Bacon's Rebellion in Virginia* (Chapel Hill, 1957), for a recent analysis of Bacon's Rebellion which devotes special attention to the complications of the Indian problem. Washburn notes that there is no evidence that Bacon's followers killed any really hostile Indians; instead, they attacked tribes which were neutral in the border disputes or nominally friendly to the whites.

48. Mooney, "Powhatan Confederacy," *Amer. Anthropologist*, 9 (1907), 141, tentatively identifies the Richeharians as Cherokee. Although this view has been questioned by other scholars, there is no agreement on any alternative identification. The Richeharians defeated the attacking party of whites and allied Indians, and the incident is worthy of notice in regard to the later events of Bacon's Rebellion as a gauge of the insecurity felt by the border settlers as early as 1656. An investigation of the affair indicated that the Richeharians probably only wanted to trade but that hostilities began before the intentions of these strange Indians were determined.

49. [The Royal Commissioners], "A True Narrative of the Late Rebellion in Virginia," in Charles M. Andrews, ed., *Narratives of the Insurrections, 1675-1690* (New York, 1915), 123 and 127; [Thomas Mathew], "The Beginning, Progress and Conclusion of Bacon's Rebellion, 1675-1676," *ibid.*, 26.

Peace was finally affirmed officially with the Virginia tribes in a treaty signed in 1677. However, the effects of the Rebellion had been devastating, and after their long history of war and defeat, the Indians of the tidelands and piedmont regions found it increasingly difficult to preserve their accustomed habits of existence. This was equally true of the Susquehanna and Algonkian tribes north of the Potomac.

Nevertheless, several tribes of the Powhatan Confederacy are represented today by groups preserving a sense of social distinctiveness, based largely on historical and racial origins rather than any cultural characteristics. These tribes are the Pamunkey, Rappahannock, Mattaponi, Chickahominy, and Nansemond.[50] The story of their survival is uncertain in its details. Often it appeared that these tribes had been swept away by the rush of history, but each time after an interval the names reappeared on contemporary documents. For example, the signatory tribes of the Confederacy in the treaty of 1677 included the Pamunkey, Appomattoc, Weanoc, Nansemond, Nantaughtacund, and Portobacco—the last a collective term for the tribes of the Eastern Shore. Also signatory to the treaty were the Iroquoian-speaking tribes of the piedmont, the Nottaway and Meherrin, as well as Powhatan's old enemies, the Monacan. Undoubtedly the Pamunkey, the largest tribe of the Confederacy, had temporarily subsumed the unlisted Chickahominy, Mattaponi, and Rappahannock.[51]

In a similarly complex process of development, many of the piedmont tribes which were still extant in the latter seventeenth century regrouped permanently under different names. The Nottaway, Meherrin, and Monacan, for example, were signatory to the treaty of 1677, but only the Nottaway and Meherrin signed the Treaty of Albany in 1722. However, the Christanna were named in the 1722 treaty, and this group had come to include remnant Monacan and other piedmont tribes as well as recent migrants from the Algonkian, Iroquoian, and Siouan groups of North Carolina. Governor Spotswood of Virginia gathered these tribes together in 1715 and settled them at Fort Christanna near the Carolina border in southwestern Virginia.[52]

50. William H. Gilbert, "Surviving Indian Groups in the Eastern United States," in Smithsonian Institution, *Annual Reports of the Board of Regents* (Washington, D. C., 1948), 417-18.

51. Mooney, "Powhatan Confederacy," *Amer. Anthropologist*, 9 (1907), 141-47, traces the course of affiliations and residence of piedmont and tidelands Indians between 1677-1722 on the basis of the two treaties and intervening documents.

52. *Ibid.*, 144-52; see also J. C. Householder, "Virginia's Indian Neighbors in 1712," Indiana Academy of Science, *Proceedings*, 55 (1946), 23-25, for a discussion of Governor Spotswood's administration of Indian affairs.

The condition of the Indians toward the end of the seventeenth century is illustrated in many contemporary documents. A letter from the Reverend Mr. Clayton provides a detailed and well-organized summary.[53] It is worth special attention for its factual data and as an illustration that both whites and Indians continued to view each other from their own culture's frame of logic, without any real understanding. Describing the populational degeneration which had resulted largely from disease, deprivation, and malnutrition, the letter states:

This is very certain that the Indian inhabitants of Virginia are now very inconsiderable as to their numbers and seem insensibly to decay though they live under the English protection and have no violence offered them. They are undoubtedly no great breeders.

Clayton, like many white observers imbued with Christian concepts of proselytization, appeared surprised that one of the most striking retentions of native patterns was the cultural aspect of religion. He noted that special structures were still set aside for temples and that the shaman or *wichiost* enjoyed a degree of prestige which was secondary only to that accorded to their "King and to their great War-Captain." The retention of this prestige illustrates secular authority distinguished from the sacred sway of the *wichiost* and shows a continuity of concepts regarding social structure. The king remained the center of authority and continued to receive homage and tribute in the form of personal services performed by other members of the tribe. Apparently the ruling position was still hereditary within a line of descent recognized as that of the chief family. None of the records are clear on this point, for lines of chieftainship are confused in the documents by the indiscriminate use of such titles as "King" and "Queen." Hereditary leadership occasionally did devolve on women, and Archer noted such a case in 1607 when he described the Queen of Appomattoc, who held her rank by virtue of some now obscure genealogical reckoning. Leadership was inherited first by the surviving male siblings and then the female siblings, and evidently passed on to the next generation only with the death of all members of the preceding generation.[54] In later years the Queen of Pamunkey was so designated by the whites because her husband, the hereditary Pamunkey ruler, had been killed in 1656 while fighting for the British. The settlers paid his widow the

53. Bushnell, "Virginia From Early Records," *Amer. Anthropologist*, 9 (1907), 41-44, prints the entire text of the letter from the original in the records of the British Museum, "A Letter from the Rev. Mr. John Clayton, afterwards Dean of Kildare in Ireland, to Dr. Green in answer to several qurys sent to him . . . A.D. 1687. . . ." All references to the condition of the Indians in this period are from Clayton unless otherwise noted.

54. Arber, ed., *Works of John Smith*, 451.

honor of the title, but it is questionable whether she exercised any traditional authority within her own group, although she was their recognized representative in dealings with the colonists.

The role of the ordinary Indian woman generally receives little notice in acculturational descriptions by untrained observers, and the Clayton letter is no exception. A brief sentence notes gardening, cooking, pottery making, and the weaving of mats. The domestic phase of Indian life was easily overlooked although it changed less than other aspects. Actually, the domesticity of the whites and Indians differed only slightly. Kingdoms might rise and fall, but housekeeping, child care, cooking, and garment making had to be regularly performed in both cultures. Like many European observers, Clayton describes hunting, a principal occupation of the Indian male, as "Exercise." This error probably contributed to an early and persistent stereotype of the Indian: the industrious, overburdened woman, the slothful, pleasure-seeking man. Like all stereotypes, it is worthy of examination and it is an especially interesting example of adjustment to change. The traditional division of labor was approximately equal, the men hunting, the women gardening. These two activities supplied the principal subsistence. The English depended on the hunt in the early stages of settlement, but as soon as it ceased to have great economic importance they reverted to the European tradition of categorizing it as sport. The Indians also had their tradition: both men and women considered agriculture to be an unmanly task. When game diminished and gardening became the primary productive activity, they found it extremely difficult to make appropriate changes in the socioeconomic role of the male.

Clayton's references to the material culture of the Indians may be augmented from many sources, as this was the most easily discerned aspect of Indian life. The natives frequently observed traditional habits of dress. They continued to use indigenous material such as deerskin for clothing, but they prized European textiles, being especially fond of linen goods and a heavy woolen cloth, called a "matchcoat," which they often used instead of fur or feather mantles. Certain changes in style, if not modesty, may be noted in the matter of dress. When the Queen of Appomattoc greeted the Europeans in 1607, she wore only a skirt and a great amount of jewelry, but "all ells was naked";[55] but the Queen of Pamunkey was clad in Indian finery from neck to ankles for an occasion of state in 1677.[56]

55. [Archer], "Relayton," *ibid.*, 1.
56. [Mathew], "Bacon's Rebellion," Andrews, ed., *Narratives of the Insurrections, 1675-1690,* 25-26; [Royal Commissioners], "Late Rebellion," *ibid.,* 126-27.

Although the blue and white shell beads known as "wampum" probably originated as a currency through the trade with the New England tribes, they were manufactured in great quantities by Europeans for use in the fur trade and by 1687 figured as a quasi currency as far south as Virginia. The Indian shaman who also acted in the capacity of physician was paid by the natives in wampum as well as in skins and other commodities. When he treated English settlers, the *wichiost* usually received his remuneration in matchcoats or rum. Further details from Clayton's letter reveal that metal armaments, tools, and utensils were in common usage by the end of the century, although the bow and arrow and native pottery continued to be available.

From Clayton's observations and comparable data it is evident that Indian adjustment to European civilization in the late seventeenth century continued to take the form of resistance whenever there remained any possibility of retaining essential elements of the old culture. Specific items were accepted, as they fitted into existing patterns and represented elaboration or improvement of familiar features. In-group recognition of the danger posed for their traditional ways is illustrated in a fragment of folklore included in Clayton's account. There was supposedly an ancient prophecy, made long before the Europeans arrived, that "bearded men . . . should come and take away their country and that there should none of the original Indians be left within a certain number of years, I think it was an hundred and fifty." This rationalization of history is a recurrent myth found among many Indian groups. It helps to preserve a degree of dignity and pride by saying in effect, "We knew it all along, but we put up an admirable fight anyway."

The cultural disorganization noted in 1687 was to be a continuing process. The prophecy of destruction has now been fulfilled, to the extent that the Indians have ceased to exist as a culturally definable entity, although remnant groups maintain their social identities and tribal names. Throughout the seventeenth and eighteenth centuries the tribes which had temporarily resided with the Pamunkey wandered back to their original territories, leaving only the Pamunkey and part of the Mattaponi on lands secured to them by colonial treaties and guaranteed today by the state of Virginia. Traditional habits were generally abandoned as it became ever more difficult to exist in the white man's world. Eventually, the only effective economic system was that practiced by the surrounding Europeans; the Indians who were not located on reservations tended to settle in neighborhoods and acquire land on an individual basis. The destruction of the native social and religious mores, almost a predictable consequence of the disastrous wars and scattering of tribes, was virtually accomplished. A civil and religious structure which had been designed to accommodate the needs and activities of thirty tribes, almost nine thousand people, was impossibly cumbersome when the population had dwindled to one thousand people who were not in regular communication with one another and who were at any rate overwhelmingly occupied with the problem of sheer physical survival. The Indians in time found social and religious satisfaction in the traditions of their white neighbors; but they remained socially distinct from them.

Despite the loss of their own culture, many Indians remain aware of their historical origins. Beginning in 1908 with the Chickahominy, the various non-reservation natives of Virginia obtained official recognition as Indian tribes from the state government. In 1923 they formed an organization known as the "Powhatan Confederacy" and included the Nanticoke, recognized by Delaware as non-reservation Indians but otherwise not historically eligible for inclusion in the Confederacy. Showing Caucasoid and Negroid ancestry, the Nanticoke are the most racially heterogeneous of the modern confederated tribes, although a blending of racial characteristics may be seen to a lesser extent in the reservation Pamunkey and Mattaponi and the non-reservation Mattaponi, Rappahannock, Chickahominy, and Nansemond. In cultural terms the modern Virginia Indians retain little more of their heritage than tribal names and a sense of common origin.[57] The value of Indian identity has been increased by the social isolation of dark-skinned peoples in American life, since Indians in contrast to other racial minorities have generally enjoyed a degree of prestige in the opinion of the dominant group. In the tidewater region this may well be due to the influence of socially prominent Virginians who trace their ancestry to Pocahontas; she was, after all, a "Princess."

The end result of European contact in the piedmont region presents a somewhat different picture. Along the western border of Virginia and in the adjoining regions there are well-defined groups who claim Indian descent but no longer recall any particular tribal affiliations. They are known locally as Ramps, Melungeons, Brown People, Issues, and other terms. In order to avoid the social disabilities of classification with Negroes, they cling to their unofficial classification as Indians and remain rooted in regions where their peculiar status is known.[58] Some of these people may very well be descendants of the historic piedmont tribes of Virginia which vanished as identifiable tribal entities. Although much research remains to be done on this point, it is probable that their almost complete loss of

57. Gilbert, "Surviving Indian Groups," Smithsonian Institution, *Annual Reports of the Board of Regents*, 418-19.
58. *Ibid.*, 419.

identity, in contrast to the tidelands tribes, which at least recall their tribal origins, may be traced to the fact that they experienced disorganizing defeats at the hands of other Indians before the tidelands groups were ultimately conquered by the Europeans. The coastal Indians were in possession of European weapons at an earlier date and in all likelihood turned them against traditional enemies in the piedmont region before they found the need to use them primarily in forays against the white settlers. Thus the piedmont groups suffered a military disadvantage almost at the outset of European contact. By the time the whites penetrated to the piedmont region these tribes had already lost much of their former power. Furthermore, by the late seventeenth century they were also harassed by native enemies to the rear.[59] Unlike the tribes further inland, the piedmont peoples did not have time to regroup effectively and take advantage of the fur trade as a means of survival by adaptation to the presence of whites. Throughout the latter part of the seventeenth century they were in the path of westward movement by the whites, northward migrations of dispossessed Carolina tribes, and southern invasions by the Seneca on warlike campaigns. Their only hope for survival was in intertribal mixture and intermarriage with racially alien populations, both Negro and white.

Although the Virginia Indians were utterly defeated by the close of the seventeenth century, the experience of that period laid the foundations for modern adjustment to the white man's culture. As a result of stubborn opposition to amalgamation, some tribes have survived into the mid-twentieth century as populational entities, although they have been unable to retain a distinctive culture. Their primary technique of adjustment to European civilization, at least as documented in the Virginia tidelands region, was, with few exceptions, one of rigid resistance to alien ways which held no particular attractions, except for disparate items. Their culture simply disintegrated under the strain of continued pressure placed upon it. In contrast, the tribes further inland, by their more flexible adaptation to Europeans, achieved a social and cultural continuity which is still impressive despite many material innovations from European and American civilization.

59. Mooney, "Siouan Tribes of The East," Bureau of American Ethnology, Smithsonian Institution, *Bulletin* 22 (Washington, D. C., 1894), 28, notes that the Monacan were "directly in the path of the Richahecrian (Rickohockan, Cherokee)," who ostensibly invaded the Virginia area in 1656. Thus, Mooney suggested that the Monacan may have been victims of attacks by tribes to their west.

PART THREE

People and Society

I always consider the settlement of America with reverence and wonder.

JOHN ADAMS

IV.

SOCIAL ORIGINS OF SOME EARLY AMERICANS

Mildred Campbell

VASSAR COLLEGE

A STUDY OF American origins must eventually lead to the structure and functioning of many Old World societies, for the national fabric is woven of many threads. But the people who came first in their sturdy ships of fifty to a hundred tons, who kept coming throughout the seventeenth century until the small seaboard settlements had moved out of their first precarious existence to a more certain future—these have a special claim upon us. Indeed, one wonders whether individuals ever meant as much to any enterprise as did those who filled the emigrant ships in that first century of colonization. Emigration across the Atlantic has never ceased from their day to ours, but only then did actual survival depend on the arrival of a relatively few people.

It was also only in the first century that those who came were a fairly homogeneous group in terms of national origins. For despite the Dutch on the Hudson, and small groups of Swiss, Swedes, Finns, and French Huguenots pocketed along the coast, the small vessels which set out on the American voyage were chiefly English built and English manned. Their cargoes, moreover, consisted largely of Englishmen and, later and in smaller numbers, Englishwomen. Even the Scots and Irish, who in the next century would crowd the harbors of the New World, were a minority in the first century.

We have long been accumulating a vast amount of information about these early settlers, and able historians have exploited the material with skill and insight. Only in more recent years, however, have serious attempts been made to push the story further back. We now try to discover their social origins. We want to know more about what they brought with them; not their material possessions—the *Susan Constant* and her sister ships provided space for only the barest minimum of necessities—but that other luggage which every individual perforce carries about with him, his heritage. That heritage was the sum total of his own experiences and the environment in which he grew up; it had made him what he was and determined, to an extent, what he would become. The impact of the New World might, and we know often did, produce marked changes in a settler which, for good or ill, would affect his whole future. It could never entirely obliterate his past.

Let us admit at the outset that we shall never know the past of these first Americans, still English in their own eyes and in the eyes of others, as well as we should like to know it; nor shall we be able to answer half the questions about them that can be asked. An appallingly large number of them never lived to play their part in the enterprise to which they were so important. Thousands either died on the voyage or during the first year after their arrival. Most of those who came never kept personal records and no records were kept about them. Except for the concern of a ship captain or his agent that there be a profitable cargo for the outgoing voyage, their homeland in most cases took little note of their leaving. And the New World soon made it clear that their past mattered less than what they could do in the "needful" present. But the search is worth while if one can know even a little more about the lives of these people in their native England: the social strata from which they sprang, the fabric of life in their home communities, the reasons why the New World made its appeal—all matters about which we have thus far little concrete information.

The scene of the search is England under the Stuarts and in the Cromwellian interlude. Recent decades have taught us much about the entire social background of this period. Professors Trevelyan and Rowse paint the larger canvas in the bold strokes they use so effectively. Wallace Notestein perhaps comes nearer than anyone else to taking up residence among seventeenth-century Englishmen and learns from his close acquaintance both big and little things about them that are revealing. Others have dealt more narrowly with special segments of society, or have done what the English scholars do so well—shown what life was like in specific localities. The Tawney-Trevor Roper controversy over the gentry has also added light as well as heat. Such studies have enabled us to read a broadside addressed to "earls, lords, knights, gentlemen, and yeomen," with a better knowledge of what those terms mean. There remains, however, a multitude of shadings to vex us, especially in the lower groups and in the more mobile and intricate relationships of urban society.

In searching for the origins of American settlers we shall not be concerned equally with all of the social strata. Yet two basic aspects of seventeenth-century social philosophy which affected everyone must be kept in mind: first, the universal acceptance of the concept of social gradation and a complete belief in its rightness; and second, the belief, held simultaneously, that differences in rank, although normally to be observed, were not unalterable. One will not, of course, forget that the period of the Civil Wars produced a handful of Diggers on St. George's Hill who espoused a doctrine of communistic living, or that John Lilburne and his fellow-soldiers turned a part of the Cromwellian army into a debating society on political democracy. The issues of these debates would one day assume great importance; but they are probably remembered more for their later significance than because of any immediate effect they had on social structure. Degree, priority, and place, as Shakespeare described it, as the clergy taught and preached it, and as the people of all ranks lived it, was the accepted social philosophy of the day. "For that infinite wisdom of God which hath distinguished his angels by degrees . . . hath also ordained kings, dukes . . . and other degrees among men."[1]

The normal expectation of the members of every class was to see their children settled and married within their own social group. On the other hand, if a man came to a position of substance and outlook more in keeping with another class above or below him, he eventually moved into its ranks. This practice had long lent a freshness and toughness to the fiber of English society. Now in the fast changing and more competitive conditions of the Tudor and Stuart era, social fluidity was greater than it had ever been. Some deplored the current development in which "Joan is as good as My Lady," where "Citizen's wives have of late growne Gallants," and "the yeoman doth gentilize it."[2] But most people considered it a source of national strength that "in England the temple of honour is bolted against none."

It worked both ways though. A man could go down as well as up. Inflationary prices, a fluctuating land market, defective land titles, precarious investments, and bad debts created a milieu which gave some men

1. Walter Raleigh, *History of the World* (London, 1614), Preface. I have modernized the spelling. There are examples to be found in all kinds of writings. Perhaps the most explicit from Shakespeare is the famous speech of Ulysses in *Troilus and Cressida*, Act I, scene 3.

2. Sir William Vaughan, *The Golden Fleece* (London, 1626), Preface. See Sebastian Brant's *Ship of Fools*, Barclay edn. (Edinburgh, 1874), I, 187; and Thomas Wilson, "The State of England, 1600," *Camden Society Publications*, 3rd ser., 52 (1936), 19.

their opportunity and brought dismal failure to others. Every social cate-gory had its crop of new men.[3] Increased competition placed a higher premium on personal initiative than had been known in an earlier England. In emphasizing the manner in which pioneer colonial life developed indi-vidual initiative, it may be that we have not sufficiently recognized that much initiative was already present in the society from which the early settlers came, that indeed this may partially explain their coming.

In England tales of discovery and exploration had enlisted the interest and stretched the imagination of people of every class. But those at the top of the social hierarchy rarely were concerned with actual settlement. In terms of patronage and investment, however, many of them were active. Lord Baltimore had able friends among his own associates to aid in the Maryland enterprise; and no fewer than eight earls, one viscount, and a bishop helped to launch the Virginia Company under its second charter in 1609.[4] Interest in colonial schemes became a favorite hobby, more than a hobby in some cases, with noblemen at the court of Charles II. But in answer to the query, "Who would venture their persons and who their purses?" the noblemen usually answered in favor of the latter, and few members of the nobility actually emigrated with the intention of remaining in the colonies.[5]

Below the nobility came the knights and country gentry: "gentlemen of the blood," of ancient lineage. But with them also were newly landed men, office holders, members of the professions, university men, and many with business and mercantile interests—these too were known as "gentle-men." Dozens of such men became involved in colonial activities. Indeed, one wonders if seventeenth-century America would have advanced much beyond the trading-post stage had it not been for their money, vision, and perseverance. They were the men who instituted, to a great extent financed, and almost wholly ran the great companies under which the first colonies were started. The wealthier and more important, men like

3. Wallace Notestein says, "What saved the nobility was a new nobility always coming on." *The English People on the Eve of Colonization* (New York, 1954), 44. The same could be said for the gentry. I have found in Professor Notestein's recent book both reassurance for my own views and much new illustrative material, particularly on the nobility and professional men, with whom I have had less to do.

4. Professor C. M. Andrews says that "even in the eighteenth century, the hope still remained strong in the minds of titled men in England of financial profit from lands in the New World." *The Colonial Period of American History* (New Haven, Conn., 1934), II, 226.

5. The Lady Arbella and her sister, the Lady Susan, daughters of the Earl of Lincoln; George Percy, Duke of Northumberland's eighth son; and the West brothers, the sons of Lord De la Warr, are among the few members of the nobility who went to the colonies. Others went to hold governorships or other offices, but not with the intent of remaining.

Sir Ferdinand Gorges, Sir John Popham, Matthew Cradock, Sir Thomas Smith, carried on their work from England. But others came in person to lead the new plantations: younger sons of the financial backers, gentry of lesser pretensions, clergymen, and merchants. This was especially true in the earlier years, partly because leadership from below had not yet had time to develop, and partly because it seems to have been the original intent that the colonies should be led by individuals of the upper classes, a policy in keeping with the philosophy of the time.[6] It is also apparent that in the beginning such men had little idea that the demands made upon them by the New World would be so different from those to which they had been accustomed at home.

More is known about these leaders than about any of the other settlers and for obvious reasons. They were the articulate ones. They themselves wrote and kept records, though not perhaps as many records as we should like, and others wrote about them. They were the clergymen about whom Perry Miller, Alan Simpson, and a host of writers tell us, those who preached *Puritanism in Old and New England* and made frequent journeys back and forth. Among them are some of Louis Wright's *First Gentlemen of Virginia* and some of John Pomfret's proprietors of *The Province of West New Jersey*. They wander through the pages of Bernard Bailyn's *New England Merchants in the Seventeenth Century*.[7] In terms of social origins, less illustrious people also belong in this group: bankrupt businessmen; ill-starred younger sons and brothers of the gentry; proverbial ne'er-do-wells whose families hoped that a change of scene would set them on a better path, youths like Lady Finch's unruly son, "whom she sent to Virginia to be tamed."[8] Sometimes family hopes for reformation were realized. Often enough, however, parents had to face the fact that the voyage across the Atlantic was not sufficient to bring about the moral transformation desired. Despite this unpromising contingent, men of the rank of knight or gentleman (whether that rank came by birth or acquisition) played a role in colonial society out of proportion to their numbers. And the more we know about them, the better off we

6. See British Museum Mss. Add. 12,496, fol. 454; Public Record Office Mss., S.P. 30/24/48. See also the order of 1622 for the adding of new adventurers to those who had been original members of the Council of New England, "provided they be persons of honour or gentlemen of the blood, except Six Western merchants"; quoted in Frances Rose Troupe, *John White, the Patriarch of Dorchester* (Putnam, N.Y., 1931), 58.

7. See also William Sachse, *The Colonial American in Britain* (Madison, Wis., 1956), for those who moved back and forth. All of these books exemplify the transatlantic character of much of the current writing in the colonial field.

8. N. E. McClure, ed., *Letters of John Chamberlain* (Philadelphia, 1939), II, 502. Sometimes the emigration of entire groups was sponsored for the purpose of moral reform.

shall be. They are recognized by the title "Sir" if they were knights, or merely by "Mr.," a term not applied below the gentry. In many colonial narratives they are spoken of as "the better sort" and in lists of ships' passengers are usually identified as the "men of quality." Thus one ship carried "eighteen men of quality and eighty-seven others." Another speaks of "seven gentlemen and sixty-four others." And again, we read of "about a score of men of quality and a hundred and four others." One becomes familiar with the pattern.

But who were "the others"? Practically nothing is known about them, although the passenger lists make it perfectly clear that they account for the overwhelming numbers in the emigrant ships. "How to people His Majesty's dominions with people?" becomes a kind of recurrent refrain in the plantation literature of the seventeenth century. It was "the others" who chiefly furnished the answer to that query. Because there were so many of them and because our information about them is so woefully scant they have perhaps a special claim to attention. Who actually were they? Did they belong chiefly to the "middling people"—yeomen and artisans? Were they largely the poor agricultural laborers whose sorry plight in this period is well known? Or were they mostly riffraff from the streets of London and Bristol, the poor who had so increased under the Tudors as to demand state action; or beggars, and condemned persons who filled the prisons?[9] We know that all of these were represented among the early colonists. But beyond that we have had little concrete information about them, and slight knowledge of the relative degree with which the various groups responded to the appeals from the New World for settlers.

Two sets of seventeenth-century manuscripts merit attention for what they have to offer about the identity of "the others." They record the departure of slightly more than 11,000 emigrants from Bristol and London in the second half of the seventeenth century. The Bristol record, the more important of the two, contains the names of some 10,000 people who shipped from that port between 1654 and 1685. It provides a small amount of data for the entire group over the whole period; but the fuller part of the record, and that part which contains information pertinent to the subject of social origins, covers approximately the first 7 years and deals with upwards of 3,000 people. The London record includes approximately 750 men and women who left for the New World in the year 1683-84. Although a smaller sample, it contains the same type of information (including several additional items) as found in the Bristol

9. It was said in the next century in regard to Georgia's attempts to bring over a great many poor from London, "The Trustees found that many of the poor who had been useless in England were inclined to be useless likewise in Georgia." A. D. Candler, ed., *Colonial Records of Georgia* (Atlanta, 1905), III, 387.

record, thus providing comparative material from another area.[10]   The London and Bristol records list only a few of the many thousands of men and women who made their beginning in the New World as indentured servants before the American Revolution.   But they originated in a period for which data are scarce; hence, though neither record is statistically perfect, both deserve careful consideration.[11]

The first significant fact about both records is that they deal entirely with people who were coming to America as indentured servants.   This is perhaps fortunate; for studies made in the last two decades have demonstrated that a far larger percentage of our colonial population entered the country under indenture than was formerly thought.   One-half of the total is held to be a conservative estimate.[12]   On the question of their social origins, moreover, almost no concrete information is available.

The plan of indenture has been so fully treated by scholars that only a brief definition is required here.   Under the indenture terms, a prospective settler agreed to serve a master in one of the colonies for a period of years (usually four or five), in return for free passage across the Atlantic and certain "Freedom dues" when his term of service was over.   One aspect of indenture, however, has not been sufficiently considered: the fact that within the framework of English society, as it actually functioned in the

10. The Bristol registers are a part of the Corporation Mss. in the archives at the Council House in Bristol. A list of names and destinations, entitled *Bristol in America* (n.d.), edited by N. Dermot Harding, was published by the Corporation of Bristol shortly after the Mss. had been discovered. But it neither gave the status and occupational terms nor indicated that they were given in the originals. The London record is among the manuscripts at the Middlesex Guild Hall in London.

Neither of these records is unknown to scholars though both have turned up since the Andrews-Osgood days.   Particulars have been drawn from them by several scholars; but no full-length analysis has been made, and the key they provide for getting something more of the background of the emigrants, has not, I think, been recognized.

11. As early as 1636 there were printed indentures containing blank spaces to be filled in with name of servant, ship's master, ship, term of service, and the like. By 1682 they were made out in duplicate, one copy of which could be left in the hands of the justice of the peace who had signed the indenture, bearing witness to the fact that the servant was going of his own volition to the plantations; the servant took the other part with him. What I have here called the London record consists of the actual indentures, the part kept by the justice of the peace of Middlesex before whom the servants appeared. *The Genealogist Magazine* of London is beginning to print them piecemeal, a project to extend over several years. Since writing this essay, I have seen sixty-six additional indentures that were made out by the justices of peace in Middlesex in the same year as those of the London record. They appear to have been at one time a part of the same Middlesex collection. They are now in the Folger Shakespeare Library in Washington.

12. See Richard B. Morris, *Government and Labor in Early America* (New York, 1946), 315; and Abbot E. Smith, *Colonists in Bondage* (Chapel Hill, 1947), 34. These books give the most thorough treatment available of the way in which the servant traffic was carried on.

seventeenth century, such a practice would be considered not only natural but salutary. This is of great importance if we look at the New World from the point of view of the prospective emigrant still in England, or of the family of a young person contemplating settlement. The whole idea of service and services in return for land, training, protection—in short, for social and economic security—was an idea basic to medieval thinking and practice and one that had by no means disappeared. The practice of apprenticeship, for example, was not legalized and specifically defined until 1563, but it had been the general practice for generations.[13]

The same mental and social outlook that found positive values in the seven-year apprenticeship for young children would see social values in a four- or five-year indenture for a young man—and even more for a young woman—who was preparing to set out on a journey of three thousand miles in the hope of eventually establishing himself. Promotion literature advised young single men—particularly those with small means—to go into service for a few years and especially recommended indenture for young women. Some tales that came back across the water about the life of an indentured servant in the American colonies made it clear that it was often very different from the version presented in the promotion literature. But stories of those settlers who had been fortunate circulated in England as well; and the practice of indenture, which was based on the long-accepted principle of service, could weather reports of abuse and failure.

Historians have long been interested in the social status of the colonists who came under indenture; but throughout the first third of the twentieth century it remained a subject of the widest conjecture, despite the tremendous amount of excellent work done in the colonial field. Professor Andrews, who often deplored our lack of sufficient knowledge on the subject, said of the indentured servants in Virginia: "Some of them, perhaps many, seem to have been in origin above the level of menials, to have good family connections in England, and in a few instances to have been even of gentle birth."[14] Marcus Jernegan believed they came chiefly from the undesirables and the agricultural class who under conditions in England had no chance to better themselves.[15] In his *First Americans,* Professor

13. In her recent study of English apprenticeship, Margaret Gay Davies concludes that the statute defined a practice which was already "the rule rather than the exception in economic and social life" and that its enforcement presented no great problem except in times of economic crisis because "it had acquired positive values suited to the social structure of the period." *The Enforcement of English Apprenticeship* (Cambridge, Mass., 1956), 257.

14. *Colonial Period of American History,* I, 208.

15. *Laboring and Dependent Classes in Colonial America, 1607-1783* (Chicago, 1931), 46-47, 52.

Wertenbaker shared this view. The bulk of the indentured servants were, he said, "poor laborers who were no longer content to work in misery and rags in England while opportunity beckoned them across the Atlantic." Fifteen years later he had accepted what Abbot Smith, Richard Morris, and others were saying, namely, that "all kinds came."[16] An analysis of the Bristol and London records helps to define that phrase and to show in what proportions different social groups were represented.

It is a matter of considerable interest that approximately twenty-five percent of the Bristol group are women. We shall have something more to say of them later. Among the men, yeomen and husbandmen are in the majority; they account for about thirty-six percent, with the yeomen outnumbering the husbandmen. Artisans and tradesmen number approximately twenty-two percent; laborers account for about ten percent; gentlemen and professional men make up a little less than one percent.[17] Thus the farmers outnumber the skilled workers almost two to one, and the combined farmers and skilled workers outnumber the laborers more than five to one.

In the smaller London sampling, the women are somewhat under the twenty-five percent of the Bristol records. The skilled workers outnumber the yeomen and husbandmen in almost the reverse proportion to the Bristol record: approximately two to one. This difference is, of course, to be expected in the records of an urban center. The husbandmen are also more numerous than the yeomen. But as in the case of the Bristol servants, the number of farmers and skilled workers in comparison with the laborers is in a ratio of about five to one.

A question may be raised concerning the authenticity of the status terms. Would not an ordinary laborer, knowing that masons, bricklayers, and carpenters were in great demand in the colonies at high wages, possibly try to assume a skill for which he had no training? Some may have tried

16. Thomas J. Wertenbaker, *The First Americans* (New York, 1927), 25, 63. Professor Wertenbaker revised his view in *The Old South* (New York, 1942), 223.

17. The status and occupational terms are not given for 31 percent of the Bristol group. If these omissions were scattered pretty well throughout, one might feel more concern about them. But for a term of years no data appear on this particular point; then it is given in full again. I was puzzled by this omission until I found in the London indentures the same block omission with the reason for it clearly apparent. Some of the printed forms that were used contained no blanks for the servant's status or occupation; hence the gaps. It is more than likely that this same thing accounts for the block gaps in the Bristol record. If so, there is every reason for taking that part of the record that is given as a fair sample for all of it. Shortly after 1662 in the Bristol record, all of the data given in the earlier years, except the name, destination, and term of years, are dropped. The record therefore is not only fuller in the early years, but often gives individual bits of information about particular servants.

this deception, and it is possible that the number of artisans should be slightly lowered to take care of self-styled craftsmen. But two factors weigh in favor of the general validity of the terms. First, the number and variety of the skills listed in the records suggest accuracy: there are ninety-eight trades, many of which, such as the tuckers, fullers, and button makers, were not those most sought after by the colonial agents. Secondly, men in the seventeenth century were still accustomed to being recorded in terms of their status or occupation. They were so listed in court records, wills, deeds, leases, and business transactions of all kinds. It would have seemed natural and prudent to give the same information for this record as for all others. Hence, allowing for a certain margin of error and even some false reporting, the evidence still points to a large majority of farmers and tradesmen over laborers.

The relatively low number of laborers was at first puzzling. According to writers of the period, the laborers' status was the lowest in the social hierarchy. They were the most numerous and poorest members of England's working population. Although their wages rose slightly during the first half of the century, they tended to remain constant, even in some places to drop a little, from then until the end of the century.[18] Those who worked by the year for an annual wage ranging from three to five pounds were perhaps the most fortunate. They had a roof over their heads and something to eat. We think it a hardship that the medieval serf could not escape the land, but neither, it may be well to remember, could the land get away from him. His life was meager, often harsh, but economically it was more secure than that of his successor, the landless laborer.

In the comments of some of their contemporaries may lie a partial explanation of the laborers' lack of enthusiasm for emigration. Thomas Ludwell, a Somerset man, received a request for servants from his brother in Virginia. He answered that there were workmen in his neighborhood to spare, but "they will live meanly and send their families to the parish to be relieved rather than hear of such a long journey to mend their condition."[19] Robert Southwell, who had had poor luck in his attempt to recruit laborers in 1669, said of them: "They are loth to leave the smoke

18. When the Somerset wage schedule was revised in 1666, 1673, and 1676, the wages dropped slightly. It is difficult to be as exact as one would wish about the general wage situation; wage schedules were fixed by the justices of the peace for each county and differed from county to county. Sample schedules can be found for workers by the year, for Dorset, Essex, Hertford, Rutland, Suffolk, and the East Riding of Yorkshire. For day and piece workers, there are sample schedules for Dorset, Essex, Suffolk, and Wiltshire in their respective county archives, except the ones for Suffolk, which are in the Cambridge University Mss. Add. XXII, 76.

19. *Wm. and Mary College Qtly.*, 1st ser., 3 (1894), 198.

of their own cabin if they can but beg neere it."[20]   There are other comments in the same vein.   The laborers were accustomed to little; they could do with little.   In times of dearth they would be hungry; but they had rarely had full stomachs, and while they might come close to starvation, the parish would not let them die.   In addition, they were a superstitious lot and quite possibly would have been frightened by the tales about the dangers of the long voyage over strange waters.

If the London and Bristol records can be taken as a fair sample (and they are in accord with other recent studies), it is clearly a mistaken assumption to think that the laborers formed the large part of those who came to America as indentured servants.[21]   The majority were farmers and skilled workers.

Most of the women in the list were not classified according to status except as "singlewoman" or "spinster," the latter term being used at this period to describe either a married or an unmarried woman.   A number of "widows" were listed, and a few women were classified according to the skill or occupation which they hoped to have in the homes of their new masters—"dairy maid," "lady's maid," and the like.   Young women often went in twos and threes from the same village, and now and then the lists show members of the same family.   It is quite possible that a larger percentage of women than men came from among the laborers.   Country folk had their own measuring rods in terms of social codes and behavior patterns; a yeoman or tradesman of some standing would feel more reluctant to see his daughter set off on such a journey than would a laborer. Yeomen and husbandmen worked alongside farm laborers getting in the crops and mingled with them in the village alehouse.   Yet it was not considered the proper thing for the daughters of yeomen to work in the fields, although the wives and daughters of laborers did so as a matter of course.   Daughters of yeomen and tradesmen, however, often went into the service of families in their neighborhoods, and in certain industries such as lacemaking, girls were apprenticed in the usual way.

There are women listed in both these records who were going in answer to personal requests from planters in Maryland and Virginia for servants of various skills.   Charles Peck of London was sending one to his brother Tom in Virginia at the latter's request.   She was to serve in his own home,

20. Shaftsbury Papers, Section IX, no. 14, in W. N. Sainsbury *et al.*, eds., *Calendar of State Papers, Colonial Series, America and West Indies, 1669-1674* (London, 1889), 40.

21. Analyses that I have made of other servant groups in the eighteenth century show a remarkably similar ratio between laborers and farmers and skilled workers. One of these has been published: "English Emigration on the Eve of the American Revolution," *Amer. Hist. Rev.*, 51 (1955), 1-20.

and "not be soulde unless to some planter for a wife."[22] It was commonly accepted that a husband was the chief inducement the New World had to offer a young girl. Nor would she have much trouble getting one, although the match was not always with the wealthy planter that the promotion literature promised. It is interesting that promoters were becoming a bit more discriminating in their advice respecting the women who were wanted. They were somewhat on the defensive about the women who had been sent over from the houses of correction: "But if they come of honest stock, and have good repute they may pick their husbands out of the better sort of people."[23] Three months, one of them thought, was as long as one could hope to keep a good maid before "some proper young fellow" would come after her.

Servants sought as wives were purchased either in pounds sterling or tobacco. This businesslike way of approaching marriage strikes a wrong note in our generation. But it would have seemed quite normal to the seventeenth century, where every girl (except those of the very lowest groups, who were not too particular about such things) was accustomed to a marriage that was largely a business arrangement. Women who went to the colonies, however, may not always have accepted husbands immediately, even if they were not under indenture; there was plenty of work at good pay for them until such time as they did marry. Later in the century when many servants were going to Pennsylvania, Gabriel Thomas lamented about the exorbitant wages women could command: "They are not as yet very numerous which makes them stand on high terms for their several services." He added, however, "They are usually marry'd before they are twenty years of age."[24]

Practically all of the servants were young. Indeed, it is clear that the whole plan for indentured service was designed for the young unmarried man and woman. It is easier for the young to be uprooted, and a newfound land across the sea would beckon to twenty-one as it would not to fifty. The Bristol record does not give ages, but they are given in the London group. The majority were between the ages of eighteen and twenty-four, with twenty-one and twenty-two predominating—just the age when the young tradesmen were finishing their apprenticeship.[25] The

22. *Tyler's Qtly. Mag.*, 1 (1919), 271.

23. William Bullock, *Virginia Impartially Examined* . . . (London, 1649), 54. Practically all of the promotion literature has something to say on this subject.

24. Gabriel Thomas, *An Account of Pennsylvania and West New Jersey* (Cleveland, 1903), 45-46. It is only fair to say that conditions from the first were very favorable in Pennsylvania.

25. There is supporting evidence from the American records to confirm the youthfulness of the group as a whole. See Wesley Frank Craven, *The Southern Colonies in the Seventeenth Century* (Baton Rouge, La., 1949), 305n, and Morris, *Government and Labor in Early America*, 390 ff.

large number of farmers and skilled workers going under indenture demonstrates the appeal which this method of emigration made to single young men of small means and even to those whose parents could perhaps have managed the passage money.

A young man just out of his apprenticeship would not, if he remained in England, set up for himself at once. Likewise, a yeoman's son, unless he were the eldest or his father were able to buy land for him, would work at home or for a neighboring yeoman or gentleman through his earlier years while he accumulated piecemeal holdings of his own. English yeomen were a canny lot. Perhaps farmers everywhere are. To be able to get to America without any expense to himself or his family would appeal to a lad brought up as these had been. Besides if a young man went to America alone without enough money to buy labor, reputed to be both high and scarce, what could he do with the fifty or a hundred acres of land that he hoped to get? Nobody knew better than a farmer's son that it took more than one pair of hands to get crops in the ground and to harvest them. These were some of the facts that would have been in the minds of the yeomen and husbandmen, carpenters, tilemakers, and weavers whose names are enrolled in the Bristol and London lists.

A few married men went without their wives, leaving them sometimes provided for, sometimes not.[26] And there were a few married couples going together, but not many, for this practice was discouraged because of complications likely to arise on the other side. Finally in 1682 an order prohibiting a married man from going as an indentured servant went into effect. But it is doubtful if recruiting agents looked into the matter too closely. There are examples in other records of groups of married people who paid their own passage, but were apparently somewhat older and better established. They took along with them single young men and women under indenture—their neighbors, friends, and kinspeople. They would thereby get the "headright" lands for having brought them over, and the young people coming as servants were with friends and kinsfolk during their early years in a strange country.[27] Hundreds who were not so fortunate left it to chance to place them in the hands of a good master or a poor one when the ship docked.

It is significant that the married people referred to above who took their families and paid their own passage were for the most part farmers and tradesmen of the same social rank as the servants they took with them.

26. See Petition of Mayor of Bristol in 1662 concerning desertions, Bristol Corporation Mss. A few cases of a whole family's going appear in the Bristol record, but they are rare.

27. See the interesting group of some five hundred people who came to Pennsylvania between 1683 and 1687. *Penn. Mag. of Hist. and Biog.*, 8 (1884), 328-40.

This was, I believe, generally the case. For one of the gratifying by-products of the information concerning status that comes from these records is that through them we are also able indirectly to determine the status of the remainder of "the others" who filled the emigrant ships. If the laborers at the bottom of the economic scale account for a relatively small number of those coming under indenture, it is certain that they were not widely represented among those who paid their own passage. The reluctance of the laborers to go as servants has already been shown. If one adds to that the crucial fact that they simply would not have had the five or six pounds required to pay their own passage, it is clear that there would be few of them in that group. Individuals or small groups sometimes came over in the personal service of men of better substance, but this would not account for many. If, therefore, the laborers at the bottom of the social and economic hierarchy were a minority, as were also the "men of quality" at the other extreme, we can but conclude that "the others," both those who came under indenture and those who paid their own fare, were drawn from the middling classes: farmers and skilled workers, the productive groups in England's working population. The difference between those who came as servants and those who paid their own fare was partly economic, with the poorer farmers and "decayed" tradesmen coming under indenture; and partly, as we have seen, it was a matter of age, experience, and marital position.[28]

Status is basic to the quest for social origins. But before attempting further to spell out its meaning in terms of actual living conditions, we must pay our respects to one other relatively small group among the Bristol servants, the children. The term of service set down in the indenture provides the key for determining their numbers. The vast majority of adult terms are for four or five years, the four-year term slightly predominating, although now and then a servant went for two or three years, or more rarely, even for one. Children, however, were sent for longer terms in order that they should reach adulthood by the time their service was over. Their average term was seven years, as was that of the ordinary apprentice in England; but in both cases it might be as high as ten or twelve years, depending on the child's age.

About eight percent of the Bristol group went for a term of six years or more, chiefly seven. But seven years or longer is also the term assigned to those recalcitrants whom the justices of the peace sent to the colonies for the punishment of minor crimes. How can we know that the emi-

28. In the emigrant list of those who left on the eve of the American Revolution, where free colonists and servants are both included, there is relatively little difference in rank or status between the two groups.

grants with terms of seven years or more were not these delinquents rather than minors? It is likely that some of them were, for delinquents of this type were sent along with other servants and we know of some who were in this group. Fortunately, the London indentures containing the actual ages for everyone are of assistance in this problem. For they show that almost all of the indentures for long terms (about six percent in this record) apply to children under fifteen. Only occasionally is an older person given a longer term. An examination of Quarter Sessions court records, where instances of forced emigration for minor crimes were documented, offers supporting evidence during the years in question that this type of punishment was apparently used sparingly by the county officials.[29] Hence, unless there was a larger percentage of delinquents in the Bristol group than among those going from London, which hardly seems likely, we may assume that the majority of Bristol's eight percent assigned to long terms were also minors.

Not infrequently, of course, some of the individuals deported for misdemeanors were likewise minors; often the children who went as servants were orphans or problem children whom someone wished to dispose of. We glimpse them now and again in the records. John Morgan, a Bristol upholsterer, appeared in July, 1659, with an uncancelled indenture that had been made out for David Thomas, a Glamorgan boy who was bound to him. He should have been registered earlier: "But in regard he was on shipboard, and could not be brought up for fear of his running away, he was not enrolled in the middle of the book." A fourteen-year-old girl in London was taken out of White Chapel jail to which she had been committed for "pilfering lace" and with the consent of her father and mother was indentured for service in America. A stray letter among the London indentures tells the story of Robert Redman. An uncle in Cambridge had sent him up to London to be put aboard *The Hopewell*. He writes that in the boy's trunk "is his best and worst cloathes, an extra shirt, 2 pr. stockins, 6 neck cloathes, 6 handkerchers, 2 caps, 1 hatt, 1 pr. shoes." Instructions are given that anything else needful is to be provided. "If 9 years or tenn yeares service be required," the uncle writes, "I am contented provided he have his bellefull of food, with cloathes to keep him warm and warm lodgin at night." He asks to be told when the boy is "disposed of" and to whom and "how to rit a letter to his master and to him." It is apparent that things have not gone well. Young Redman is not to be given the keys to his trunk for fear he will either sell or give away his belongings. "I could keep him no longer," the uncle says; yet he hopes he will have a good voyage, and has sent along "Balsome and

29. The justice of the peace did not deal with serious criminals.

salve" for the ship's surgeon to use in treating an injury on the boy's leg. After a somewhat formal ending according to the fashion of the day, a postscript adds that "Thers a Rage to dress his wounded leg with."[30]

Aside from the delinquents, both minor and adult, sent by the justices, two groups of indentured servants entered into their contracts under compulsion: convicts and, during both the Commonwealth and Restoration period, political prisoners. Neither group will be considered here; for with the few possible exceptions which have been considered among those holding long terms, it seems clear that these records deal with the ordinary men and women who went to America under indenture of their own volition.[31] Therefore, we turn again to the two basic records for additional clues which will make possible at least a fragmentary reconstruction of the environment they were leaving behind them.

Next in importance to the status term is that part of the record which gives the emigrant's place of origin; for without this information, it would be impossible to enlarge our understanding of the American settler's background. Both records show how widely the New World ventures were known in England. The Bristol names include representatives from every English county except Rutland, and many from Wales. An overwhelming majority are from the West, with Somerset, Gloucestershire, and Wiltshire taking the lead among the English counties and Monmouthshire first among the Welsh. Proximity to Bristol undoubtedly accounts partly for this concentration; but it is significant that some western counties are much more sparsely represented. Outside the heavy concentration in London

30. This letter is dated from Cambridge, July 8, 1684.

31. The term of years called for in the indentures is the best evidence. Several women in the London record appear to have been freed from the house of correction to emigrate. But the percentage of long terms in both records is very small; and where the matter can be confirmed in the London record with the actual ages, it is clear that the majority of the long-term emigrants are minors. Moreover, the whole point of the Bristol registration was to prevent anyone's being taken abroad as a servant who did not go of his own volition. The convicts, except those guilty of minor misdemeanors, who were handled at the Quarter Sessions courts, were tried at the Assizes and handed over to the sheriff. The convict lists are usually so designated. In later years the prisoners were sent under special contract with merchants, who were compelled to give strict account for delivery to their destinations. All of the more recent studies account for larger numbers of convicts coming than was once thought to have been the case and smaller numbers of political prisoners. Abbot E. Smith gives a definitive account of convict emigrants although he rather neglected the ordinary men and women. See his *Colonists in Bondage*, Chaps. V-IX. See also Morris, *Government and Labor in Early America*, 323-47. Older but useful still is James D. Butler, "British Convicts Shipped to the American Colonies," *Amer. Hist. Rev.*, 2 (1896), 12-83. Also see Ian C. C. Graham, *Colonists from Scotland: Emigrants to North America, 1707-1783* (Ithaca, N. Y., 1956), on political prisoners.

and Middlesex, Yorkshire furnished the largest number to the London group.

The place of origin carries significance beyond the servant group; for if large numbers of servants were coming from certain centers, it is almost certain that there were also large numbers from these same centers who paid their own passage. The largest number of servants recorded in the Bristol group, slightly more than half, booked for Virginia. One is therefore not surprised to come upon the following passage from James Southall's sketch of a Virginia family, in which he discusses the section in England that was the source of so many of Virginia's early settlers. He describes an area

about thirty miles north of Bristol in the west of England, running due north and south for a distance of about ten miles and with an average breadth of three miles, where a . . . ridge of the Malvern Hills divides the county of Hereford from the county of Worcester and on the southeast of these, on the south bank of the upper Severn, with yet ampler dimensions stretches the county of Gloucester, all three counties touching each other at a common point near the city of Gloucester.

It was in this district, the author says,

and from Somersetshire, and the neighboring counties of Wales . . . from Warwick on the north, Devon in the southwest, Herts and the Isle of Wight in the south, and across the Bristol Channel from the coast of Ireland, that in Virginia, the counties of Henrico, James City, Charles City, Isle of Wight, Gloucester, Surrey, and Prince George were largely settled.[32]

Except for including Ireland and the Isle of Wight, he has described almost exactly the area chiefly represented by the Bristol record. Along with East Anglia, and Lincolnshire and Yorkshire in the north, the West Country was the homeland of thousands of the early settlers. From the beginning there was in the West a strong tradition for the American adventure. The New World would not seem so far away to West Country boys, many of whose fathers and brothers earned their living as mariners and seamen on ships that plied between Plymouth, Bristol, and lesser ports to the New World. They were not, said a contemporary, of "the In-land sort," who were "wedded to their native soils like a Snaile to his shell, or . . . a mouse to his chest."[33] Their grandfathers would have sailed or known people who sailed with Drake and Raleigh—and grandfathers are

32. "The Cocke Family," *Va. Mag. of Hist. and Biog.*, 3 (1896), 285-86. The founder of this family was one of the West Country gentry who came over in the first half of the century.

33. Richard Eburne, *A Plaine Path-way to Plantations* (London, 1624), 59.

all alike. It was natural that Hugh Peter, telling the House of Lords in 1665 about his departure to New England, should say that he "by birth in Cornwall was not altogether ignorant of that place." It is then to the West Country that we must turn. For here lay the farm lands and villages from which almost eighty-five percent of the Bristol emigrants came.

Three centuries have inevitably changed the West Country. The most conspicuous difference is the growth of modern urban centers; yet there has been less change than in some parts of England, and one can drive through miles of rural Gloucestershire, Wiltshire, and Somerset, where the country must look much the same as it did three centuries and a half ago when many of its humbler people were preparing to leave. There are evidences now of more intensive agriculture, but the contours of hills and green sloping meadows remain the same. It is a good land to look upon. So also they must have thought who were departing from it. For it is a great mistake to assume that emigration, for whatever purpose, meant that people left home and familiar surroundings with no regrets. Even the most rabid of the New England Puritan clergy, full of spleen and invective, frequently expressed devotion to old England and the "mistaken ones" who stayed behind.[34] These folk who left the West Country were not very articulate; they could not have said what they felt as did a later West Country man:

> 'Tis time, I think, by Wenlock town
> The golden broom should blow.

But chance words and phrases that appear in prosaic colonial records betray the same nostalgia. It was probably sheer homesickness that overcame the boy from a Gloucestershire village who went to Bristol with a friend intent on shipping to Virginia—he let the other boy go on without him, the record says, and "came back home."

The houses they lived in, especially the homes of the lesser folk, were made of whatever natural building materials the locality afforded. Some of the small stone houses that can be seen today in Cotswold villages were there then, some newly built, some already old—all evidence of the prosperity that Cotswold wool had brought to the locality. Beyond the Cotswolds to the west in the Severn Valley, a redder sandstone furnished excellent building material, but it was hard to quarry and in general was reserved for churches and the houses of great men. Farmers and trades-

34. Even Winthrop, wrapped up though he was in the cause he led, was not sure that he wanted his son to settle in New England. See also examples in B. M. Sloane Mss. 922, 106, and Nathaniel Ward, *The Simple Cobler of Aggawam in America* (London, 1647), 25.

men built their houses mostly of a combination of wood and some kind of plaster spread often over a wattle framework. "Cob," as it was called, used largely in Devon farmhouses, was a mixture of mud, straw, gravel, and chalk. These houses were small, varying from the two to three rooms of the less well-to-do to as many as eight or nine in the houses of wealthy yeomen, small clothiers, and tradespeople of some substance.[35] The homes of the laborers have not survived; they were probably little more than hovels and, except for some very newly built, were almost certainly without much light. John Aubrey, himself a West Country man, wrote of Wiltshire in 1671 and remarked that within his remembrance the use of glass had been restricted: "Copyholders and ordinary poor people had none."[36] The inventories attached to wills supply details of the interiors of these crude homes. Trestled furniture was still being used, although sometimes "joined" tables are mentioned. Pewter dishes were by now a commonplace in the cupboards of the middling people, but wooden trenchers were still in everyday use. Occasionally there were a few prized silver teaspoons. Their standards of both comfort and cleanliness would, of course, be scorned by people of like position in modern society.[37]

It is understandable that promoters found these middling people of the West Country satisfactory settlers and made special efforts to induce them to go to the colonies. It was not merely their skills that were wanted. They had other qualities born of the kind of lives they had lived that would stand them in good stead. They were not, it is true, accustomed to the peculiar type of pioneer hardship that prevailed in America, but their lives in England had known little comfort or ease. The craftsmen were accustomed to working from five in the morning until seven or eight at night. Farmers labored outside from daylight until dark and carried on indoor tasks by fire and candlelight. A man could not be idle and hold his own in the demanding world in which they lived. Idlers there were, of course, but lower and middle class families did not have the means to care for loafers.

35. Arthur Broadbent and Anthony Monoprio, *Minor Domestic Architecture in Gloucestershire* (Gloucester, 1931); "Richard Symonds' Diary of the Marches of the Royal Army During the Great Civil War, 1644," *Camden Society Publications*, 74 (1889), 151 ff. Miscellaneous information on these points crops up here and there in wills, deeds, inventories, and the like. Some West Country farmers and tradesmen were sufficiently prosperous to have their wills proved in the Prerogative Court of Canterbury; these are now at Somerset House in London. But the early wills of the common folk are usually still in the local probate registries of their respective county towns. There are also some in diocesan directories.

36. John Aubrey, *Natural History of Wiltshire* (London, 1847), 14.

37. See the quotation from Baxter in Notestein, *The English People on the Eve of Colonization*, 78.

Men of the West Country like those elsewhere were forced to adapt themselves to the competitive and acquisitive society common to their age. Those with a greater margin of wealth could weather the crises better. Because of their fairly simple standard of living and the fact that they were practically self-supporting, the farmers were less affected by the high prices of outside products than almost any other group. Despite market fluctuations, they could usually sell their sheep and grain at a very good profit.

Wealthy yeomen of the West Country not only had glass and chimneys in their houses, but were now installing wainscoting in their "halls" and "parlours." The members of this class were aggressive, and if they held their land in a good tenure—that is, if it were freehold or of that particular kind of copyhold which carried similar security—they were most probably affluent. But circumstances which brought success to many meant failure for others. Land hunger was rife among all classes. Wealthy clothiers, drapers, and merchants who had done well and wished to set themselves up in land were avidly watching the market, ready to pay almost any price for what was offered. Even prosperous yeomen often could not get the land they desired for their younger sons; and indeed those who did not hold their own land in a good tenure ran the risk of losing it.

The West Country was good farming country, especially for sheep raising. Somerset in particular also had excellent land for tillage, and its farmers were noted for their skill. Yet even if the title to his land were clear, a West Country farmer could fare badly compared with farmers in some sections of England. For the West was a conservative part of the country. Change came slowly there, and only a beginning had been made with inclosures. More than a century later George Turner, writing of farming conditions in the vale of Gloucestershire, could still say: "I know one acre which is divided into eight lands, and spread over a large common field, so that a man must travel two or three miles to visit it all. . . . But this is not the worst. . . ." And he continued to recite the woes that West Country farmers were still enduring.[38]

A great deal of the land was still copyhold, and large landholders kept the village economy almost on a feudal basis. The farmers from Tetbury, Chipping Sodbury, and other Gloucestershire villages were still performing services that had long since been discarded in many parts of England.[39]

38. "Gloucestershire," in *Reports to the Board of Agriculture* (London, 1794), 39, 49.

39. Conditions were much the same on the manors of the hundred of Berkeley as they had been when John Smyth of Nibley described them earlier in the century. *Lives of the Berkeleys* (Gloucester, 1885), III. See W. B. Willcox, *Gloucestershire, 1590-1640* (New Haven, Conn., 1940), Chap. X. There are good manorial

The tendency, moreover, to retain long leases (ninety-nine years was the most common), once an advantage to the leaseholders, was now catching up with western farmers. Many leases which had been made out in Elizabeth's reign were now "falling in," leaving the tenant to face increased fines and rents or the likelihood of seeing his land go to someone else. It is not surprising if farmers facing these and similar conditions lent a sympathetic ear to the tales of ship captains and their agents, colonial promoters, and returned travellers—tales of a country where land was to be had for the asking, or nearly so, where leases did not "fall in," nor rents come due, where, in short, a man was his own landlord. That these promises were often highly exaggerated, that there was not land in many places, at any rate, suitable land, to be had for the asking did not alter the landlord dream. It is a commonplace to say that land was the greatest inducement the New World had to offer; but it is difficult to overestimate its psychological and social importance to people in whose minds land had always been identified with security, success, and the good things of life. "Now we can get few English servants," said a member of the Barbados Assembly in 1665, "having no lands to give them at the end of their time which formerly was their main allurement."[40]   Tradesmen as well as yeomen and husbandmen looked forward to becoming landholders. Richard Norton was a Bristol millwright and John Hatten a watchmaker, but they, no less than John Rose, a Wiltshire husbandman, and Morgan Jones, son of a Monmouthshire yeoman, carried with them indentures that called for fifty acres of land in Virginia or Maryland. This was in 1655.[41]   In later years the Carolinas and Pennsylvania would make even more attractive land offers.

---

records for Gloucestershire in the Gloucester Public Library; and the "Views and Surveys" of manors in British Museum Mss. Harl. 71 includes good material for Devon, Somerset, and Wiltshire. For Somerset, see also British Museum Mss. Eng. 2223. P. R. O., C. O. 1/35, no. 45. See also W. N. Sainsbury et al., eds., Cal. State Papers, Col., 1677-1680, no. 1334.

40. Another thing that irked the Somerset and Gloucestershire farmers was the Act of 1652, restricting the growth of tobacco. They were beginning to do quite well with it. As late as 1662, militia were still being called out in Somerset to destroy the tobacco planted there.

41. The question whether servants going to Virginia in the fifties and early sixties actually got land, even if their indenture called for it, has been a vexing one. It was not a legal right. See Morris and Smith on the subject; also see Wertenbaker, The Old South, 312, and Andrews, The Colonial Period of American History, I, 209, n. 1. It is quite clear from the records in the Land Office in Annapolis that the servant who went to Maryland was getting his land if he wanted it "for performing his time of service in this province." Abbot Smith has pointed out the fact that only a relatively small number of them did take it. Carolina and Pennsylvania from the beginning offered land on very attractive terms. See Robert Beverley's comment on the situation in Virginia in 1705, in The History and Present State of Virginia, ed. by Louis B. Wright (Chapel Hill, 1947), 274, 277.

With the bulk of the family land going to the eldest son, it had been the traditional pattern for farmers in every section of England to apprentice one or more of their other sons to trade. This was especially true in the West Country, where the cloth trade had for generations been a source of employment. Hard times among the East Anglian clothworkers made it easier for Winthrop and the other Puritan leaders to gain recruits for New England. The exodus of West Country clothworkers to America in the second half of the century is less well known but merits equal attention. The plight of the West Country was made considerably worse by economic disruption during and after the Civil Wars. No part of the nation was unaffected by this conflict, but the West was especially hard hit. As a key city Bristol early became a major objective and was successively under the control of both armies. The neighboring countryside suffered accordingly. "This England," said one, "is merely the ghost of that England which it was lately."[42] Ships rotted in Bristol harbor; Gloucestershire woolen mills were plundered; clothworkers in Somerset were left without employment for months.

Nor did matters improve when the wars were over. Returned soldiers found themselves without work. Slack periods in the cloth business came in close succession. Prices fluctuated. Problems growing out of the plight of war widows, disabled soldiers, and an increasing number of poor rose to plague local officials and cast a pall of gloom over village communities. "I wish I could hear what condition you live in," an Essex tradesman had written a few years earlier to his Virginia kinsman, "for I fear if these times hold long amongst us we must be all faine come to Virginia."[43] If the emigrant records can be taken as a key, many West Country men and women were now thinking the same thing. The annual exodus of servants shipping from Bristol rose from slightly less than 300 in 1655 to almost 800 in 1659, and hundreds more emigrants were going with their families and paying their own fare.

Discontent in the West Country cloth towns was not new. The trade had suffered somewhat earlier in the century, but it was not until after the Civil Wars that the complaints so increased in volume and bitterness. Modern scholars are inclined to think that the depression in the cloth trade traditionally assigned to the late Commonwealth and early Restoration years was not as damaging to the industry as was earlier thought. They tend to see the complaints from clothiers as disgruntlement over a shift to new men and new methods rather than a decline in the industry

42. Letter from Citizens of Bristol to the King, 1643, quoted in Samuel Seyer, *Memoirs Historical and Topographical of Bristol* (Bristol, 1821-23), II, 316.
43. *Wm. and Mary College Qtly.*, 1st ser., 8 (1899), 239.

itself.[44]   But they all agree on the bad effects of the situation for the workers.   The local records at Taunton and Trowbridge and Gloucester are filled with the hardships of the clothworkers: those who "toiled in their cottages from Castle Colne and Malmsbury on the edge of the Cotswold country" and in the industrial towns on the Avon, "to Westbury, Edington and the other villages under the plain."[45]   And it was from Castle Colne, Malmsbury, Westbury, and other villages under the plain that John Niblett, the clothmaker, Thomas Allen, the worsted comber, Edward Webb, the feltmaker, and John Davis, the tailor, with dozens of their friends and neighbors, made their way to Bristol during the late fifties and early sixties, to sign the indentures which assured their free passage to America.   Other tradesmen and farmers in the nearby countryside were likewise affected, for hard times cannot come to a basic industry in a rural area without affecting auxiliary trades and the whole working population.

Tradesmen, like farmers, were worried not merely by present uncertainties but by the lack of future opportunity.   It had once been the expectation of journeymen that they would advance their status three or four years after apprenticeship.   Many were beginning now to find that they would have to be wage earners all their lives.[46]   Skilled workers of certain kinds much needed in the colonies could sometimes get special favors written into their agreements.   John Walker and Samuel Minor, both carpenters, had made such arrangements.   Walker's term was only three years, with a wage of forty pounds per annum while he was still in service.   Minor, probably younger, was bound for five years, to receive twenty pounds the first three years and twenty-five the last two.   Most of the servants, however, were either not that forehanded or their skills were not such as would be so much needed in America.   Land and high wages were counted on to make up for that.

Despite the fact that industry and the land had each its peculiar character and concerns, their interaction in the general economy was very

44. The best work on the western cloth trade is George Ramsay, *Wiltshire Woollen Industry in the Sixteenth and Seventeenth Centuries* (Bristol, 1945).   See also R. Perry, "The Gloucester Woollen Industry," in *Bristol and Gloucestershire Transactions* (1947); and Miss Mann's chapters in the *Victoria County History, Wiltshire*, in process of publication.

45. Ramsay, *Wiltshire Woollen Industry*, 126, 138. See also Petition from Mayor and Aldermen of Gloucester, November, 1659, in John Washburn, ed., *Collection of Scarce and Curious Tracts Relating to the County and City of Gloucester During the Civil Wars* (Gloucester, 1825), Appendix 21.

46. George Unwin, *Industrial Organization in the Sixteenth and Seventeenth Centuries* (Oxford, 1904), continues to be one of the best analyses that has yet been made of the change in status of skilled workers, esp. 198-200.   For conditions in Wiltshire, see Historical Manuscripts Commission, *Report on Manuscripts in Various Collections* (London, 1901), I, 132 ff.

marked. What each could offer or failed to offer to the individual was of paramount importance. Together they provided the economic framework within which West Country farmers and tradesmen shaped the course of their lives. The laborers, whether agricultural or urban, were perhaps most immediately affected by the current fluctuations common to both Cromwellian and Restoration years. They eked out a meager living on their daily wage if there was work for them.[47] If the cloth works were "still" or harvests were thin, they became a public charge; the local records bear eloquent testimony to the efforts of harassed parish officials to look after their poor.[48] For such among them as were ambitious there was little or no opportunity. Emigration offered it and, as we know, there were some who took advantage of the offer. But most of them were not ambitious. Their niche in the social and economic scale was not threatened as was often that of small landed men or craftsmen.

It would, however, be a great error to assume that these West Country people thought only of economic matters. It should also be remembered that numerous though the emigrants were from any region, far more people stayed at home than left. To think otherwise would be to distort the view of the background of American immigration. There had long been a good deal of mobility among England's working population, particularly among young single men who moved around in search of work when times were bad in their own communities.[49] In some cases families whose sons emigrated to America were already accustomed to having them away from home. The life of country communities would not be markedly changed because here and there a young person or a few families left. Those at home would carry on with the normal pursuits of daily life as dictated by their rank and position in the community and by individual and group interests.

Aside from the demands of daily occupations, perhaps the central focus of their activities was religion. Their scale of values was in large part

47. Hist. Mss. Comm., *Report on Manuscripts in Various Collections*, I, 131-36, 155; Hist. Mss. Comm., *Twelfth Report, Appendix: The Manuscripts of the Duke of Beaufort, K. G., . . . and Others* (London, 1891), Part IX, 78.

48. See the various petitions for aid in the Somerset Records at Taunton, and the Wiltshire local records at Trowbridge; see also Washburn, ed., *Collections of Scarce and Curious Tracts*, Appendix I.

49. See E. E. Rich, "The Population of Elizabethan England," *Econ. Hist. Rev.*, 2nd ser., 2 (1950), 247-66. Of the English movement overseas in the first century, Mr. Rich says: "The quietly pervasive essence of the movement was that it was accomplished by ordinary men and women who for the most part were not conscious that they were doing anything remarkable." He upholds the point of view that there was not much difference to the individual concerned between migration at home and emigration to America. I cannot quite go all the way with him on that view, though it may have been true of some.

determined by it, and it profoundly affected the shape and substance of their mental and social outlook. To the middling people of the West Country, as to many of their kind elsewhere, religion meant non-conformity. It was not, of course, all of one brand—that is the essence of non-conformity. "How many ways do you make it to heaven in this place?" a royalist chaplain had asked in 1647 as he deplored the "rabble of heresies" around Bristol.[50] The years under Cromwell had not eased their troubles as much as many had hoped for. There was probably not much actual religious persecution, although it was not wholly absent; Quakers were cruelly treated at Bristol in 1654-56 and hundreds of them went to America in the following years. A comparison of the Bristol list with Besse's "Sufferers" shows an identity of almost five hundred names.[51] Granting the error which may originate in the prolific repetition among West Country names, these figures cannot be entirely without significance. And not only Quakers were troubled. The West was indeed as the royalist chaplain had found, a hotbed of activity of the various sects. The rise in the Bristol emigration for 1659 has already been indicated. It is significant that the largest annual exodus came in 1662, when the first Restoration statutes against dissenters went into effect. Between eight and nine hundred servants went to America in that year from this one port. If the non-conformists of the West Country had not fared too well in the Commonwealth, they certainly did not expect the return of the Stuarts to help matters. Nor did it.

George Herbert, earlier tracing the cycle through which he thought religion ran her course, startled some of his friends by saying:

> Religion stands on tiptoe in our land
> Readie to pass to the American strand.

Nor had he been unaware of the social and economic implications:

> Then shall Religion to America flee;
> .   .   .   .
> My God, Thou dost prepare for them a way,
> By carrying first their gold from them away,
> For gold and grace did never yet agree
> Religion alwaies sides with povertie.[52]

50. Quoted in Seyer, *Memoirs . . . of Bristol*, 466.

51. Joseph Besse, *A Collection of the Sufferings of the People Called Quakers* (2 vols.; London, 1753).

52. "The Church Militant," Alexander Grosart, ed., *Complete Works of George Herbert* (London, 1874), II, 11-12; Josiah Child, *A New Discourse of Trade* (London, 1694), 184-85.

Josiah Child was only the best known of various writers in the second half of the century who pointed out the "great swarms of new inhabitants" whom the New World received because of the restrictions placed on dissenters in England.

Nowhere were non-conformity and the ferment which it bred more deeply rooted than in the clothmaking centers. Richard Baxter, a Puritan clergyman of yeoman origins, pointed out this relationship as he looked back upon the part played by the various classes in the Civil Wars. Writing in 1683, he said,

On the side of Parliament were the smaller part (as some thought) of the gentry in most of the countries and the greatest part of the Tradesmen and Freeholders, and the Middle sort of men; especially in those corporations and countries [counties] which depend on Cloathing and such Manufactures.[53]

The preoccupation of the middling classes with non-conformity has often been noted. It was, says Alan Simpson, "weavers at their looms, tradesmen in their shops, and yeoman farmers in their homes" among whom Puritanism chiefly took root.[54] Certainly non-conformity, clothmaking, and emigration were active influences in East Anglia in the first half of the century. It was also a combination that was active in the West Country in the second half. Restrictions on non-conformity and the impoverishment of the clothmaking industry gave the New World a double appeal. By no means, of course, were all of these Somerset farmers and Wiltshire and Gloucestershire clothworkers deeply religious people. Far from it. But most of them had been brought up in non-conformist groups which had, to a great extent, shaped the pattern of their lives. As Oscar Handlin has said about the effect of the church on later comers to America, it was not so much that they "rationally accepted doctrines" as that their beliefs were "closely wrapped in the day-to-day events of their existence."[55] And as was true of most people in seventeenth-century England, whatever their religious persuasion they accorded it intense loyalty and were ready to defend it with all of the energy—to say nothing of the invective—at their disposal. Religious controversy was in the very air they breathed; and it inevitably colored personal and neighborhood activities which often had nothing to do with religion.

With certain Puritan clergymen, religious conviction may well have

53. *Reliquiae Baxterianae* (London, 1696), 30.
54. *Puritanism in Old and New England* (Chicago, 1955), 11-12. George Homans has recognized the relationship noted above in his article, "The Puritans and the Clothing Industry," *New Eng. Qtly.*, 13 (1940), 519-29.
55. *The Uprooted* (Boston, 1951), 118-19.

been the primary motive for emigration. It may have motivated some other people, but this would not, I think, have been true of most. Among the farmers and tradesmen who left their native villages, religion was a kind of cement which gave unity and security to those who were thinking of moving to a new life in strange surroundings. Families would be readier to permit their young people to make the voyage if they went with neighbors of the same religious persuasion as their own. Threats and discrimination, moreover, were no balm to people already disgruntled; hence one more factor was added to the existing restiveness, one that provided the emotional and psychological stimulus sometimes needed to translate economic wants and needs into action.

The New World was the beneficiary of this state of mind. For many it seemed to provide the best answer to their needs and hopes. "They say there's bread and work for all, and the sun shines always there." The gospel of this line from an emigrant song of a later period was at the heart of the movement from its beginning. For West Country men and women Bristol was the nearest port from which ships went almost weekly during the summer months. For others it was London or one of the lesser ports. Laborers went if they could be persuaded. Convicts and, on several occasions, political prisoners were forced to go. But over the course of the years, the majority of "the others" who found shipping in the trading vessels that regularly plied the western waters were England's middling people—the most valuable cargo that any captain carried on his westbound voyage.

V.

POLITICS AND SOCIAL STRUCTURE
IN VIRGINIA

Bernard Bailyn
HARVARD UNIVERSITY

By the end of the seventeenth century the American colonists faced an array of disturbing problems in the conduct of public affairs. Settlers from England and Holland, reconstructing familiar institutions on American shores, had become participants in what would appear to have been a wave of civil disobedience. Constituted authority was confronted with repeated challenges. Indeed, a veritable anarchy seems to have prevailed at the center of colonial society, erupting in a series of insurrections that began as early as 1635 with the "thrusting out" of Governor Harvey in Virginia. Culpeper's Rebellion in Carolina, the Protestant Association in Maryland, Bacon's Rebellion in Virginia, Leisler's seizure of power in New York, the resistance to and finally the overthrow of Andros in New England—every colony was affected.

These outbursts were not merely isolated local affairs. Although their immediate causes were rooted in the particular circumstances of the separate colonies, they nevertheless had common characteristics. They were, in fact, symptomatic of a profound disorganization of European society in its American setting. Seen in a broad view, they reveal a new configuration of forces which shaped the origins of American politics.

In a letter written from Virginia in 1623, George Sandys, the resident treasurer, reported despondently on the character and condition of the leading settlers. Some of the councilors were "no more then Ciphers," he wrote; others were "miserablie poore"; and the few substantial planters lived apart, taking no responsibility for public concerns. There was, in fact, among all those "worthie the mencioninge" only one person deserving of full approval. Lieutenant William Peirce "refuses no labour, nor sticks at anie expences that may aduantage the publique." Indeed, Sandys added, Peirce was "of a Capacitie that is not to bee expected in a man of his breedinge."[1]

The afterthought was penetrating. It cut below the usual complaints of the time that many of the settlers were lazy malcontents hardly to be preferred to the Italian glassworkers, than whom, Sandys wrote, "a more damned crew hell never vomited."[2] What lay behind Sandys' remark was not so much that wretched specimens were arriving in the shipments of servants nor even that the quality of public leadership was declining but that the social foundations of political power were being strangely altered.

All of the settlers in whatever colony presumed a fundamental relationship between social structure and political authority. Drawing on a common medieval heritage, continuing to conceive of society as a hierarchical unit, its parts justly and naturally separated into inferior and superior levels, they assumed that superiority was indivisible; there was not one hierarchy for political matters, another for social purposes. John Winthrop's famous explanation of God's intent that "in all times some must be rich some poore, some highe and eminent in power and dignitie; others meane and in subieccion" could not have been more carefully worded. Riches, dignity, and power were properly placed in apposition; they pertained to the same individuals.[3]

So closely related were social leadership and political leadership that experience if not theory justified an identification between state and society. To the average English colonist the state was not an abstraction existing above men's lives, justifying itself in its own terms, taking occasional human embodiment. However glorified in monarchy, the state in ordinary form was indistinguishable from a more general social authority; it was woven into the texture of everyday life. It was the same squire or manorial lord who in his various capacities collated to the benefice, set the rents, and enforced the statutes of Parliament and the royal decrees. Nothing could have been more alien to the settlers than the idea that competition for political leadership should be open to all levels of society or that obscure social origins or technical skills should be considered valuable qualifications

1. Sandys to John Ferrar, April 11, 1623, Susan M. Kingsbury, ed., *The Records of the Virginia Company of London* (4 vols.; Washington, D. C., 1906-35), IV, 110-11.

2. Sandys to "Mr. Farrer," March 1622/23, *ibid.*, 23.

3. John Winthrop, "Modell of Christian Charity," *Winthrop Papers* (5 vols.; Boston, 1929-47), II, 282.

for office. The proper response to new technical demands on public servants was not to give power to the skilled but to give skills to the powerful.[4] The English gentry and landed aristocracy remained politically adaptable and hence politically competent, assuming when necessary new public functions, eliminating the need for a professional state bureaucracy. By their amateur competence they made possible a continuing identification between political and social authority.

In the first years of settlement no one had reason to expect that this characteristic of public life would fail to transfer itself to the colonies. For at least a decade and a half after its founding there had been in the Jamestown settlement a small group of leaders drawn from the higher echelons of English society. Besides well-born soldiers of fortune like George Percy, son of the Earl of Northumberland, there were among them four sons of the West family—children of Lord de la Warr and his wife, a second cousin of Queen Elizabeth. In Virginia the West brothers held appropriately high positions; three of them served as governors.[5] Christopher Davison, the colony's secretary, was the son of Queen Elizabeth's secretary, William Davison, M.P. and Privy Councilor.[6] The troublesome John Martin, of Martin's Brandon, was the son of Sir Richard Martin, twice Lord Mayor of London, and also the brother-in-law of Sir Julius Caesar, Master of the Rolls and Privy Councilor.[7] Sir Francis and Haute Wyatt were sons of substantial Kent gentry and grandsons of the Sir Thomas Wyatt who led the rebellion of 1554 against Queen Mary.[8] George Sandys' father was the Archbishop of York; of his three older brothers, all knights and M.P.'s, two were eminent country gentlemen, and the third, Edwin, of Virginia Company fame, was a man of great influence in the city.[9] George Thorpe was a former M.P. and Gentleman of the Privy Chamber.[10]

More impressive than such positions and relationships was the cultural level represented. For until the very end of the Company period, Virginia remained to the literary and scientific an exotic attraction, its settlement an

4. Cf. J. H. Hexter, "The Education of the Aristocracy in the Renaissance," *Jour. of Modern Hist.*, 22 (1950), 1-20.

5. *Dictionary of National Biography*, 1908-9 edn. (New York), XV, 836-37; Annie L. Jester and Martha W. Hiden, comps. and eds., *Adventurers of Purse and Person: Virginia 1607-1625* ([Princeton, N. J.], 1956), 349-50.

6. *D.N.B.*, V, 632; Richard B. Davis, *George Sandys: Poet-Adventurer* (London, 1955), 112-13n.

7. Alexander Brown, *Genesis of the United States* (Boston, 1890), II, 943-44.

8. Jester and Hiden, comps., *Adventurers*, 372; *D.N.B.*, XXI, 1092-93, 1102-4.

9. Davis, *Sandys*, Chap. I.

10. Brown, *Genesis*, II, 1031.

important moment in Christian history.[11] Its original magnetism for those in touch with intellectual currents affected the early immigration. Of the twenty councilors of 1621, eight had been educated at Oxford, Cambridge, or the Inns of Court. Davison, like Martin trained in the law, was a poet in a family of poets. Thorpe was a "student of Indian views on religion and astronomy." Francis Wyatt wrote verses and was something of a student of political theory. Alexander Whitaker, M.A., author of *Good Newes from Virginia*, was the worthy heir "of a good part of the learning of his renowned father," the master of St. John's College and Regius Professor of Divinity at Cambridge. John Pory, known to history mainly as the speaker of the first representative assembly in America, was a Master of Arts, "protege and disciple of Hakluyt," diplomat, scholar, and traveler, whose writings from and about America have a rightful place in literary history. Above all there was George Sandys, "poet, traveller, and scholar," a member of Lord Falkland's literary circle; while in Jamestown he continued as a matter of course to work on his notable translation of Ovid's *Metamorphoses*.[12]

There was, in other words, during the first years of settlement a direct transference to Virginia of the upper levels of the English social hierarchy as well as of the lower. If the great majority of the settlers were recruited from the yeoman class and below, there was nevertheless a reasonable representation from those upper groups acknowledged to be the rightful rulers of society.

It is a fact of some importance, however, that this governing elite did not survive a single generation, at least in its original form. By the thirties their number had declined to insignificance. Percy, for example, left in 1612. Whitaker drowned in 1617. Sandys and Francis Wyatt arrived only in 1621, but their enthusiasm cooled quickly; they were both gone by 1626. Of the Wests, only John was alive and resident in the colony a decade after the collapse of the Company. Davison, who returned to England in 1622 after only a year's stay, was sent back in 1623 but died within a year of his return. Thorpe was one of the six councilors slain in the massacre of 1622. Pory left for England in 1622; his return as investigating commissioner in 1624 was temporary, lasting only a few months. And the cantankerous Martin graced the Virginia scene by his

11. Perry Miller, *Errand into the Wilderness* (Cambridge, Mass., 1956), 99-140; Howard Mumford Jones, *The Literature of Virginia in the Seventeenth Century* (*Memoirs of the American Academy of Arts and Sciences*, XIX, Part 2, Boston, 1946), 3-7.

12. Davis, *Sandys*, especially 190-92; Harry C. Porter, "Alexander Whitaker," *Wm. and Mary Qtly.*, 3rd ser., 14 (1957), 336; Jones, *Literature of Virginia*, 14n, 5-6, 26-28.

absence after 1625; he is last heard from in the early 1630's petitioning for release from a London debtor's prison.[13]

To be sure, a few representatives of important English families, like John West and Edmund Scarborough, remained. There were also one or two additions from the same social level.[14] But there were few indeed of such individuals, and the basis of their authority had changed. The group of gentlemen and illuminati that had dominated the scene during the Company era had been dispersed. Their disappearance created a political void which was filled soon enough, but from a different area of recruitment, from below, from the toughest and most fortunate of the surviving planters whose eminence by the end of the thirties had very little to do with the transplantation of social status.[15]

The position of the new leaders rested on their ability to wring material gain from the wilderness. Some, like Samuel Mathews, started with large initial advantages,[16] but more typical were George Menefie and John

13. Davis, *Sandys*, 195-97, 112-13n; Jester and Hiden, comps., *Adventurers*, 350-51; Brown, *Genesis*, II, 1031, 970; *Va. Mag. of Hist. and Biog.*, 54 (1946), 60-61; Jones, *Literature of Virginia*, 14n.

14. Scarborough was a well-educated younger son of an armigerous Norfolk family. Among the additions were Charles Harmar (who died in 1640), nephew of the warden of Winchester College and brother of the Greek Reader, later the Greek Professor, at Oxford; and Nathaniel Littleton, whose father was Chief Justice of North Wales, two of whose brothers were Fellows of All Souls and a third Chief Justice of Common Pleas and Lord Keeper of the Great Seal. Susie M. Ames, ed., *County Court Records of Accomack-Northampton, Virginia, 1632-1640* (Washington, D. C., 1954), xxvii, xxix-xxx, xxxv.

15. The difficulty of maintaining in Virginia the traditional relationship between social and political authority became in 1620 the basis of an attack by a group of "ancient planters," including Francis West, on the newly appointed governor, Sir George Yeardley. Although Yeardley had been knighted two years earlier in an effort to enhance his personal authority, the petitioners argued that his lack of eminence was discouraging settlement. "Great Actions," they wrote, "are carryed wth best successe by such Comanders who haue personall Aucthoritye & greatness answerable to the Action, Sithence itt is nott easye to swaye a vulgar and seruile Nature by vulgar & seruile Spiritts." Leadership should devolve on commanders whose "Eminence or Nobillitye" is such that "euerye man subordinate is ready to yeild a willing submission wthout contempt or repyning." The ordinary settlers, they said, would not obey the same authority "conferrd vpon a meane man . . . no bettar than selected owt of their owne Ranke." If, therefore, the Company hoped to attract and hold colonists, especially of "the bettar sorte," it should select as leaders in Virginia "some eythar Noble or little lesse in Honor or Dower . . . to maintayne & hold vp the dignitye of so Great and good a cawse." Kingsbury, ed., *Records of the Virginia Company*, III, 231-32.

16. For Mathews' twenty-three servants and his "Denbigh" plantation, described in 1649 as a self-sufficient village, see John C. Hotten, ed., *Original List of Persons of Quality* . . . (London, 1874), 233-34; Jester and Hiden, comps., *Adventurers*, 244-45; *A Perfect Description of Virginia* . . . , in Peter Force, comp., *Tracts and Other Papers Relating Principally to the Origin, Settlement, and Progress of the Colonies in North America* (4 vols., Washington, D. C., 1836-46), II, no. 8, 14-15.

Utie, who began as independent landowners by right of transporting themselves and only one or two servants. Abraham Wood, famous for his explorations and like Menefie and Utie the future possessor of large estates and important offices, appears first as a servant boy on Mathews' plantation. Adam Thoroughgood, the son of a country vicar, also started in Virginia as a servant, aged fourteen. William Spencer is first recorded as a yeoman farmer without servants.[17]

Such men as these—Spencer, Wood, Menefie, Utie, Mathews—were the most important figures in Virginia politics up to the Restoration, engrossing large tracts of land, dominating the Council, unseating Sir John Harvey from the governorship. But in no traditional sense were they a ruling class. They lacked the attributes of social authority, and their political dominance was a continuous achievement. Only with the greatest difficulty, if at all, could distinction be expressed in a genteel style of life, for existence in this generation was necessarily crude. Mathews may have created a flourishing estate and Menefie had splendid fruit gardens, but the great tracts of land such men claimed were almost entirely raw wilderness. They had risen to their positions, with few exceptions, by brute labor and shrewd manipulation; they had personally shared the burdens of settlement. They succeeded not because of, but despite, whatever gentility they may have had. William Claiborne may have been educated at the Middle Temple; Peirce could not sign his name; but what counted was their common capacity to survive and flourish in frontier settlements.[18] They were tough, unsentimental, quick-tempered, crudely ambitious men concerned with profits and increased landholdings, not the grace of life. They roared curses, drank exuberantly, and gambled (at least according to deVries) for their servants when other commodities were lacking.[19] If the worst of Governor Harvey's offenses had been to knock out the teeth of an offending councilor with a cudgel, as he did on one occasion, no one would have questioned his right to the governorship.[20] Rank had

17. Jester and Hiden, comps., *Adventurers*, 248-49, 321, 329, 339-40; Hotten, ed., *Persons of Quality*, 226, 237, 233, 253, 228; Clarence W. Alvord and Lee Bidgood, *The First Explorations of the Trans-Alleghany Region . . . 1650-1674* (Cleveland, 1912), 34 ff.

18. *Wm. and Mary Qtly.*, 2nd ser., 19 (1939), 475n; Davis, *Sandys*, 158n.

19. Ames, ed., *Accomack-Northampton Recs.*, xxxiv, xxxix-xl; Susie M. Ames, *Studies of the Virginia Eastern Shore in the Seventeenth Century* (Richmond, Va., 1940), 181, 183. DeVries wrote of his astonishment at seeing servants gambled away: "I told them that I had never seen such work in Turk or Barbarian, and that it was not becoming Christians." David P. deVries, *Short Historical . . . Notes of several Voyages . . .* (Hoorn, 1655), reprinted in the New York Hist. Soc., *Collections*, 2nd ser., 3 (1857), 36, 125.

20. Harvey readily confessed to the deed, offering as an official justification the fact that it had all taken place outside the Council chamber, and anyhow the

its privileges, and these men were the first to claim them, but rank itself was unstable and the lines of class or status were fluid. There was no insulation for even the most elevated from the rude impact of frontier life.

As in style of life so in politics, these leaders of the first permanently settled generation did not re-create the characteristics of a stable gentry. They had had little opportunity to acquire the sense of public responsibility that rests on deep identification with the land and its people. They performed in some manner the duties expected of leaders, but often public office was found simply burdensome. Reports such as Sandys' that Yeardley, the councilor and former governor, was wholly absorbed in his private affairs and scarcely glanced at public matters and that Mathews "will rather hazard the payment of fforfeitures then performe our Injunctions" were echoed by Harvey throughout his tenure of office. Charles Harmar, justice of the peace on the Eastern Shore, attended the court once in eight years, and Claiborne's record was only slightly better. Attendance to public duties had to be specifically enjoined, and privileges were of necessity accorded provincial officeholders. The members of the Council were particularly favored by the gift of tax exemption.[21]

The private interests of this group, which had assumed control of public office by virtue not of inherited status but of newly achieved and strenuously maintained economic eminence, were pursued with little interference from the traditional restraints imposed on a responsible ruling class. Engaged in an effort to establish themselves in the land, they sought as specific ends: autonomous local jurisdiction, an aggressive expansion of settlement and trading enterprises, unrestricted access to land, and, at every stage, the legal endorsement of acquisitions. Most of the major public events for thirty years after the dissolution of the Company—and especially the overthrow of Harvey—were incidents in the pursuit of these goals.

From his first appearance in Virginia, Sir John Harvey threatened the interests of this emerging planter group. While still in England he had identified himself with the faction that had successfully sought the collapse of the Company, and thus his mere presence in Virginia was a threat to the legal basis of land grants made under the Company's charter. His demands for the return as public property of goods that had once belonged to the

fellow had "assailed him with ill language." *The Aspinwall Papers*, Mass. Hist. Soc., *Collections*, 4th ser., 9 (1871), 133n.

21. Kingsbury, ed., *Records of the Virginia Company*, IV, 110-11; *Va. Mag. of Hist. and Biog.*, 8 (1900-1), 30; Ames, ed., *Accomack-Northampton Recs.*, xxv, xxix; William W. Hening, ed., *The Statutes-at-Large . . . of Virginia (1619-1792)* (New York, 1823), I, 350, 454; Philip A. Bruce, *Institutional History of Virginia in the Seventeenth Century* (2 vols.; New York, 1910), II, Chaps. XV, XXIX.

Company specifically jeopardized the planters' holdings. His insistence that the governorship was more than a mere chairmanship of the Council tended to undermine local autonomy. His conservative Indian policy not only weakened the settlers' hand in what already seemed an irreconcilable enmity with the natives but also restricted the expansion of settlement. His opposition to Claiborne's claim to Kent Island threatened to kill off the lucrative Chesapeake Bay trade, and his attempt to ban the Dutch ships from the colony endangered commerce more generally. His support of the official policy of economic diversification, together with his endorsement of the English schemes of tobacco monopoly, alienated him finally and completely from the Council group.[22]

Within a few months of his assuming the governorship, Harvey wrote home with indignation of the "waywardnes and oppositions" of the councilors and condemned them for factiously seeking "rather for their owne endes then either seekinge the generall good or doinge right to particuler men." Before a year was out the antagonisms had become so intense that a formal peace treaty had to be drawn up between Harvey and the Council. But both sides were adamant, and conflict was inescapable. It exploded in 1635 amid comic opera scenes of "extreame coller and passion" complete with dark references to Richard the Third and musketeers "running with their peices presented." The conclusion was Harvey's enraged arrest of George Menefie "of suspicion of Treason to his Majestie"; Utie's response, "And wee the like to you sir"; and the governor's forced return to England.[23]

Behind these richly heroic "passings and repassings to and fro" lies not a victory of democracy or representative institutions or anything of the sort. Democracy, in fact, was identified in the Virginians' minds with the "popular and tumultuary government" that had prevailed in the old Company's quarter courts, and they wanted none of it; the Assembly as a representative institution was neither greatly sought after nor hotly resisted.[24] The victory of 1635 was that of resolute leaders of settlement stubbornly fighting for individual establishment. With the reappointment of Sir Francis Wyatt as governor, their victory was assured and in the

22. The charges and countercharges are summarized, together with supporting documents, in the profuse footnotes of *Aspinwall Papers*, 131-52.

23. *Va. Mag. of Hist. and Biog.*, 8 (1900-1), 30, 43-45; 1 (1893-94), 418, 419, 427, 420.

24. *Ibid.*, 1 (1893-94), 418; Hening, ed., *Va. Stat. at L.*, I, 232-33. For a balanced statement of the importance attached by contemporaries to Virginia's representative Assembly, see Wesley Frank Craven, *Dissolution of the Virginia Company* (New York, 1932), 71 ff., 330 ff. Cf. Charles M. Andrews, *The Colonial Period of American History* (4 vols.; New Haven, Conn., 1934-38), I, 181 ff., and Davis, " 'Liberalism' in the Virginia Company and Colony," *Sandys*, Appendix G.

Commonwealth period it was completely realized. By 1658, when Mathews was elected governor, effective interference from outside had disappeared and the supreme authority had been assumed by an Assembly which was in effect a league of local magnates secure in their control of county institutions.[25]

One might at that point have projected the situation forward into a picture of dominant county families dating from the 1620's and 1630's, growing in identification with the land and people, ruling with increasing responsibility from increasingly eminent positions. But such a projection would be false. The fact is that with a few notable exceptions like the Scarboroughs and the Wormeleys, these struggling planters of the first generation failed to perpetuate their leadership into the second generation. Such families as the Woods, the Uties, the Mathews, and the Peirces faded from dominant positions of authority after the deaths of their founders. To some extent this was the result of the general insecurity of life that created odds against the physical survival in the male line of any given family. But even if male heirs had remained in these families after the death of the first generation, undisputed eminence would not. For a new emigration had begun in the forties, continuing for close to thirty years, from which was drawn a new ruling group that had greater possibilities for permanent dominance than Harvey's opponents had had. These newcomers absorbed and subordinated the older group, forming the basis of the most celebrated oligarchy in American history.

Most of Virginia's great eighteenth-century names, such as Bland, Burwell, Byrd, Carter, Digges, Ludwell, and Mason, appear in the colony for the first time within ten years either side of 1655. These progenitors of the eighteenth-century aristocracy arrived in remarkably similar circumstances. The most important of these immigrants were younger sons of substantial families well connected in London business and governmental circles and long associated with Virginia; family claims to land in the colony or inherited shares of the original Company stock were now brought forward as a basis for establishment in the New World.

Thus the Bland family interests in Virginia date from a 1618 investment in the Virginia Company by the London merchant John Bland, supplemented in 1622 by another in Martin's Hundred. The merchant never touched foot in America, but three of his sons did come to Virginia in the forties and fifties to exploit these investments. The Burwell fortunes derive from the early subscription to the Company of Edward Burwell, which was inherited in the late forties by his son, Lewis I. The first Wil-

25. Wesley Frank Craven, *The Southern Colonies in the Seventeenth Century, 1607-1689* (Baton Rouge, La., 1949), 288-94.

liam Byrd arrived about 1670 to assume the Virginia properties of his mother's family, the Steggs, which dated back to the early days of the Company. The Digges's interests in Virginia stem from the original investments of Sir Dudley Digges and two of his sons in the Company, but it was a third son, Edward, who emigrated in 1650 and established the American branch of the family. Similarly, the Masons had been financially interested in Virginia thirty-two years before 1652, when the first immigrant of that family appeared in the colony. The Culpeper clan, whose private affairs enclose much of the history of the South in the second half of the seventeenth century, was first represented in Virginia by Thomas Culpeper, who arrived in 1649; but the family interests in Virginia had been established a full generation earlier: Thomas' father, uncle, and cousin had all been members of the original Virginia Company and their shares had descended in the family. Even Governor Berkeley fits the pattern. There is no mystery about his sudden exchange in 1642 of the life of a dilettante courtier for that of a colonial administrator and estate manager. He was a younger son without prospects, and his family's interests in Virginia, dating from investments in the Company made twenty years earlier, as well as his appointment held out the promise of an independent establishment in America.[26]

Claims on the colony such as these were only one, though the most important, of a variety of forms of capital that might provide the basis for secure family fortunes. One might simply bring over enough of a merchant family's resources to begin immediately building up an imposing estate, as, presumably, did that ambitious draper's son, William Fitzhugh. The benefits that accrued from such advantages were quickly translated into landholdings in the development of which these settlers were favored by the chronology of their arrival. For though they extended the area of cultivation in developing their landholdings, they were not obliged to initiate settlement. They fell heirs to large areas of the tidewater region that had already been brought under cultivation. "Westover" was not the creation of William Byrd; it had originally been part of the De la Warr estate, passing, with improvements, to Captain Thomas Pawlett, thence to Theodorick Bland, and finally to Byrd. Lewis Burwell inherited not only his father's land, but also the developed estate of his stepfather,

26. Nell M. Nugent, *Cavaliers and Pioneers* (Richmond, Va., 1934), I, 160; Jester and Hiden, comps., *Adventurers*, 97, 108, 154-55, 288; Louis B. Wright, *The First Gentlemen of Virginia* (San Marino, Calif., 1940), 312-13; *Va. Mag. of Hist. and Biog.*, 35 (1927), 227-28; Helen Hill, *George Mason, Constitutionalist* (Cambridge, Mass., 1938), 3-4; Fairfax Harrison, "A Key Chart of the . . . Culpepers . . . ," *Va. Mag. of Hist. and Biog.*, 33 (1925), f. 113, 339, 344; *D.N.B.*, II, 368; Kingsbury, ed., *Records of the Virginia Company*, II, 75, 90, 391.

Wingate. Some of the Carters' lands may be traced back through John Utie to a John Jefferson, who left Virginia as early as 1628. Abraham Wood's entire Fort Henry property ended in the hands of the Jones family. The Blands' estate in Charles City County, which later became the Harrisons' "Berkeley" plantation, was cleared for settlement in 1619 by servants of the "particular" plantation of Berkeley's Hundred.[27]

Favored thus by circumstance, a small group within the second generation migration moved toward setting itself off in a permanent way as a ruling landed gentry. That they succeeded was due not only to their material advantages but also to the force of their motivation. For these individuals were in social origins just close enough to establishment in gentility to feel the pangs of deprivation most acutely. It is not the totally but the partially dispossessed who build up the most propulsive aspirations, and behind the zestful lunging at propriety and status of a William Fitzhugh lay not the narcotic yearnings of the disinherited but the pent-up ambitions of the gentleman *manqué*. These were neither hardhanded pioneers nor dilettante romantics, but ambitious younger sons of middle-class families who knew well enough what gentility was and sought it as a specific objective.[28]

The establishment of this group was rapid. Within a decade of their arrival they could claim, together with a fortunate few of the first generation, a marked social eminence and full political authority at the county level. But their rise was not uniform. Indeed, by the seventies a new circumstance had introduced an effective principle of social differentiation among the colony's leaders. A hierarchy of position within the newly risen gentry was created by the Restoration government's efforts to extend its control more effectively over its mercantile empire. Demanding of its colonial executives and their advisors closer supervision over the external aspects of the economy, it offered a measure of patronage necessary for enforcement. Public offices dealing with matters that profoundly affected the basis of economic life—tax collection, customs regulation, and the bestowal of land grants—fell within the gift of the governor and tended to form an inner circle of privilege. One can note in Berkeley's administration the growing importance of this barrier of officialdom. Around its privileges there formed the "Green Spring" faction, named after Berkeley's plantation near Jamestown, a group bound to the governor not by royalist sympathies so much as by ties of kinship and patronage.

27. Wright, *First Gentlemen*, 155 ff.; Jester and Hiden, comps., *Adventurers*, 98, 108, 339-41, 363-64, 97, 99.

28. Fitzhugh's letters, scattered through the *Va. Mag. of Hist. and Biog.*, I-VI, cannot be equalled as sources for the motivation of this group.

Thus Colonel Henry Norwood, related to Berkeley by a "near affinity in blood," was given the treasurership of the colony in 1650, which he held for more than two decades. During this time Thomas Ludwell, a cousin and Somerset neighbor of the governor, was secretary of state, in which post he was succeeded in 1678 by his brother Philip, who shortly thereafter married Berkeley's widow. This Lady Berkeley, it should be noted, was the daughter of Thomas Culpeper, the immigrant of 1649 and a cousin of Thomas Lord Culpeper who became governor in 1680. Immediately after her marriage to Berkeley, her brother Alexander requested and received from the governor the nomination to the surveyor-generalship of Virginia, a post he filled for twenty-three years while resident in England, appointing as successive deputies the brothers Ludwell, to whom by 1680 he was twice related by marriage. Lady Berkeley was also related through her mother to William Byrd's wife, a fact that explains much about Byrd's prolific office-holding.[29]

The growing distinctiveness of provincial officialdom within the landed gentry may also be traced in the transformation of the Council. Originally, this body had been expected to comprise the entire effective government, central and local; councilors were to serve, individually or in committees, as local magistrates. But the spread of settlement upset this expectation, and at the same time as the local offices were falling into the hands of autonomous local powers representing leading county families, the Council,

29. Colonel [Henry] Norwood, *A Voyage to Virginia* (1649), in Force, ed., *Tracts*, III, 49, 50; *Va. Mag. of Hist. and Biog.*, 33 (1925), 5, 8; Harrison, "Key Chart," *ibid.*, 351-55, 348; *Wm. and Mary Qtly.*, 1st ser., 19 (1910-11), 209-10. It was after Culpeper's appointment to the governorship that Byrd was elevated to the Council and acquired the auditor- and receiver-generalships. William G. and Mary N. Stanard, comps., *The Colonial Virginia Register* (Albany, N. Y., 1902), 22-23.

The Berkeley-Norwood connection may be followed out in other directions. Thus the Colonel Francis Moryson mentioned by Norwood as his friend and traveling companion and whom he introduced to the governor was given command of the fort at Point Comfort upon his arrival in 1649, replacing his brother, Major Richard Moryson, whose son Charles was given the same post in the 1660's. Francis, who found the command of the fort "profitable to him," was elevated by Berkeley to the Council and temporarily to the deputy-governorship, "wherein he got a competent estate"; he finally returned to England in the position of colony agent. Norwood, *Voyage*, 50; *Va. Mag. of Hist. and Biog.*, 9 (1900-1), 122-23; Ella Lonn, *The Colonial Agents of the Southern Colonies* (Chapel Hill, 1945), 21 ff.

The inner kinship core of the group enclosed the major provincial positions mentioned above. But the wider reaches of the clique extended over the Council, the collectorships, and the naval offices as well as minor positions within the influence of the governor. On these posts and their holders, see Stanard and Stanard, comps., *Va. Register*, 38-40; Bruce, *Institutional History*, II, Chaps. XXXVIII-XLII. On the limitations of the gubernatorial influence after 1660, see Craven, *Southern Colonies*, 293.

appointed by the governor and hence associated with official patronage, increasingly realized the separate, lucrative privileges available to it.[30]

As the distinction between local and central authority became clear, the county magistrates sought their own distinct voice in the management of the colony, and they found it in developing the possibilities of burgess representation. In the beginning there was no House of Burgesses; representation from the burghs and hundreds was conceived of not as a branch of government separate from the Council but as a periodic supplement to it.[31] Until the fifties the burgesses, meeting in the Assemblies with the councilors, felt little need to form themselves into a separate house, for until that decade there was little evidence of a conflict of interests between the two groups. But when, after the Restoration, the privileged status of the Council became unmistakable and the county magnates found control of the increasingly important provincial administration pre-empted by this body, the burgess part of the Assembly took on a new meaning in contrast to that of the Council. Burgess representation now became vital to the county leaders if they were to share in any consistent way in affairs larger than those of the counties. They looked to the franchise, hitherto broad not by design but by neglect, introducing qualifications that would ensure their control of the Assembly. Their interest in provincial government could no longer be expressed in the conglomerate Assembly, and at least by 1663 the House of Burgesses began to meet separately as a distinct body voicing interests potentially in conflict with those of the Council.[32]

Thus by the eighth decade the ruling class in Virginia was broadly based on leading county families and dominated at the provincial level by a privileged officialdom. But this social and political structure was too new, too lacking in the sanctions of time and custom, its leaders too close to humbler origins and as yet too undistinguished in style of life, to be accepted without a struggle. A period of adjustment was necessary, of which Bacon's Rebellion was the climactic episode.

Bacon's Rebellion began as an unauthorized frontier war against the Indians and ended as an upheaval that threatened the entire basis of social and political authority. Its immediate causes have to do with race relations and settlement policy, but behind these issues lay deeper elements related to resistance against the maturing shape of a new social order. These elements explain the dimensions the conflict reached.

30. Craven, *Southern Colonies*, 167-69, 270, 288; Bruce, *Institutional History*, II, Chap. XV.

31. For the Assembly as "the other Counsell," see the "Ordinance and Constitution" of 1621 in Kingsbury, ed., *Records of the Virginia Company*, III, 483-84.

32. Andrews, *Colonial Period*, I, 184-85; Craven, *Southern Colonies*, 289 ff.

There was, first, resistance by substantial planters to the privileges and policies of the inner provincial clique led by Berkeley and composed of those directly dependent on his patronage. These dissidents, among whom were the leaders of the Rebellion, represented neither the downtrodden masses nor a principle of opposition to privilege as such. Their discontent stemmed to a large extent from their own exclusion from privileges they sought. Most often their grievances were based on personal rebuffs they had received as they reached for entry into provincial officialdom. Thus—to speak of the leaders of the Rebellion—Giles Bland arrived in Virginia in 1671 to take over the agency of his late uncle in the management of his father's extensive landholdings, assuming at the same time the lucrative position of customs collector which he had obtained in London. But, amid angry cries of *"pittyfull fellow, puppy* and *Sonn of a Whore,"* he fell out first with Berkeley's cousin and favorite, Thomas Ludwell, and finally with the governor himself; for his "Barbarous and Insolent Behaviors" Bland was fined, arrested, and finally removed from the collectorship.[33] Of the two "chiefe Incendiarys," William Drummond and Richard Lawrence, the former had been quarreling with Berkeley since 1664, first over land claims in Carolina, then over a contract for building a fort near James City, and repeatedly over lesser issues in the General Court; Lawrence "some Years before . . . had been partially treated at Law, for a considerable Estate on behalfe of a Corrupt favorite." Giles Brent, for his depredations against the Indians in violation of official policy, had not only been severely fined but barred from public office.[34] Bacon himself could not have appeared under more favorable circumstances. A cousin both of Lady Berkeley and of the councilor Nathaniel Bacon, Sr., and by general agreement "a Gent:man of a Liberall education" if of a somewhat tarnished reputation, he had quickly staked out land for himself and had been elevated, for reasons "best known to the Governour," to the Council. But being "of a most imperious and dangerous hidden Pride of heart . . . very ambitious and arrogant," he wanted more, and quickly. His alienation from and violent opposition to Berkeley were wound in among the animosities created by the Indian problem and were further complicated by his own unstable personality; they were related also to the fact that Berkeley finally turned down the

33. Jester and Hiden, comps., *Adventurers*, 98-99; H. R. McIlwaine, ed., *Minutes of the Council and General Court . . . 1622-1632, 1670-1676* (Richmond, Va., 1924), 399, 423.

34. Charles M. Andrews, ed., *Narratives of the Insurrections, 1675-1690* (New York, 1915), 96, 27; Wilcomb E. Washburn, "The Humble Petition of Sarah Drummond," *Wm. and Mary Qtly.*, 3rd ser., 13 (1956), 368-69; H. R. McIlwaine, ed., *Journals of the House of Burgesses of Virginia 1659/60-1693* (Richmond, Va., 1914), 14.

secret offer Bacon and Byrd made in 1675 for the purchase from the governor of a monopoly of the Indian trade.[35]

These specific disputes have a more general aspect. It was three decades since Berkeley had assumed the governorship and begun rallying a favored group, and it was over a decade since the Restoration had given this group unconfined sway over the provincial government. In those years much of the choice tidewater land as well as the choice offices had been spoken for, and the tendency of the highly placed was to hold firm. Berkeley's Indian policy—one of stabilizing the borders between Indians and whites and protecting the natives from depredation by land-hungry settlers—although a sincere attempt to deal with an extremely difficult problem, was also conservative, favoring the established. Newcomers like Bacon and Bland and particularly landholders on the frontiers felt victimized by a stabilization of the situation or by a controlled expansion that maintained on an extended basis the existing power structure. They were logically drawn to aggressive positions. In an atmosphere charged with violence, their interests constituted a challenge to provincial authority. Bacon's primary appeal in his "Manifesto" played up the threat of this challenge:

Let us trace these men in Authority and Favour to whose hands the dispensation of the Countries wealth has been commited; let us observe the sudden Rise of their Estates [compared] with the Quality in wch they first entered this Country... And lett us see wither their extractions and Education have not bin vile, And by what pretence of learning and vertue they could [enter] soe soon into Imployments of so great Trust and consequence, let us ... see what spounges have suckt up the Publique Treasure and wither it hath not bin privately contrived away by unworthy Favourites and juggling Parasites whose tottering Fortunes have bin repaired and supported at the Publique chardg.

Such a threat to the basis of authority was not lost on Berkeley or his followers. Bacon's merits, a contemporary wrote, "thretned an eclips to there riseing gloryes. . . . (if he should continue in the Governours favour) of Seniours they might becom juniours, while there younger Brother . . .

---

35. Wilcomb E. Washburn, *The Governor and the Rebel, A History of Bacon's Rebellion in Virginia* (Chapel Hill, 1957), 17-19; Andrews, ed., *Narratives*, 74, 110. For the offer to buy the monopoly and Berkeley's initial interest in it, see Bacon to Berkeley, September 18, 1675, and William and Frances Berkeley to Bacon, September 21, 1675, Coventry Papers, Longleat Library of the Marquises of Bath, LXXVII, 6, 8 (microfilm copy, Library of Congress); for the refusal, see *Aspinwall Papers*, 166. Mr. Washburn, who first called attention to these Bacon letters at Longleat, is editing them for publication by the Virginia Historical Society.

might steale away that blessing, which they accounted there owne by birthright."[36]

But these challengers were themselves challenged, for another main element in the upheaval was the discontent among the ordinary settlers at the local privileges of the same newly risen county magnates who assailed the privileges of the Green Spring faction. The specific Charles City County grievances were directed as much at the locally dominant family, the Hills, as they were at Berkeley and his clique. Similarly, Surry County complained of its county court's highhanded and secretive manner of levying taxes on "the poore people" and of setting the sheriffs' and clerks' fees; they petitioned for the removal of these abuses and for the right to elect the vestry and to limit the tenure of the sheriffs. At all levels the Rebellion challenged the stability of newly secured authority.[37]

It is this double aspect of discontent behind the violence of the Rebellion that explains the legislation passed in June, 1676, by the so-called "Bacon's Assembly." At first glance these laws seem difficult to interpret because they express disparate if not contradictory interests. But they yield readily to analysis if they are seen not as the reforms of a single group but as efforts to express the desires of two levels of discontent with the way the political and social hierarchy was becoming stabilized. On the one hand, the laws include measures designed by the numerically predominant ordinary settlers throughout the colony as protests against the recently acquired superiority of the leading county families. These were popular protests and they relate not to provincial affairs but to the situation within the local areas of jurisdiction. Thus the statute restricting the franchise to freeholders was repealed; freemen were given the right to elect the parish vestrymen; and the county courts were supplemented by elected freemen to serve with the regularly appointed county magistrates.

On the other hand, there was a large number of measures expressing the dissatisfactions not so much of the ordinary planter but of the local leaders against the prerogatives recently acquired by the provincial elite, prerogatives linked to officialdom and centered in the Council. Thus the law barring office-holding to newcomers of less than three years' residence struck at the arbitrary elevation of the governor's favorites, including Bacon; and the acts forbidding councilors to join the county courts, outlawing the governor's appointment of sheriffs and tax collectors, and nullifying tax exemption for councilors all voiced objections of the local chieftains

36. Craven, *Southern Colonies*, 362-73; *Va. Mag. of Hist. and Biog.*, I (1893-94), 56-57; Andrews, ed., *Narratives*, 53.

37. *Va. Mag. of Hist. and Biog.*, 3 (1895-96), 132 ff. (esp. 142-46), 239-52, 341-49; IV, 1-15; II, 172.

to privileges enjoyed by others. From both levels there was objection to profiteering in public office.[38]

Thus the wave of rebellion broke and spread. But why did it subside? One might have expected that the momentary flood would have become a steady tide, its rhythms governed by a fixed political constellation. But in fact it did not; stable political alignments did not result. The conclusion to this controversy was characteristic of all the insurrections. The attempted purges and counterpurges by the leaders of the two sides were followed by a rapid submerging of factional identity. Occasional references were later made to the episode, and there were individuals who found an interest in keeping its memory alive. Also, the specific grievances behind certain of the attempted legal reforms of 1676 were later revived. But of stable parties or factions around these issues there were none.

It was not merely that in the late years of the century no more than in the early was there to be found a justification for permanently organized political opposition or party machinery, that persistent, organized dissent was still indistinguishable from sedition; more important was the fact that at the end of the century as in 1630 there was agreement that some must be "highe and eminent in power and dignitie; others meane and in subieccion."[39] Protests and upheaval had resulted from the discomforts of discovering who was, in fact, which, and what the particular consequences of "power and dignitie" were.

But by the end of the century the most difficult period of adjustment had passed and there was an acceptance of the fact that certain families were distinguished from others in riches, in dignity, and in access to political authority. The establishment of these families marks the emergence of Virginia's colonial aristocracy.

It was a remarkable governing group. Its members were soberly responsible, alive to the implications of power; they performed their public obligations with notable skill.[40] Indeed, the glare of their accomplishments is so bright as occasionally to blind us to the conditions that limited them. As a ruling class the Virginian aristocracy of the eighteenth century was unlike other contemporary nobilities or aristocracies, including the English. The differences, bound up with the special characteristics of the society it ruled, had become clear at the turn of the seventeenth century.

38. Hening, ed., *Va. Stat. at L.*, II, 341-65.

39. Thus the Burgesses, proposing in 1706 that the vestries be made elective, did not dispute the Council's assertion that the "men of Note & Estates" should have authority and assured them that the people would voluntarily elect the "best" men in the parish. H. R. McIlwaine, ed., *Legislative Journals of the Council of Colonial Virginia* (Richmond, Va., 1918-19), I, 468.

40. Charles S. Sydnor, *Gentlemen Freeholders: Political Practices in Washington's Virginia* (Chapel Hill, 1952), Chaps. I, VI-IX.

Certain of these characteristics are elusive, difficult to grasp and analyze. The leaders of early eighteenth-century Virginia were, for example, in a particular sense, cultural provincials. They were provincial not in the way of Polish *szlachta* isolated on their estates by poverty and impassable roads, nor in the way of sunken *seigneurs* grown rustic and old-fashioned in lonely Norman chateaux. The Virginians were far from uninformed or unaware of the greater world; they were in fact deeply and continuously involved in the cultural life of the Atlantic community. But they knew themselves to be provincials in the sense that their culture was not self-contained; its sources and superior expressions were to be found elsewhere than in their own land. They must seek it from afar; it must be acquired, and once acquired be maintained according to standards externally imposed, in the creation of which they had not participated. The most cultivated of them read much, purposefully, with a diligence the opposite of that essential requisite of aristocracy, uncontending ease. William Byrd's diary with its daily records of stints of study is a stolid testimonial to the virtues of regularity and effort in maintaining standards of civilization set abroad.[41]

In more evident ways also the Virginia planters were denied an uncontending ease of life. They were not *rentiers*. Tenancy, when it appeared late in the colonial period, was useful to the landowners mainly as a cheap way of improving lands held in reserve for future development. The Virginia aristocrat was an active manager of his estate, drawn continuously into the most intimate contacts with the soil and its cultivation. This circumstance limited his ease, one might even say bound him to the soil, but it also strengthened his identity with the land and its problems and saved him from the temptation to create of his privileges an artificial world of self-indulgence.[42]

But more important in distinguishing the emerging aristocracy of Virginia from other contemporary social and political elites were two very specific circumstances. The first concerns the relationship between the integrity of the family unit and the descent of real property. "The English political family," Sir Lewis Namier writes with particular reference to the eighteenth-century aristocracy,

41. Albert Goodwin, ed., *The European Nobility in the Eighteenth Century* (London, 1953), *passim;* John Clive and Bernard Bailyn, "England's Cultural Provinces: Scotland and America," *Wm. and Mary Qtly.*, 3rd ser., 9 (1954), 200-13; Louis B. Wright and Marion Tinling, eds., *The Secret Diary of William Byrd of Westover 1709-1712* (Richmond, Va., 1941).

42. Willard F. Bliss, "The Rise of Tenancy in Virginia," *Va. Mag. of Hist. and Biog.*, 58 (1950), 427 ff.; Louis B. Wright, *Cultural Life of the American Colonies, 1607-1763* (New York, 1957), 5-11.

is a compound of "blood," name, and estate, this last . . . being the most important of the three. . . . The name is a weighty symbol, but liable to variations. . . . the estate . . . is, in the long run, the most potent factor in securing continuity through identification. . . . Primogeniture and entails psychically preserve the family in that they tend to fix its position through the successive generations, and thereby favour conscious identification.

The descent of landed estates in eighteenth-century England was controlled by the complicated device known as the strict settlement which provided that the heir at his marriage received the estate as a life tenant, entailing its descent to his unborn eldest son and specifying the limitations of the encumbrances upon the land that might be made in behalf of his daughters and younger sons.[43]

It was the strict settlement, in which in the eighteenth century perhaps half the land of England was bound, that provided continuity over generations for the landed aristocracy. This permanent identification of the family with a specific estate and with the status and offices that pertained to it was achieved at the cost of sacrificing the younger sons. It was a single stem of the family only that retained its superiority; it alone controlled the material basis for political dominance.

This basic condition of aristocratic governance in England was never present in the American colonies, and not for lack of familiarity with legal forms. The economic necessity that had prompted the widespread adoption of the strict settlement in England was absent in the colonies. Land was cheap and easily available, the more so as one rose on the social and political ladder. There was no need to deprive the younger sons or even daughters of landed inheritances in order to keep the original family estate intact. Provision could be made for endowing each of them with plantations, and they in turn could provide similarly for their children. Moreover, to confine the stem family's fortune to a single plot of land, however extensive, was in the Virginia economy to condemn it to swift decline. Since the land was quickly worn out and since it was cheaper to acquire new land than to rejuvenate the worked soil by careful husbandry, geographical mobility, not stability, was the key to prosperity. Finally, since land was only as valuable as the labor available to work it, a great estate was worth passing intact from generation to generation only if it had annexed to it a sufficient population of slaves. Yet this condition imposed severe rigidities in a plantation's economy—for a labor force bound to a

43. Lewis B. Namier, *England in the Age of the American Revolution* (London, 1930), 22-23; H. J. Habakkuk, "Marriage Settlements in the Eighteenth Century," Royal Hist. Soc., *Transactions*, 4th ser., 32 (1950), 15-30.

particular plot was immobilized—besides creating bewildering confusions in law.

The result, evident before the end of the seventeenth century, was a particular relationship between the family and the descent of property. There was in the beginning no intent on the part of the Virginians to alter the traditional forms; the continued vitality of the ancient statutes specifying primogeniture in certain cases was assumed.[44] The first clear indication of a new trend came in the third quarter of the century, when the leading gentry, rapidly accumulating large estates, faced for the first time the problem of the transfer of property. The result was the subdivision of the great holdings and the multiplication of smaller plots while the net amount of land held by the leading families continued to rise.[45]

This trend continued. Primogeniture neither at the end of the seventeenth century nor after prevailed in Virginia. It was never popular even among the most heavily endowed of the tidewater families. The most common form of bequest was a grant to the eldest son of the undivided home plantation and gifts of other tracts outside the home county to the younger sons and daughters. Thus by his will of 1686 Robert Beverley, Sr., bequeathed to his eldest son, Peter, all his land in Gloucester County lying between "Chiescake" and "Hoccadey's" creeks (an unspecified acreage); to Robert, the second son, another portion of the Gloucester lands amounting to 920 acres; to Harry, 1,600 acres in Rappahannock County; to John, 3,000 acres in the same county; to William, two plantations in Middlesex County; to Thomas, 3,000 acres in Rappahannock and New Kent counties; to his wife, three plantations including those "whereon I now live" for use during her lifetime, after which they were to descend to his daughter Catherine, who was also to receive £200 sterling; to his daughter Mary, £150 sterling; to "the childe that my wife goeth with, be it male or female," all the rest of his real property; and the residue of his personal property was "to be divided and disposed in equall part & portion betwix my wife and children." Among the bequests of Ralph Wormeley, Jr., in 1700 was an estate of 1,500 acres to his daughter Judith as well as separate plantations to his two sons.

Entail proved no more popular than primogeniture. Only a small minority of estates, even in the tidewater region, were ever entailed. In fact, despite the extension of developed land in the course of the eighteenth

44. Clarence R. Keim, Influence of Primogeniture and Entail in the Development of Virginia (unpublished Ph.D. dissertation, University of Chicago, 1926), Chap. I.
45. E.g., Ames, *Eastern Shore*, 29-32.

century, more tidewater estates were docked of entails than were newly entailed.[46]

Every indication points to continuous and increasing difficulty in reproducing even pale replicas of the strict settlement. In 1705 a law was passed requiring a special act of the Assembly to break an entail; the law stood, but between 1711 and 1776 no fewer than 125 such private acts were passed, and in 1734 estates of under £200 were exempted from the law altogether. The labor problem alone was an insuperable barrier to perpetuating the traditional forms. A statute of 1727, clarifying the confused legislation of earlier years, had attempted to ensure a labor force on entailed land by classifying slaves as real property and permitting them to be bound together with land into bequests. But by 1748 this stipulation had resulted in such bewildering "doubts, variety of opinions, and confusions" that it was repealed. The repeal was disallowed in London, and in the course of a defense of its action the Assembly made vividly clear the utter impracticality of entailment in Virginia's economy. Slaves, the Assembly explained, were essential to the success of a plantation, but "slaves could not be kept on the lands to which they were annexed without manifest prejudice to the tenant in tail. . . . often the tenant was the proprietor of fee simple land much fitter for cultivation than his intailed lands, where he could work his slaves to a much greater advantage." On the other hand, if a plantation owner did send entailed slaves where they might be employed most economically the result was equally disastrous:

the frequent removing and settling them on other lands in other counties and parts of the colony far distant from the county court where the deeds or wills which annexed them were recorded and the intail lands lay; the confusion occasioned by their mixture with fee simple slaves of the same name and sex and belonging to the same owner; the uncertainty of distinguishing one from another after several generations, no register of their genealogy being kept and none of them having surnames, were great mischiefs to purchasers, strangers, and creditors, who were often unavoidably deceived in their purchases and hindered in the recovery of their just debts. It also lessened the credit of the country; it being dangerous

46. Keim, Primogeniture and Entail, 44 ff., 113-14. Keim found that only 1 of a sample of 72 wills in Westmoreland (1653-72) contained provisions for entailing; by 1756-61 the proportions had risen to 14 out of 39, but these entails covered only small parts of the total estates. Typical of his other tidewater samples are Middlesex, 1698-1703, 16 out of 65, and 1759-72, 7 out of 48; Henrico, 1677-87, 2 out of 29, and no increase for the later periods. The piedmont samples show even smaller proportions; ibid., 54-62. The Beverley will is printed in Va. Mag. of Hist. and Biog., 3 (1895-96), 47-51; on Wormeley, see ibid., 36 (1928), 101.

for the merchants of Great Britain to trust possessors of many slaves for fear the slaves might be intailed.[47]

A mobile labor force free from legal entanglements and a rapid turn-over of lands, not a permanent hereditary estate, were prerequisites of family prosperity. This condition greatly influenced social and political life. Since younger sons and even daughters inherited extensive landed properties, equal often to those of the eldest son, concentration of authority in the stem family was precluded. Third generation collateral descendants of the original immigrant were as important in their own right as the eldest son's eldest son. Great clans like the Carters and the Lees, though they may have acknowledged a central family seat, were scattered through-out the province on estates of equal influence. The four male Carters of the third generation were identified by contemporaries by the names of their separate estates, and, indistinguishable in style of life, they had an equal access to political power.[48]

Since material wealth was the basis of the status which made one eligible for public office, there was a notable diffusion of political influence throughout a broadening group of leading families. No one son was predestined to represent the family interest in politics, but as many as birth and temperament might provide. In the 1750's there were no fewer than seven Lees of the same generation sitting together in the Virginia Assembly; in the Burgesses they spoke for five separate counties. To the eldest, Philip Ludwell Lee, they conceded a certain social superiority that made it natural for him to sit in the Council. But he did not speak alone for the family; by virtue of inheritance he had no unique authority over his brothers and cousins.

The leveling at the top of the social and political hierarchy, creating an evenness of status and influence, was intensified by continuous intermarriage within the group. The unpruned branches of these flourishing family trees, growing freely, met and intertwined until by the Revolution the aristocracy appeared to be one great tangled cousinry.[49]

As political power became increasingly diffused throughout the upper stratum of society, the Council, still at the end of the seventeenth century a repository of unique privileges, lost its effective superiority. Increasingly

47. Hening, ed., *Va. Stat. at L.*, III, 320, IV, 399-400, 222 ff., V, 441-42n (quoted). In 1765 the legal rigors of entailment were permanently relaxed by a law permitting the leasing of entailed land for up to three lives, a move made necessary, the Assembly said, because "many large tracts of entailed lands remain uncultivated, the owners not having slaves to work them. . . ." *Ibid.*, VIII, 183. For a striking ex-ample of the difficulties of maintaining entailed lands, see *ibid.*, VI, 297-99; Keim, Primogeniture and Entail, 108.

48. Louis Morton, *Robert Carter of Nomini Hall* (Williamsburg, 1941), 11.

49. Burton J. Hendrick, *The Lees of Virginia* (Boston, 1935), 97.

through the successive decades its authority had to be exerted through align-ments with the Burgesses—alignments made easier as well as more neces-sary by the criss-crossing network of kinship that united the two houses. Increasingly the Council's distinctions became social and ceremonial.[50]

The contours of Virginia's political hierarchy were also affected by a second main conditioning element, besides the manner of descent of family property. Not only was the structure unusually level and broad at the top, but it was incomplete in itself. Its apex, the ultimate source of legal de-cision and control, lay in the quite different society of England, amid the distant embroilments of London, the court, and Parliament. The levers of control in that realm were for the most part hidden from the planters; yet the powers that ruled this remote region could impose an arbitrary authority directly into the midst of Virginia's affairs.

One consequence was the introduction of instabilities in the tenure and transfer of the highest offices. Tenure could be arbitrarily interrupted, and the transfer to kin of such positions at death or resignation—uncertain in any case because of the diffusion of family authority—could be quite dif-ficult or even impossible. Thus William Byrd II returned from England at the death of his father in 1704 to take over the family properties, but though he was the sole heir he did not automatically or completely succeed to the elder Byrd's provincial offices. He did, indeed, become auditor of Virginia after his father, but only because he had carefully arranged for the succession while still in London; his father's Council seat went to someone else, and it took three years of patient maneuvering through his main Lon-don contact, Micajah Perry, to secure another; he never did take over the receivership. Even such a power as "King" Carter, the reputed owner at his death of 300,000 acres and 1,000 slaves, was rebuffed by the resident deputy governor and had to deploy forces in England in order to transfer a Virginia naval office post from one of his sons to another. There was family continuity in public office, but at the highest level it was uncertain, the result of place-hunting rather than of the absolute prerogative of birth.[51]

Instability resulted not only from the difficulty of securing and trans-ferring high appointive positions but also and more immediately from the presence in Virginia of total strangers to the scene, particularly governors and their deputies, armed with extensive jurisdiction and powers of en-forcement. The dangers of this element in public life became clear only after Berkeley's return to England in 1677, for after thirty-five years of

50. Percy S. Flippin, *The Royal Government in Virginia, 1624-1775* (New York, 1919), 166-67, 169; Herbert L. Osgood, *The American Colonies in the Eighteenth Century* (4 vols.; New York, 1924-25), IV, 231-32.

51. John S. Bassett, ed., *The Writings of "Colonel William Byrd of Westover in Virginia Esqr"* (New York, 1901), xlviii-ix; Morton, *Carter*, 28n.

residence in the colony Sir William had become a leader in the land independent of his royal authority. But Howard, Andros, and Nicholson were governors with full legal powers but with at best only slight connections with local society. In them, social leadership and political leadership had ceased to be identical.

In the generation that followed Berkeley's departure, this separation between the two spheres created the bitterest of political controversies. Firmly entrenched behind their control of the colony's government, the leading families battled with every weapon available to reduce the power of the executives and thus to eliminate what appeared to be an external and arbitrary authority. Repeated complaints by the governors of the intractable opposition of a league of local oligarchs marked the Virginians' success. Efforts by the executives to discipline the indigenous leaders could only be mildly successful. Patronage was a useful weapon, but its effectiveness diminished steadily, ground down between a resistant Assembly and an office-hungry bureaucracy in England. The possibility of exploiting divisions among the resident powers also declined as kinship lines bound the leading families closer together and as group interests became clearer with the passage of time. No faction built around the gubernatorial power could survive independently; ultimately its adherents would fall away and it would weaken. It was a clear logic of the situation that led the same individuals who had promoted Nicholson as a replacement for Andros to work against him once he assumed office.[52]

Stability could be reached only by the complete identification of external and internal authority through permanent commitment by the appointees to local interests. Commissary Blair's extraordinary success in Virginia politics was based not only on his excellent connections in England but also on his marriage into the Harrison family, which gave him the support of an influential kinship faction. There was more than hurt pride and thwarted affection behind Nicholson's reported insane rage at being spurned by the highly marriageable Lucy Burwell; and later the astute Spotswood, for all his success in imposing official policy, fully quieted the controversies of his administration only by succumbing completely and joining as a resident Virginia landowner the powers aligned against him.[53]

52. For the classic outcry against "the party of Malecontents," see Spotswood's letter to the Board of Trade, March 25, 1719, in R. A. Brock, ed., *The Official Letters of Alexander Spotswood* (Richmond, Va., 1882-85), II, 308 ff.; cf. 285. On patronage, see Flippin, *Royal Government*, 208-214; Leonard W. Labaree, *Royal Government in America* (New Haven, Conn., 1930), 102; Worthington C. Ford, "A Sketch of Sir Francis Nicholson," *Mag. of Amer. Hist.*, 29 (1893), 508-12.

53. Peter Laslett, "John Locke . . . ," *Wm. and Mary Qtly.*, 3rd ser., 14 (1957),

But there was more involved than instability and conflict in the discontinuity between social and political organization at the topmost level. The state itself had changed its meaning. To a Virginia planter of the early eighteenth century the highest public authority was no longer merely one expression of a general social authority. It had become something abstract, external to his life and society, an ultimate power whose purposes were obscure, whose direction could neither be consistently influenced nor accurately plotted, and whose human embodiments were alien and antagonistic.

The native gentry of the early eighteenth century had neither the need nor the ability to fashion a new political theory to comprehend their experience, but their successors would find in the writings of John Locke on state and society not merely a reasonable theoretical position but a statement of self-evident fact.

I have spoken exclusively of Virginia, but though the histories of each of the colonies in the seventeenth century are different, they exhibit common characteristics. These features one might least have expected to find present in Virginia, and their presence there is, consequently, most worth indicating.

In all of the colonies the original transference of an ordered European society was succeeded by the rise to authority of resident settlers whose influence was rooted in their ability to deal with the problems of life in wilderness settlements. These individuals attempted to stabilize their positions, but in each case they were challenged by others arriving after the initial settlements, seeking to exploit certain advantages of position, wealth, or influence. These newcomers, securing after the Restoration governmental appointments in the colonies and drawn together by personal ties, especially those of kinship and patronage, came to constitute colonial officialdom. This group introduced a new principle of social organization; it also gave rise to new instabilities in a society in which the traditional forms of authority were already being subjected to severe pressures. By the eighth decade of the seventeenth century the social basis of public life had become uncertain and insecure, its stability delicate and sensitive to disturbance. Indian warfare, personal quarrels, and particularly the temporary confusion in external control caused by the Glorious Revolution became the occasions for violent challenges to constituted authority.

398; Daniel E. Motley, *Life of Commissary James Blair* . . . (Baltimore, 1901), 10, 43 ff.; William S. Perry, ed., *Historical Collections Relating to the* . . . *Church* ([Hartford], 1870-78), I, 69, 72-73, 88, 90, 102, 135; Leonidas Dodson, *Alexander Spotswood* (Philadelphia, 1932), 251 ff.

By the end of the century a degree of harmony had been achieved, but the divergence between political and social leadership at the topmost level created an area of permanent conflict. The political and social structures that emerged were by European standards strangely shaped. Everywhere as the bonds of empire drew tighter the meaning of the state was changing. Herein lay the origins of a new political system.

PART FOUR

Church and State

The seventeenth century in America as well as in England was a *saeculum theologicum*.

VERNON LOUIS PARRINGTON

VI.

THE ANGLICAN PARISH IN VIRGINIA

William H. Seiler

KANSAS STATE TEACHERS COLLEGE, EMPORIA

ON JANUARY 23, 1677, the Anglican minister and six vestrymen met to conduct the affairs of Petsoe Parish in Gloucester County, Virginia. The minutes of this meeting, which begin one of the oldest continuous colonial vestry records still in existence, show that ordinary business was transacted. In no way do they suggest the turbulence which had affected the colony during the previous year. Bacon's Rebellion had ended officially just the week before and the county had been one of the main theaters in which that dramatic event had taken place. Indeed, it is believed that during the previous October the rebel had died at the home of Major Thomas Pate, who attended the meeting as a churchwarden, with Philip Lightfoot, and vestrymen John Buckner, William Thornton, Thomas Royston, Robert Lee, and William Pritchett.

Major Pate and the vestrymen of Petsoe Parish possessed the combination of wealth, political influence, and family connections which increasingly characterized the Virginia vestries in the closing years of the seventeenth century. Pate was a justice of the peace and military officer of the county. A nephew of John Pate, who had served on the Virginia Council, he became the administrator of his uncle's estate in 1682, when it was valued at £1,221 11s. 11d. plus a tobacco crop of 23,714 pounds. John Pate, presumably a son of Thomas, owned 1,000 acres of county land in 1704, and a son (John?) married into the prominent Reade family of neighboring Kingston Parish.

John Buckner came to Gloucester County as an emigrant from

England in 1669 and patented 1,000 acres, including his own headright. He became a prosperous businessman and agent for English merchants and a burgess from the county. In 1682 he brought the first printing press and printer to Virginia. Along with Thomas Royston, another vestryman at the meeting of January, 1677, he patented 2,000 acres on the south side of the Rappahannock River, a tract which later became the site of the town of Fredericksburg. Buckner served as a Petsoe vestryman from 1677 until 1694. Thomas Buckner, later a captain, began his service as a churchwarden the following year. By 1704 he owned 850 acres of land in Gloucester County and 1,000 acres in Essex. For many years he served on the county court.

Philip Lightfoot and his brother John, later a councilor, emigrated from England to Gloucester County, where Philip became one of the most influential men in the colony. In 1675 he joined with John Buckner, Thomas Royston, John Lewis, and Lieutenant Colonel John Smith in patenting 10,000 acres in New Kent County. He served as surveyor-general, a member of the county court, collector of the duties for the Upper District of the James River, and vestryman of Petsoe until his removal to James City County in 1690. He married Alice Corbin, the daughter of Henry Corbin of "Buckingham House," Middlesex County— a name of consequence throughout the eighteenth century in that county and in Christ Church Parish. By 1737 a granddaughter with a fortune set at £5,000 was the wife of Beverley Randolph, eldest son of William Randolph of the Council.

William Thornton, who was in the colony as early as 1646, possessed large landholdings along the Rappahannock River. William, Jr., became a member of the vestry in 1680 and for a time father and son served together. Later, grandsons Seth and Francis continued the Thornton name on the vestry records. The names of Pate, Buckner, Lightfoot, and Thornton are accompanied by other prominent family names in this seventeenth-century vestry book—the Bernards, after whose origins in England the parish was probably named, the Carters, Greens, Throck-mortons, and Wyatts. Vestryman Conquest Wyatt was the largest land-holder in the county and a descendant of former Governor Sir Francis Wyatt.

Presiding at the meeting in 1677 was the Reverend Thomas Vicaris. Like his fellow-clergymen, he served a rural parish, although Petsoe, with its 40,000 acres of rich farmland, was among the wealthier and more populous ones. Very little is known about him or any of the Anglican clergy in Virginia in the later seventeenth century. He was probably serving the parish as early as 1666, when he received a grant of 650 acres of land in the county. He continued to serve it faithfully until his death in 1696. His length of service, which was the average that prevailed among the clergy in 1724, indicates that in Petsoe Parish there was an early beginning of the stability that later characterized the ministers' employment in the more substantial parishes of the tidewater.

The business of the vestry meeting was routine, suggesting some of the usual duties undertaken by the Anglican parish within the framework of Virginia's state-church. The vestry approved Mr. Vicaris' salary of 12,000 pounds of tobacco—below the Assembly's recommendation of 13,333 pounds to allow £80 sterling for the year, but Gloucester County raised sweet-scented tobacco, the most valuable type. It also allotted 500 pounds of tobacco to the parish clerk, 100 pounds to Mr. Lightfoot for furnishing the communion wine, and another 2,150 pounds to him "for 33 cedar posts and cariage by 6 oxen and 4 men," evidently in connection with the building of the new church at Poplar Spring. Another 500 pounds was assigned to the parishioner who handled the subscription for the new church. Allowances were made for the care of parish indigents, and a bastard child was bound out as an apprentice until he reached the age of twenty-one. Here in Petsoe, as in the other Virginia parishes—whether in normal times or in the wake of an event as momentous as Bacon's Rebellion—the vestry carried on its duties.[1]

By the close of the seventeenth century the Anglican state-church had been firmly set in its colonial mold, the result of nearly one hundred years of existence in the New World. The Church of England was one of the numerous English institutions transferred to America in the founding of the Virginia colony in 1607. It was one of the most important, for an alliance between church and state, holding dominion over the affairs of

1. C. G. Chamberlayne, ed., *The Vestry Book of Petsworth Parish, Gloucester County, Virginia, 1677-1793* (Richmond, Va., 1933). The parish was originally known as Petsoe. On Thomas Pate, see *Va. Mag. of Hist. and Biog.*, 4 (1897), 249; 19 (1911), 255-57; on John Buckner, see *ibid.*, 1 (1894), 406; 10 (1903), 236; 31 (1923), 233-34; on Thomas Royston, see *ibid.*, 31 (1923), 233-34, and *Wm. and Mary Qtly.*, 1st ser., 9 (1901), 260; 12 (1904), 121-22; on Philip Lightfoot, see *Va. Mag. of Hist. and Biog.*, 1 (1894), 244, and *Wm. and Mary Qtly.*, 1st ser., 2 (1894), 204-7; 3 (1895), 104-11; on William Thornton, see *Va. Mag. of Hist. and Biog.*, 1 (1894), 480, and *Wm. and Mary Qtly.*, 1st ser., 4 (1896), 89-91; little is known about Robert Lee and William Pritchett. Robert Lee was a kinsman of Richard and Henry Lee, and the vestry book in 1680 shows that by his last will and testament he gave £10 to the poor of the parish. His widow married Edward Porteus, a vestryman of the parish; *Wm. and Mary Qtly.*, 1st ser., 24 (1916), 47, and *Va. Mag. of Hist. and Biog.*, 13 (1906), 311. William Pritchett evidently came to the colony in 1644; *Va. Mag. of Hist. and Biog.*, 28 (1920), 144. On the Reverend Thomas Vicaris, see Chamberlayne, ed., *Vestry Book of Petsworth Parish*, xii; for the landholdings, see Thomas J. Wertenbaker, *The Planters of Colonial Virginia* (Princeton, N. J., 1922), Appendix.

men, was the commonly accepted pattern of European society at that time. Absolute control by the state and its true church existed as an aid to worldly and sinful men; governments exercised civil authority to restrain the evil that men might do to one another, and a disciplined conformity in religious affairs promoted that obedience and rectitude necessary for man's ultimate goal—the earthly journey to eternal salvation.[2]

The harsh conditions imposed by a foreign and hostile environment, geographical separation from the mother country, and the absence of a competent episcopal form of organization led the colonists to apply their own distinctive modifications to the structure and operation of the church in Virginia. In the absence of direct English control a colonial control was substituted. The Assembly, the governor, and, most important in the development of local self-government, the parish vestry, assumed essential roles in the emergence of the Anglican Church in Virginia.

The association of church and state, accepted as a normal institutional arrangement, was clearly set forth in the chartering of the Virginia Company when James I ordered that the religious Establishment should conform "to the doctrine, rights, and religion now professed and established within our realme of England."[3] Take along "one or twoo preachers," the worldly Hakluyt had counseled, "that God may be honoured, the people instructed, mutinies the better avoided, and obedience the better used."[4] During the first years of the colony, the piety of the age was manifest in frequent divine services and prayers, and later in a period of discontent and doubt, Governor Dale's regime presented rigorous rules enforcing the Establishment as an aid to civil order and discipline.[5]

At its first meeting in 1619 the Assembly endorsed the Church of England as the legally authorized religious organization in the colony.[6]

2. Perry Miller, "The Religious Impulse in the Founding of Virginia," *Wm. and Mary Qtly.*, 3rd ser., 5 (1948), 498; 6 (1949), 27-28, 32-33; Evarts B. Greene, *Religion and the State* (New York, 1941), 8-9.

3. William W. Hening, ed., *The Statutes-at-Large . . . of Virginia (1619-1792)* (13 vols.; Richmond, Va., 1809-23), I, 69.

4. Wesley Frank Craven, *The Southern Colonies in the Seventeenth Century, 1607-1689* (Baton Rouge, La., 1949), 64.

5. "Yet wee had daily Common Prayer morning and evening, every Sunday two Sermons, and every three months the holy Communion, till our Minister died; but our Prayers daily, with an Homily on Sundaies, we continued two or three yeares after, till more Preachers came." John Smith, *Advertisements for the unexperienced Planters of New-England*, in Edward Arber, ed., *Works of Capt. John Smith* (Westminster, Eng., 1895), 957-58; [W. Strachey], comp., *Lawes Divine, Morall and Martiall*, in Peter Force, comp., *Tracts and Other Papers Relating Principally to the Origin, Settlement, and Progress of the Colonies in North America* (4 vols.; Washington, D. C., 1836-46), III, no. 2, 10.

6. H. R. McIlwaine, ed., *Journals of the House of Burgesses of Virginia, 1619-1658/59* (Richmond, Va., 1914), 13, 36.

An act of 1624 stated that there should be "uniformity in our church as neere as may be to the canons in England; both in substance and circumstance, and that all persons yield readie obedience unto them under paine of censure."[7]   The phrase "as neere as may be" represented orthodoxy's concession to the practical difficulties confronting the colonial church: geographical separation from the mother church, hazardous local conditions, the shortage of ministers, absence of a resident bishop or even direct association with an English diocese, and recognition of the disputes within the church at home.

Certainly the Virginia Establishment reflected the religious disputations occurring in England.   During the early years of the colony, "the Puritan movement in its broad aspects embraced all sorts and conditions of religious and moral discontent, from the Brownists or Separatists to the non-conforming clergyman and low churchman of the Anglican Church."[8] Predominant in the company's membership at home and among the first Virginia settlers were those individuals of Puritan belief who would reform the Church of England from within, rather than become Separatists.   As far as is known, all of the clergy in the colony during the early years of settlement belonged to this Puritan school within the church.   But this designation was not one which would create a schism.[9]

There is this fact to be noted: while the Virginia Company professed adherence to the Church of England, its ecclesiastical complexion always shows itself more "low" than "high," and therefore not radically different from many Puritans'.   Virginians enacted the canons of England, creating a state church, but the quality of their piety, their sense of their relation to God, was so thoroughly Protestant as to be virtually indistinguishable from the Puritan.[10]

The seventeenth-century Virginia church denied Separatism, but continued to meet the demands of the low churchman by keeping the Establishment "sufficiently mild to provide room for all forms of Protestant faith except [those that] showed themselves disloyal to the king or hostile

7. Hening, ed., *Va. Stat. at L.,* I, 123.

8. Charles M. Andrews, *The Colonial Period of American History* (4 vols.; New Haven, Conn., 1934-38), I, 228.

9. Miller, "The Religious Impulse in the Founding of Virginia," *Wm. and Mary Qtly.,* 3rd ser., 5 (1948), 499-500; G. M. Brydon, *Virginia's Mother Church and the Political Conditions Under Which It Grew* (Richmond, Va., 1947), I, 18, 25-27, 29.

10. Miller, "The Religious Impulse in the Founding of Virginia," *Wm. and Mary Qtly.,* 3rd ser., 5 (1948), 499. See also Harry Culverwell Porter, "Alexander Whitaker: Cambridge Apostle to Virginia," *ibid.,* 3rd ser., 14 (1957), 342.

to the government of the colony."[11]   The Puritan movement found expression in the institutional organization of the church, where parishes and their vestries effectively developed local political and social control.[12]

During the period of the English Civil War the stature of the Established Church remained unimpaired within the colony.   Only to a small minority of radical Puritan dissidents did the political aspect of the state-church association become a basic issue.   This Puritan faction appealed to Boston for Puritan ministers to serve non-conformist congregations in Virginia, but Governor Berkeley opposed this measure and in 1643 legislation was passed which required conformity of all ministers, with the governor and Council ordered to expel all dissenting clergymen.[13]   Two of the three Puritan clergymen who had come to the colony departed, but William Thompson remained.   This was apparently the first time that a stringent law had been enacted against non-conforming ministers.   These measures, however, "were far more immediately intended to prevent the presence in Virginia of dissenting ministers as fomenters of sedition and disloyalty to their king than they were to interfere with the holding of other forms of religious belief."[14]   In 1649 increasing pressure against the anti-monarchical forces caused more than three hundred Puritans to leave Virginia in one group and go to Maryland at the invitation of Lord Baltimore—an invitation which may have been regretted in the light of future developments there.[15]

Although Virginia submitted to the government of the Commonwealth in 1651, the new instructions pertaining to religious affairs were never completely effective in the colony.   There was no displacement of clergymen, and the Book of Common Prayer, so odious to the Cromwellians, was permitted for one year with the stipulation that references to the monarchy be deleted; in actuality it was probably used until the Restoration.[16]

11. Brydon, *Virginia's Mother Church*, I, x; Hugh Jones, *The Present State of Virginia*, ed. by Richard L. Morton (Chapel Hill, 1956), 11, 182, 223.

12. "Home rule by the vestry, the isolation of churches, and the weakness of external authority gave American Anglicanism an independence somewhat suggestive of Congregationalism."   Curtis P. Nettels, *The Roots of American Civilization* (New York, 1939), 479; see also Max Savelle, *Seeds of Liberty* (New York, 1948), 4-5, 21-22, 23-24.   The Puritan influence present in the Virginia church throughout the colonial period is a subject worth further investigation.

13. Hening, ed., *Va. Stat. at L.*, I, 239-43.

14. Brydon, *Virginia's Mother Church*, I, 444; see also Craven, *Southern Colonies*, 229.

15. Brydon, *Virginia's Mother Church*, I, 119-21.

16. "Articles of Surrender," in Hening, ed., *Va. Stat. at L.*, I, 363-68; see also W. N. Sainsbury *et al.*, eds., *Calendar of State Papers, Colonial Series, America and West Indies*, I, *1574-1660* (London, 1860), 376.

Although Anglicanism is not mentioned as the authorized religion during the Commonwealth period, the phrasing of the statutes indicates that the church organization was utilized in Virginia.[17] As in the legislation of 1643, the Assembly delegated control to the local parishes, which strengthened more than ever the colonial foundation of the church. Most of the influential Virginia planters remained loyal to the Anglican Church and the cause of monarchy, while supporting parochial control. There is little suggestion that a Parliamentary party in the colony was seeking to turn the parishes into united Puritan citadels.[18]

Full legal status of the Anglican state-church was resumed after the Restoration. The legislation of 1662 concerning ecclesiastical affairs was similar to the enactments of 1643 and defined the church organization and policy which would prevail until the American Revolution, with the exception of modifications introduced by the Toleration Act.[19] This legislation of 1662 showed an awareness of the lack of complete ecclesiastical organization in the Virginia church. "In the very hesitation with which [the] preamble speaks of 'rules' for the government of the Church instead of 'laws,' " the historiographer of the diocese of Virginia has pointed out, "they seem to show the realization that, as a civil legislature, they were, because of circumstances beyond their control, performing the duties of an ecclesiastical synod, and their understanding that these rules were to continue in force until a proper ecclesiastical organization had been secured seems to indicate that plans were being formulated through which this might be obtained. Certainly such apparent hesitation to enact laws for the Church had never appeared in any previous code."[20]

The failure of English authorities to complete the ecclesiastical organization left the House of Burgesses as the primary determinant of ecclesiastical policy: it established new parishes and consolidated others, defined parish boundaries, fixed the salaries of ministers, outlined requirements for collection of parish taxes, and, in substance, fulfilled those responsibilities which, in England, would have rested with an established diocesan organization or ecclesiastical synod.

The governor's position was also an important one in the church-state association of the seventeenth century. From the first settlement he had been instructed to uphold religion according to the Established faith "as neere as may be." Thus the interests of the church were represented by a secular executive; whether or not the church benefitted by this representation depended upon the personal attitudes and professional abilities of

17. Hening, ed., *Va. Stat. at L.*, I, 399-400.
18. Craven, *Southern Colonies*, 265-66.
19. Hening, ed., *Va. Stat. at L.*, II, 44-46.
20. Brydon, *Virginia's Mother Church*, I, 177.

the incumbent. In his office, as lay ordinary, were vested such important episcopal functions as receiving the ministers' orders upon their entrance into the colony, recommending them to parish assignment, inducting clergymen into their livings, issuing licenses for marriages, and probating wills. The royal governor was the principal colonial representative of English ecclesiastical government, and it is always pertinent to ask what he did to advance the cause of the church in Virginia.

Two factors explain the generally ineffective role of the governors in ecclesiastical leadership during the seventeenth century. One reason was the events occurring in England; careful attention to church affairs in the colony was diverted by more important matters at home. A second and equally significant reason was the internal situation in Virginia, which contributed to a lack of continuity in the governorship. From the beginning of royal control in 1624 until the Cromwellian period when Governor Berkeley was deposed in 1652, Virginia had seven different governors or acting governors in eleven administrations. Any governor seeking to enhance his own status or espouse the imperial viewpoint met with colonial opposition, as Sir John Harvey discovered early in the century. Later governors, such as Lord Howard, Nicholson, Andros, and Spotswood, found an entrenched local self-government in church affairs which they challenged at their peril.

The parish vestry, therefore, was the third vital element in the colonial organization of the church. The parish was the local unit for the administration of ecclesiastical affairs throughout the colonial period, and because of the church-state connection it also served as the local unit for the administration of certain civil affairs. Settlers from many different sections of England had drawn on their common experience to create in this unit "a mark of the exclusive supremacy of Anglicanism in Virginia."[21] Although closely modeled upon the English parish, the colonial parish went beyond it in two vital characteristics. First, the English parish, whether ecclesiastical or civil, never became an autonomous and independent entity; it was "merely the base of a more or less elaborate hierarchy of government." In Virginia, however, the lack of strong diocesan control and the absence of a resident bishop throughout the colonial period made rigid adherence to the hierarchical structure an impossibility. Secondly, custom and law alike had given the parish a considerable degree of power; "the right and power of the parish to provide for its inhabitants

21. Herbert L. Osgood, *The American Colonies in the Seventeenth Century* (3 vols.; New York, 1904-6), III, 82.

. . . was so vaguely extensive as to be practically without . . . limits."[22] Freedom of action, which became an inherent principle in the development of the Virginia parish, brought about the predominance of the laity in determining church policy.[23]

The parish vestry was the only permanent group which dealt continuously with the affairs of the parishioners in their daily lives. In the beginning the minister appointed churchwardens and the county court evidently appointed vestrymen, but by 1645 the custom of the parish freemen's voting for vestrymen had come into use. In 1662, the Assembly granted to the vestries the right to select replacements in their membership when vacancies occurred.[24] This principle of co-optation was continued throughout the rest of the colonial period, with the possible exception of 1676, the year of Bacon's Rebellion, and on those occasions when new parishes were organized or old ones divided or when the Assembly ordered the dissolution of a vestry and a new election.

The record of creation, subdivision, and consolidation of parishes illuminates the rapid spread of population in the colony. By 1634, with settlements scattered along the shores of the James and York rivers, Virginia was divided into eight shires or counties. In four of them there is reasonable evidence to assume that counties and parishes were coterm-

22. Sidney James Webb and Beatrice Webb, *English Local Government from the Revolution to the Municipal Corporations Act: The Parish and the County* (London, 1906), 4, 5-6, 40-41; for the ecclesiastical origins and development of the English parish, *ibid.*, 37-39, n. 6; A. R. Powys, *The English Parish Church* (London, 1930), 1; Sir Frederick Pollock and Frederic William Maitland, *The History of English Law*, 2nd edn. (2 vols.; Cambridge, Eng., 1923), I, 560-61; Edward Ingle, *Local Institutions of Virginia* (Baltimore, 1885), 51.

23. This was to be an important contribution to the polity of the Protestant Episcopal Church of the United States. G. M. Brydon, "The Origins of the Rights of the Laity in the American Episcopal Church," *Hist. Mag. of the Protestant Episcopal Church*, 12 (1943), 313; G. M. Brydon, "New Light Upon the History of the Church in Colonial Virginia," *ibid.*, 10 (1941), 4; G. C. Mason, "Historic Parishes of America: Bruton Parish," *Wm. and Mary Qtly.*, 2nd ser., 14 (1934), 276. See Daniel J. Boorstin, *The Americans* (New York, 1958), 123-39.

24. Force, *Tracts*, III, no. 2, 11; Hening, ed., *Va. Stat. at L.*, I, 155-56, 185, 227, 240-41; Susie M. Ames, ed., *County Court Records of Accomack-Northampton County, Virginia, 1632-1640* (Washington, D. C., 1954), I, 1, 39. In 1645 the Assembly passed an act that allowed "the major part of the parishioners . . . to make choice of such men as by pluralities of voices shall be fitt." Hening, ed., *Va. Stat. at L.*, I, 290-91. No vestry books exist for this period, and county court records have not yet revealed the vestryman's term of office; it is not stated in the legislation of 1643 or 1645. The assumption is that elections were held when a vacancy occurred. For the legislation of 1662, see Hening, ed., *Va. Stat. at L.*, III, 296; H. R. McIlwaine, ed., *Executive Journals of the Council of Colonial Virginia* (5 vols.; Richmond, Va., 1925-30), II, 98.

inous; in the other four it is possible that six or even ten parishes existed.[25] Soon coterminous parishes and counties ceased to exist. Governor Berkeley reported twenty counties and forty-eight parishes in 1671, the same number recorded in the first official list of 1680. Commissary Blair found that the number had increased to fifty by 1697.[26]

The character of Virginia society in these tidewater parishes of the seventeenth century was determined primarily by the tobacco economy, which had fostered a diversified population. Increasing from about 8,000 in 1640 to more than 40,000 in 1671, the population included influential planters, small farmers, indentured servants, and Negro slaves, whose numbers had increased from 150 in the earlier year to 2,000 in the latter. Many of the parishes were large, making the work of the minister rigorous as he traveled over poor roads to outlying chapels. In Virginia, as in the other colonies, life was an arduous struggle for survival against sickness and death. It was a stratified as well as a highly acquisitive society, with keen striving for status and titles and economic rewards. Compulsory attendance at church, introduced for religious reasons, served secular purposes as well, because the church service furnished the typical rural pattern of relief from the isolation of life on widely separated farms. Church and churchyard became the center for the Sunday meeting of neighbors, exchange of news, and transaction of business. Until the introduction in the following century of the *Virginia Gazette,* this weekly service provided the widest possible hearing for official notices, governmental proclamations, and publication of laws and orders.

In addition to Sunday services, the ceremonies of the church touched the lives of the people at baptism, marriage, and death. The churchwardens were brought into a direct association with the social mores of·the colonists through their responsibilities for overseeing the moral conduct of the parishioners. The Assembly made them responsible for presentment to the county court

of such misdemeanors as to their knowledge have been committed the year before . . . namely, swearing, prophaning God's name, and his holy Sabboths, abuseing his holy word and commandments, conteming his holy sacrements or anything belonging to his service or worship. . . . [and of] any person or persons of what degree or condition soever shall

25. If the point of view is sustained that original counties and parishes were coterminous, then older divisions, represented in earlier Assemblies and qualifying as parishes in previous assignments, were evidently assigned, in 1634, a temporary status corresponding to the precinct.

26. Hening, ed., *Va. Stat. at L.,* II, 517; *Va. Mag. of Hist. and Biog.,* I, 242-44; *Wm. and Mary Qtly.,* 2nd ser., 17 (1937), 466-68; William Stevens Perry, ed., *Historical Collections Relating to the American Colonial Church* (3 vols.; Hartford, Conn., 1870-73), I, 11.

abuse themselves with the high & foule offences of adultery, whoredome or fornication or with the loathesome sinne of drunkenness in the abuse of God's creatures.[27]

Grand juries became more active in the presentments for violations at a later date, but throughout the colonial era this was a fundamental duty of the churchwardens.

Within these isolated parishes of the colony the clergyman carried on the duties of his office, numerous but for the most part routine. Usually removed from any outside intellectual or spiritual challenge, he was mainly confined to parochial affairs. The character of the Anglican parish clergy deserves attention because of the social influence of the minister. There is a tendency among scholars to generalize about the colonial Anglican clergy in Virginia; apologists of the church overlook their defects and hostile critics allow them no personal goodness. It is evident that the colonial clergy, as a group, went through a number of distinct periods and changes of character. Ability and intense dedication, for example, were typical of the ministers during the years of the Virginia Company. Then came a time when the clergy were "such as wore Black Coats, and could babble in a Pulpit, roare in a Tavern . . . and rather by their dissoluteness destroy than feed their Flocks."[28] The description of the clergy during this period reflected the colonial situation at that time. In the contest for power following the dissolution of the company, a new group emerged, "tough, unsentimental, quick tempered, crudely ambitious men," who "roared curses, drank exuberantly, and gambled for their servants when other commodities were lacking."[29]

A relatively small number of Anglican clergymen, royalist ministers of high caliber, left England for the colonies during Cromwell's regime, and Virginia apparently welcomed them. Yet by 1662 there were only ten clergymen to serve forty-five to forty-eight parishes.[30] Indeed, the most significant fact about the clergy at this time is their scarcity; to debate their character is to obscure the major issue. The usual explanation for this lack of numbers from about 1624 to 1660 is the inadequate supply from England, but the very high mortality rate among those ministers who

27. Hening, ed., *Va. Stat. at L.*, I, 240-41.
28. John Hammond, *Leah and Rachel* (London, 1656), in Force, *Tracts*, III, no. 14, 9. The Reverend Nicholas Moreau in a letter to the bishop of Lichfield in 1697 also commented on the unworthiness of ministers after the Company period. Perry, ed., *Historical Collections*, I, 2-3.
29. See the preceding essay by Bernard Bailyn, and his n. 19.
30. R[oger] G[reen], *Virginia's Cure* (London, 1662), in Force, *Tracts*, III, no. 15, 2; "R. G." reports about fifty parishes, but it appears that there were between forty-five and fifty-eight parishes at this time.

came to the colony should not be discounted. The extremes of climate were great, and the heat of the Virginia summer carried with it the threat of malaria and other diseases.[31] Nevertheless, the number of ministers had increased by 1680 to thirty-five; by 1702 there were thirty-seven clergymen and fifty-one parishes.[32]

Although a few lists of ministers licensed to the colony have been printed with short biographical sketches, a study is needed of the Anglican clergy in seventeenth-century Virginia after the company period.[33] Further information and a competent appraisal are necessary to clarify many questions. For example, what was the minister's status in the community during the seventeenth century? Most analyses of the clergy in Virginia are based on observations of the eighteenth century, but there is no assurance that considerable differences did not exist one hundred years earlier. The law required the minister to live within his cure and to perform divine service on Sunday, either at the parish church or at one of the outlying chapels. If the minister was absent, or the parish vacant, a lay reader was authorized to give the lessons and a homily. Services were to be conducted in full conformity with the doctrine and ceremonies of the Church of England, in so far as this was locally feasible. Officiating at baptisms, weddings, and funerals, catechizing the young, and visiting the sick were all customary duties. Holy Communion was to be administered three times a year.[34]

31. John Clement, "Clergymen Licensed Overseas by the Bishops of London, 1696-1710 and 1715-1716," *Hist. Mag. of the Protestant Episcopal Church,* 16 (1947), 321. On sickness of British-born clergymen in a neighboring colony, see John Duffy, "Eighteenth-Century Carolina Health Conditions," *Jour. of So. Hist.,* 18 (1952), 289-302.

32. List of 1680 in *Va. Mag. of Hist. and Biog.,* 1 (1894), 242-44, with corrections in *Wm. and Mary Qtly.,* 2nd ser., 17 (1937), 466-68; and the list of 1702 in *Va. Mag of Hist. and Biog.,* 1 (1894), 373-77, where Accomack and Kingston parishes, omitted from this list, were probably vacant. For 1714, see *ibid.,* 2 (1894), 1-15; for 1717, see Governor Spotswood's estimate, R. A. Brock, ed., *The Official Letters of Alexander Spotswood . . . 1710-1722* (2 vols.; Richmond, Va., 1882-85), II, 254; the count for 1726 is in *Va. Mag. of Hist. and Biog.,* 48 (1940), 141-52; that for 1754 is in Perry, ed., *Historical Collections,* I, 411-13; that for 1774 is in *Wm. and Mary Qtly.,* 1st ser., 5 (1897), 200-3.

33. N. W. Rightmyer, "List of Anglican Clergymen Receiving a Bounty for Overseas Service, 1680-1688," *Hist. Mag. of the Protestant Episcopal Church,* 17 (1948), 174-82; Clement, "Clergymen Licensed Overseas," *ibid.,* 16 (1947), 321.

34. Local conditions forced some irregularities in the performance of these duties. For example, the bishop of London in 1677 referred to several of them, including the "profane custom of burying in their gardens and orchards," rather than in the churchyards; Sainsbury *et al.,* eds., *Cal. State Papers, Col., 1677-1680,* 117. The replies to the queries of 1724 indicate a wide variety of times of the year for teaching the catechism. Perry, ed., *Historical Collections,* I, 216-318 *passim.* Frequently the clergyman would consecrate a church, because no bishop was available. Brydon, *Virginia's Mother Church,* I, 407, n. 8.

Practically no specific information exists about sermons preached in Virginia's first century. Did the ministers put into practice the lessons of their English training, where polemics predominated, theological disputation was interwoven with political argument, and splendor of diction was praised?[35] It is known that Governor Sir William Berkeley commented that ministers "should be better if they would pray oftener and preach less."[36] The Reverend Hugh Jones reported in the early part of the eighteenth century that Virginians were opposed to "quarrelsome and litigious ministers, who would differ with the parishioners about insignificant trifles" and that "in words and actions they should be neither too reserved nor too extravagant"—attitudes which applied to sermons also, it may be presumed.[37]

Christianizing the natives, so strongly urged in the charters authorizing the planting of the colony, was not carried on extensively in later years except at the Indian School of the College of William and Mary. As the colony became more stabilized and Indians were removed from the tidewater area, this duty was generally neglected. Missionary zeal showed "a Christian and humanitarian concern for the welfare of the natives" in Virginia and Maryland, but the results too often were "a harvest of Indian wars rather than converts."[38]

The religious training of the Negro was left almost totally to the masters of the plantations, and the results were generally inadequate. In 1667 the Assembly made it clear that the baptism of Negro slaves did not remove them from bondage, although masters were urged to encourage their slaves to accept Christianity and have them baptized.[39] Reports to the bishop of London in 1724, however, stated that parsons usually neglected the baptism of slaves because of the opposition of planters. With few exceptions this attitude prevailed throughout the colonial period.[40]

35. Significant clues to interest in sermons can be found in libraries of the colonial period, mainly for the eighteenth century, which have been discussed in a great number of periodical articles. See the bibliography and comments in Louis B. Wright, *The Cultural Life of the American Colonies, 1607-1763* (New York, 1957), especially 11-12, 138-39, 146-47.

36. Philip Alexander Bruce, *Institutional History of Virginia in the Seventeenth Century* (2 vols., New York, 1910), I, 206.

37. *Present State of Virginia*, ed. by Morton, 117.

38. Craven, *Southern Colonies*, 231; W. Stitt Robinson, Jr., "Indian Education and Missions in Colonial Virginia," *Jour. of So. Hist.*, 18 (1952), 152-68.

39. Hening, ed., *Va. Stat. at L.*, II, 260. In 1682 an act removed the basis for a claim to freedom from bondage even on the ground of conversion before importation, *ibid.*, 490; see also Craven, *Southern Colonies*, 403.

40. Replies of ministers in 1724 to the question, "What Means are Used for the Conversion of Negro 'Infidels'?" have been collected in Brydon, *Virginia's Mother Church*, I, 392-93.

Many of the parochial clergy were schoolmasters; from the beginning clergymen served on the teaching staff of the College of William and Mary. After 1686 schoolmasters in the colony were required to have a license from the bishop of London attesting that they would conform to the doctrine and forms of the Church of England, but this requirement was difficult to enforce.[41] With Virginia custom requiring that each householder look after the educational needs of his family, some parents sent their children to England and others had private tutors, but the greatest number of students received their training in private neighborhood schools, taught in many cases by the local minister. Many of these men made an outstanding contribution to the intellectual and spiritual life of the colony.[42]

An appraisal of the income of the seventeenth-century clergy suggests that it was generally above that of the great majority of small landholders and appreciably below that of the larger planters who were the leading members of the tidewater vestries. By the legislation of 1662 the annual income of the individual clergyman was set at £80, with 13,333 pounds of tobacco allotted to meet this sum. Whether extra allotments were made to adjust his salary in times of depressed tobacco prices depended upon the wishes of each vestry. By 1696 the Assembly approved a 16,000 pound allotment, but in juggling the collection fees and cost of cask, the net gain to the minister was only 650 pounds. From 1727 to the Revolution the stated allotment was 17,240 pounds of tobacco. Throughout the colonial period the cash value depended, however, upon the market price and type of tobacco planted in the parish: the difference between Oronoco or sweet-scented varied from £35 to £40. If a minister's salary reached £80 sterling plus perquisites for marriages (20 shillings for licenses, 5 shillings for banns), churchings (10 shillings), funerals (40 shillings), and a glebe of 200 to 250 acres, he earned enough "to enable . . . [himself] and his family to live upon the plane of an educated man and a gentleman, but it was also true that the extreme fluctuation of the purchasing value of tobacco bore much more hardly upon the minister than upon the average planter of the same social class."[43] An enterprising preacher in an acquisitive, land-dominated society could obtain extended holdings on his own initiative. Some of the clergy married into the more important

41. McIlwaine, ed., *Journals of the House of Burgesses, 1659/60-1693*, 270, 274, 455; Leonard W. Labaree, ed., *Royal Instructions to British Colonial Governors, 1670-1776* (2 vols., New York, 1935), II, 492.

42. G. F. Wells, *Parish Education in Colonial Virginia* (New York, 1923), *passim*; Bruce, *Institutional History*, I, 293-361; Brydon, *Virginia's Mother Church*, I, 390-91.

43. A full discussion may be found in Brydon, *Virginia's Mother Church*, I, 311-19 (318 quoted), and in Bruce, *Institutional History*, I, 145-62.

families; Commissary James Blair is one of the illustrious examples. Moreover, the clergymen's university training gave them an educational claim to the status of gentlemen as soon as they arrived in America. If they did not forfeit this social rank by misconduct, there is reason to believe that it gave them a secure position in the social hierarchy of Virginia.

After the dissolution of the Virginia Company, the power to select a minister for a parish was claimed by the governor, the Council, and the vestries. In England the right to nominate a clergyman belonged to the patron of the parish, the owner of the advowson; the bishop confirmed the selection by inducting the rector. Induction assured permanent tenure unless charges of moral laxity or dereliction of duty were proved before an ecclesiastical court. In the colony, if induction was administered by the governor, there was a definite prospect of long and tedious proceedings to remove an unworthy rector, because no bishop or ecclesiastical court was available. Vestries had adopted, therefore, what Commissary James Blair later called "a contrary Custom of making annual Agreements with the Ministers, which they call by a name coarse enough, *viz.* Hiring of the Ministers."[44]

The significant legislation of 1643 regularized this arrangement by granting the vestries the right to choose their own ministers, and they never relinquished it. Instituted during a period when there was valid criticism of the character of many of the clergy, annual appointments prevailed throughout the colonial period. The Assembly recognized that the procedure, although necessary when instituted, was defective and authorized the minister to become a member of the vestry and its presiding officer with "all the spiritual rights of the rectorship, both in his ministry to the people and in his possession and use of the church buildings, as well as the glebe."[45] Robert Beverley said that this method of employment presented no grave problem and that no qualified clergyman ever returned to England for want of preferment in Virginia. Brydon has shown that the twenty-nine clergymen serving in Virginia in 1724 spent, on the average, twenty-five years in the colony and twenty-one years in the parish where they were then located. Only five were inducted, the others serving on annual agreements with their vestries. Ames has suggested that the later seventeenth century would probably show a similar condition if sufficient statisti-

44. Henry Hartwell, James Blair, and Edward Chilton, *The Present State of Virginia and the College*, ed. by Hunter D. Farish (Williamsburg, 1940), 67; also see the comment by a contemporary, anonymous observer in Louis B. Wright, ed., *An Essay Upon the Government of the English Plantations on the Continent of America* (San Marino, Calif., 1945), 22.

45. Brydon, *Virginia's Mother Church*, I, 100-1.

cal data were available.[46]   If true, this would indicate that annual agreements did not endanger the tenure of the great majority of ministers in the earlier period.

How much independence of action did this leave the clergyman? Philip Alexander Bruce believed it fostered the desired qualities of energy, faithfulness, and circumspection.   Brydon argues that independence of action is a personal moral quality.   Spencer Ervin has recently noted that "there are men of ability and character who will in time give way under the nagging of domineering laymen.   Like a judge, a parson needs an independence secured by law."[47]   The answer, of course, is necessarily uncertain, for it lies partially in the personality of the individual clergyman and in his particular situation.

But by the later years of the seventeenth century, a familiar pattern had been created for the clergyman in Virginia society.   The views of colonial Virginians were liberal in regard to moderate pleasures, and an extremely emotional approach to religion was not countenanced.   Low church attitudes prevailed; the moderate Puritanism of the company period developed into a tolerant latitudinarian approach in theological matters, and the more severe injunctions against immorality were directed in support of a stabilized class system.   No doubt a few evangelical crusaders criticized these views and a few of the clergy went beyond the bounds of moderation, but the great majority were "men of good character and conduct, living according to the standards of their day and time."[48]   Within this milieu the clergy acted as leaders of the spiritual community and clerical representatives of a parish-centered state-church.

Customs and events had placed the English plantations of North America within the diocesan control of the bishop of London, who had been a member of the original Virginia Company.[49]   As bishop of London and archbishop of Canterbury, William Laud encouraged the idea of including colonies overseas within his jurisdiction, and he went so far as

46. Robert Beverley, *The History and Present State of Virginia*, ed. by Louis B. Wright (Chapel Hill, 1947), 213; Brydon, *Virginia's Mother Church*, I, 377; Susie M. Ames, *Reading, Writing and Arithmetic in Virginia, 1607-1699* (Williamsburg, Va., 1957), 36-37.

47. Bruce, *Institutional History*, I, 141; Brydon, *Virginia's Mother Church*, I, 101-2; Spencer Ervin, "Establishment, Government, and Functioning of the Church in Colonial Virginia," *Hist. Mag. of the Protestant Episcopal Church*, 26 (1957), 106.

48. Jones, *Present State of Virginia*, ed. by Morton, 254; Edward L. Goodwin, *The Colonial Church in Virginia* (Milwaukee and London, 1927), xix quoted.

49. A. L. Cross, *The Anglican Episcopate and the American Colonies* (Cambridge, Mass., 1920), 4; Hening, ed., *Va. Stat. at L.*, I, 57 ff., for the charters; Susan M. Kingsbury, ed., *Records of the Virginia Company of London* (4 vols.; Washington, D. C., 1906-35), I, 34; III, 583.

to propose a bishop for New England. Events at home, however, interfered with his promotion of stricter diocesan control of overseas settlements.[50]

After the Restoration, the Virginia Assembly, encouraged by Governor Berkeley, attempted to strengthen the colonial church by defining more carefully its connection with the mother church. Provision was made for each clergyman to present a testimonial of ordination to the governor from "some bishop in England," though not expressly the bishop of London.[51] Bishop Compton, who assumed the See of London in 1675, worked actively for control over the colonial clergy, and this limited jurisdiction was included in instructions to the governor following 1679.[52] In 1686 schoolmasters were licensed, and in 1688 the Council of Virginia ordered that ministers have a certificate from the bishop of London, who was named chancellor of the College of William and Mary when it was founded in 1693.[53]

In 1689 Dr. James Blair was appointed commissary of the bishop of London and he served in the colony for fifty-three years. There were distinct limitations on his authority, and his attempt to introduce a commissary's court with lay jurisdiction was effectively suppressed by the Assembly.[54] The commissary did not have the right to confirm, to ordain, or to consecrate. The right of induction of ministers remained with the governor and the right of presentation belonged to the vestries. Thus, the essential duties of the commissary resolved into overseeing the clergy as individuals and promoting the cause of the church in his capacity as a member of the Council.

The idea of a resident bishop was advanced several times during the seventeenth century. The most notable example concerned the appointment of the Reverend Alexander Moray [Murray], who served in Ware Parish, Gloucester County. In 1672 a charter was drawn up in England for the creation of a diocese of Virginia, and by 1675 Moray, an "old

50. Sainsbury *et al.*, eds., *Cal. State Papers, Col., 1675-1676*, 337-38. In 1633 the authority was specifically applied to merchant adventurers in Delft and Hamburg. No other colonies were designated. John Bruce *et al.*, eds., *Cal. State Papers, Domestic Series: Charles I, 1625-1649* (23 vols. to date; London, 1858—), II, *1633-34*, 225-26; see also 74, 153. For general discussion, see J. S. M. Anderson, *The History of the Church of England in the Colonies*, 2nd edn. (3 vols.; London, 1856), I, 411; Simeon E. Baldwin, "The American Jurisdiction of the Bishop of London in Colonial Times," Amer. Antiq. Soc., *Proceedings*, N.S., 13 (1900), 181-82; Cross, *Anglican Episcopate*, 21.

51. Hening, ed., *Va. Stat. at L.*, II, 46.

52. Labaree, ed., *Royal Instructions*, II, 489-90.

53. McIlwaine, ed., *Journals of the House of Burgesses, 1659/60-1693*, 270, 274, 455; Labaree, ed., *Royal Instructions*, II, 492; McIlwaine, ed., *Executive Journals of the Council*, I, 515; Hartwell, Blair, and Chilton, *Present State of Virginia*, ed. by Farish, 84.

54. Brydon, *Virginia's Mother Church*, I, 280-89.

friend of the king," was selected as the bishop-designate. Hearings were held on his qualifications for the position, and then suddenly the book is closed. The records are too fragmentary; the plan for a Virginia bishop failed, but the reasons are not known.[55]

The failure of the ecclesiastical authorities in England to complete the organization of the church in Virginia by the appointment of a bishop was keenly felt by the parish minister in his catechetical instruction leading to confirmation and explains in great measure the relatively small number of communicants among a predominantly Anglican population. In the eighteenth century, the candidate for holy orders, if native-born, felt the lack of a resident bishop in a most personal way when he was required to go three thousand miles for ordination.

Perhaps more attention should be given to the investigation of why the colonists and the royal governors did not press more urgently for a bishop who would reside in the colony or send a suffragan bishop. On this problem the colonial sources are remarkably uninformative. In comparison with the voluminous records available on political affairs and jurisdiction of the bishop of London, there are very few statements by the colonials about a resident bishop. Tentative reasons may be offered. Internal upheavals in England precluded forthright action in the early years, when the status of the young colony was too unimpressive to suggest the leadership of a resident bishop. The difficulty was compounded during the Restoration period, when clergy were in such short supply that a resident bishop for Virginia seemed out of the question. Bishop Compton then worked successfully for the connection between the bishop of London and the colonial clergy, and a commissary was sent to represent him. By the close of the seventeenth century, however, vestries had substituted local control for the hierarchy of the English church.

The importance of the laity's place in the Virginia church was sometimes disputed by the clergy, but in the main it became accepted as a well-entrenched adjunct of other local governmental influences in the seventeenth century. The many duties performed by the parish vestries constitute a measure of the importance of the laity. As we have seen, selection of a minister was a primary duty of the vestry. Of comparable importance was its power to tax for all church-state purposes, a duty which emphasized its role in local government. This levy, like the county and other public levies, was a poll tax assessed upon the basis of tithables. Thus the assess-

55. Mary F. Goodwin, "The Reverend Alexander Moray, M.A., D.D., The First Bishop-Designate of Virginia, 1672-3," *Hist. Mag. of the Protestant Episcopal Church*, 12 (1943), 59-68. It is believed that Moray died in London shortly after 1675.

ments brought the vestries into close association with the parishioners. The salary of the minister of the Established Church was the largest single continuing item in the parish budget; other large expenditures occurred periodically for church buildings and glebe.

Sufficient attention has not been given to the importance of this parish tax in the colony. Elizabeth City County records for the last decade of the seventeenth century indicate that "in a large number of instances the amount of the parish levy exceeded that of either the county or the public."[56] The yearly average for all three levies—public, county, and parish—has been computed at about one hundred pounds of tobacco per tithable, with the average annual public levy adjudged to be between fifteen and twenty pounds.[57] This appears to be substantially correct. The average from two of the four parishes whose vestry books are extant from the latter seventeenth century show that about forty-five pounds was the average parochial levy.[58] This would make the county levy between thirty-five and forty pounds, the public levy fifteen to twenty. If this is generally true, it is certain that taxation helped to emphasize the importance of the parish as a religious and secular institution in the colony. Further work in the tax records would provide an increased understanding of local governmental operations.

The collection of the parish levy was originally assigned as one of the duties of the churchwardens. The general practice after the middle of the seventeenth century, it has been reported, was to transfer collection of the parish taxes to the sheriff, who could combine it with his collections of the quitrents, county, and other public levies assigned by law. The numerous vestry books show no uniformity in this practice, however, and exceptions should be carefully noted. The allotment for collecting the

56. Bruce, *Institutional History*, I, 77; a brief study of the parish tax rates in the eighteenth century is included in William H. Seiler, "The Anglican Parish Vestry in Colonial Virginia," *Jour. of So. Hist.*, 22 (1956), 325-29.

57. Bruce, *Institutional History*, II, 557; Percy Scott Flippin, *The Royal Government in Virginia, 1624-1775* (New York, 1919), 242-44.

58. C. G. Chamberlayne, ed., *The Vestry Book and Register of St. Peter's Parish, New Kent and James City Counties, Virginia, 1684-1786* (Richmond, Va., 1937), 7-66 *passim*, gives the levy from 1686 to 1699: the average annual per tithable assessment was 42.1 pounds of tobacco. Chamberlayne, ed., *Vestry Book of Petsworth Parish*, 2-55 *passim*, gives the levy from 1676 to 1699: the average annual per tithable assessment was 48.8 pounds of tobacco. Using three parishes as a cross-section reference for eighteenth-century parochial tax rates, I found that if the average payment for all three poll tax levies was about 100 pounds per tithable for the colonial period, the general statement that the parish levy exceeded either the county or public levy is a valid conclusion for most of the eighteenth century also. During the last two decades before the Revolution, the county rate was probably higher than the parish. Further detailed studies on the tax rates are needed.

levy was a substantial amount in comparison with the individual payments authorized for parochial expenses.[59]

Church edifices, chapels of ease, glebe lands and buildings, and interior "ornaments" for the church were all provided by the vestries as a part of their duties concerning the management of church property. Building and repair of churches and chapels were major tasks confronting these officials. It was their duty to purchase land for the minister's glebe, furnish the glebe house, and provide outbuildings and livestock. These perquisites were allowed in addition to the minister's salary. The vestry books record payments in lieu of a glebe and many show the sincerity of the vestries in obtaining land if none was provided. In parishes so parsimonious that no glebe was furnished, the clergy protested strongly, and these communities were long left without ministers.

Charity to the poor was a parochial problem. As the population grew, there was a corresponding increase in the numbers receiving relief. Parish levies provided for orphans, the blind, the infirm, the insane, and the sick. The vestry books remain a constant reminder that the vestrymen did not close the church doors against the appeals of those deserving help. Fines for offenses against the moral law were used in support of the parish poor, but these did little to alleviate the total cost. With the disestablishment of the church in the eighteenth century, this became a secular function of the overseers of the poor.[60]

One of the most important secular duties of the vestry was supervision of land processioning. An act of 1662 declared that on the order of the county courts, the vestries were to divide the parishes into precincts every four years, and freeholders of adjoining lands were to examine and renew the boundary marks. During the seventeenth century this practice was not widely followed, but after legislation in 1705 and 1710 land processioning became an important part of the land policy of the colony.[61] In 1662, also, the county courts were ordered to appoint annually surveyors of highways. Each parish vestry, upon request of the surveyor, was to furnish sufficient workmen from tithables in the parish to clear the roads and make

59. Hening, ed., *Va. Stat. at L.*, I, 155, 160, 180, 240, 241; Flippin, *Royal Government*, 312-17; Bruce, *Institutional History*, I, 92. By an act of 1696 the fee was set at five percent of the levy, and was increased to ten percent in 1727, with an additional amount allowable if remoteness made it more difficult to get the tobacco to the landing for shipment. Before 1748 there was a wide range of percentage payments regardless of the law. In 1748 the fee was stabilized at six percent for the remainder of the colonial period. Hening, ed., *Va. Stat. at L.*, III, 152; IV, 205; VI, 89.

60. Hening, ed., *Va. Stat. at L.*, XII, 29-30.

61. William H. Seiler, "Land Processioning in Colonial Virginia," *Wm. and Mary Qtly.*, 3rd ser., 6 (1949), 416-36.

and repair bridges. This duty of the vestry continued throughout the colonial period.[62]

The significant church legislation in the revision of the laws of 1662 recognized the substantial place of the parish vestry in the local government of colonial Virginia. It confirmed the legislation of 1643 giving the vestry the right to choose its own minister and its own churchwardens.[63] For the first time it specifically set the number of vestrymen at twelve, with the original choice by election of the parishioners, and then provided for the right of vestries to fill their own vacancies, a procedure which was followed for the remainder of the colonial period, with the exceptions previously noted.[64] This legislation of 1662 provided what one scholar has aptly called "the whole armory of vestry power"; by "supplying its own vacancies, the vestry was to become a ruling class capable of passing on its power from one generation to another."[65]

By the closing years of the seventeenth century, affluent tidewater planters were prominent in the guidance of local affairs; in the following century they became a controlling class, in part through self-perpetuation in the vestry system. It would be inaccurate, however, to say that the co-optation procedure was introduced originally to perpetuate the control of a few. Rather, it was a current solution to the problem of sustaining parochial organization. The decision to do this was based on the scarcity of ministers in the colony—there were only ten in 1662—and the need for effective church organization in newly formed parishes and counties.[66]

62. Hening, ed., *Va. Stat. at L.*, II, 103. Examples concerning assignments by the vestries to work on highways and bridges may be found in Chamberlayne, ed., *Vestry Book, St. Peter's*, 9, 14, 38-39, and in Chamberlayne, ed., *The Vestry Book of St. Paul's Parish, Hanover County, Virginia, 1706-1786* (Richmond, 1940), 3, 18, 23.

63. Unlike common English practice, the Virginians did not allow the minister to choose one churchwarden and the vestry the other. The vestry, including the minister in its membership, chose both. There was no designation of senior and junior wardens, but one of the two in practice often held over for the following year. Often, one or both of the churchwardens served for several years, although they were selected annually by the vestry.

64. Hening, ed., *Va. Stat. at L.*, II, 44-45.

65. James Kimbrough Owen, The Virginia Vestry: A Study in the Decline of a Ruling Class (Unpublished Ph.D. dissertation, Princeton University, 1948), 26. Through the courtesy of Mrs. Owen, the notes and collected materials of the late Dr. Owen have been given to the writer to aid in the preparation of a study of the Anglican parish in colonial Virginia.

66. Wilcomb Washburn has recently suggested in *The Governor and the Rebel, A History of Bacon's Rebellion in Virginia* (Chapel Hill, 1957), 122, that "it is very probable that the vestry law was merely carelessly drawn without consideration of long-term effects of having the vestry and minister fill vacancies." He absolves Governor Berkeley of the responsibility for this law, pointing out that the revision was passed during the acting governorship of Francis Moryson. I think that it

Bacon's Rebellion in 1676 was only indirectly related to ecclesiastical matters. There was no desire to uproot the Anglican Establishment; sources of discontent rested elsewhere.[67] Governor Berkeley and his associates had steadily increased their influence; they controlled the Council, elections, and legislation, and they dominated the social life of the colony. According to one interpretation, they formed a "political phalanx, held together by the spirit of loyalty and advantage of office."[68] Planters out of power focused their attacks upon the governor and his associates. Because these officials handled church affairs, the vestries were also brought under attack.

The only matter pertaining to ecclesiastical affairs in the legislation of 1676, however, was the amendment of the Vestry Act of 1662 which allowed the election of vestrymen every three years by "the freeholders and freemen of every parish." With the downfall of Bacon and his rebels, the legislation of 1676 was annulled.[69] Triennial election of vestrymen was never reinstituted in the colony, although requests for such a law were mentioned by three counties in the lists of grievances submitted to the government.[70]

Why was this periodic election of vestrymen never reinstituted? Several answers are possible: a lack of dissenters in the population during the seventeenth century, and later adjustments which accommodated the vestry system to dissenters on the frontier; the fact that the duties of the vestry basically took the form of service; the changing purpose of co-optation. By the close of the century it was clear that self-perpetuating vestries served to benefit another group of planters in their control of local government against the pressing demands of later governors, particularly those of Lord Howard of Effingham in the seventeenth century. Men of influential social position opposed Effingham's promotion of royal prerogatives—and his own. Colonel Philip Ludwell and Robert Beverley were examples of the old Green Spring loyalist faction of Governor Berkeley's

---

was specifically introduced to meet the problem of sustaining parochial organization. It later became apparent that self-perpetuation of vestrymen served a useful purpose in the cause of local control by the planters.

67. Thomas J. Wertenbaker, *Virginia Under the Stuarts, 1607-1688* (Princeton, N. J., 1914), 115-45, and his *Torchbearer of the Revolution, the Story of Bacon's Rebellion and Its Leader* (Princeton, N. J., 1940); Washburn, *The Governor and the Rebel*.

68. Osgood, *Colonies in the Seventeenth Century*, III, 244.

69. Hening, ed., *Va. Stat. at L.*, II, 356, 380. As a concession to popular control, an act authorized each parish to elect six voting delegates to sit with the vestry in levying taxes. In 1684 this act was disallowed by the king. *Ibid.*, II, 396; *Legislative Journals of the Council*, III, 1505.

70. McIlwaine, ed., *Journals of the House of Burgesses, 1659/60-1693*, 99, 102; *Va. Mag. of Hist. and Biog.*, 2 (1894), 172.

time who now emerged in opposition to Effingham's pretensions. Co-optation of vestrymen allowed a measure of control on the parochial level, and men came to recognize that this local expression of their views was a bulwark against extension of the royal prerogative. This fact became increasingly clear in the following century during the disputes over the attempts of several governors to collate clergymen to vacant parishes and induct them into their livings.

By the closing years of the seventeenth century the aristocratic dominance of tidewater was complete: a community of like-thinking men dictated the organization of Virginia society. In colonial Virginia the Anglican parish system had already established a large measure of unrestricted control on the local level, and the introduction of religious toleration was not difficult, for dissenters were few and the state-church remained intact. Later, in the eighteenth century, the story would be different.

The General Assembly recognized the Toleration Act in 1699.[71] A survey of Virginia in 1697 listed the number of dissenters as "very inconsiderable" and mentioned only "three or four Meetings" of Quakers. There were a few Presbyterian congregations on the Eastern Shore and near Norfolk, but the small number of conflicting views is in contrast with the religious development in neighboring Maryland.[72] As Francis Nicholson remarked on leaving the governorship of Virginia in 1692, "The inhabitants are for Monarchy and the Religion Established in the Church of England."[73]

The position of the Establishment in Virginia was not disturbed by the statute of 1699, although qualified dissenters were released from enforced worshipping within the parish church. All residents of the parish remained subject to parish taxation, however, to pay the salary of the Anglican clergyman, church building expenses, and other levies of a more secular nature, such as care of the poor, administered by the Anglican vestrymen. Licenses were necessary before dissenting sects could set up places of worship. Each county court was required to submit a full report to the Council of all "Public or Private Meetings of any other Religion than the Church of England," with supplementary data on the type of meeting, how long it had been held, how many and what persons attended, the religion represented, the qualifications of their preachers, and "whether any

71. Hening, ed., *Va. Stat. at L.*, III, 170-71.

72. Hartwell, Blair, and Chilton, *Present State of Virginia*, ed. by Farish, 65; Goodwin, *Colonial Church in Virginia*, 100; Nelson Waite Rightmyer, *Maryland's Established Church* (Baltimore, 1956); George B. Scriven, "Religious Affiliation in Seventeenth Century Maryland," *Hist. Mag. of the Protestant Episcopal Church*, 25 (1956), 220-29; Spencer Ervin, "The Established Church of Colonial Maryland," *ibid.*, 24 (1955), 232-92.

73. McIlwaine, ed., *Executive Journals of the Council*, I, 269.

wandering Strangers come into their Counties as Preachers or upon any other pretence of Religion whatsoever."[74]   Marriages had to be solemnized by orthodox ministers, although in counties where no ordained minister was available, a lay official, usually a reader, performed these ceremonies without sanction of legislative enactment.[75]   Obligatory financial support of the state-church and the requirement that marriage ceremonies be conducted by Anglican clergymen were the two important objections of dissenters after the colonial Toleration Act of 1699.

The Anglican Establishment in Virginia had been founded at a time when the church-state association was the accepted condition of English society; it was designed to represent the prevailing view in the mother country.   But disagreement developed in England as to the direction the church should take; there was no definite plan for the colonial development of the church throughout most of the century, and the episcopal organization was not completed.   By the time men such as Bishop Compton had become deeply concerned, the Virginia church had developed its separate characteristics.   Fundamental in the state-church development of seventeenth-century Virginia was the growth and influence of the Anglican parish.   Here, in the contribution of worthy parsons, in the worship of its people at the country church services, in the personnel and functions of the vestries, was the true basis of the colonial church.   The Anglican parish, with its underlying religious influence, became as much a spirit of control as it was a definable unit of administration, emphasizing throughout its colonial existence the importance of local attitudes and actions.

74. Hening, ed., *Va. Stat. at L.*, III, 170-171; McIlwaine, ed., *Executive Journals of the Council*, I, 456.

75. Cromwell's Civil Marriage Act of 1653 was answered in Virginia in 1661 by the continuation of marriage ceremonies conducted by Anglican clergymen. Hening, ed., *Va. Stat. at L.*, II, 54, 55, 281.   Licenses issued by the governor had increased in volume, and the county courts were authorized to issue them in the name of the governor after 1661.   Increased emphasis on the functions of local government in the expanding colony is thus evident.   Only in 1780 was there a deviation from this procedure, although it had been evaded before that date, especially in the valley.   A statute in that year authorized each county court to license four ministers of any religious denomination to solemnize marriages.   In 1784 all except itinerant ministers were approved by the legislature.   See G. E. Howard, *A History of Matrimonial Institutions* (3 vols.; Chicago, 1904), II, 228-39.

VII.

THE CHURCH IN NEW ENGLAND SOCIETY

Emil Oberholzer, Jr.

COLLEGE OF THE CITY OF NEW YORK

ECCLESIASTICAL CENSORIOUSNESS was an important element in the life of the Puritan of colonial Massachusetts. Although the avowed purpose of the churches' disciplinary action was to safeguard the purity of the churches and to secure the repentance and restoration of fallen church members, there can be little doubt that the churches' control of the conduct of their own members had considerable influence on all the people. Colonial Massachusetts was dominated by Puritanism, and the ecclesiastical regulation of the behavior of the saints necessarily tended to establish standards of behavior for the entire community.

The exercise of ecclesiastical discipline was based on the church covenant, an agreement between the church members and God and among the members themselves. In Richard Baxter's words it was "a contract between God and man, through the mediation of Jesus Christ, for the return and reconciliation of sinners unto God, and by their Justification, Adoption, Sanctification and Glorification by him, to his glory."[1] Precisely when or where the covenant theology was first introduced into Protestant thought is unknown.[2] Even if, as some modern scholars believe, covenant theology

---

1. Richard Baxter, *A Christian Directory* (London, 1673), 688. Portions of this essay have previously appeared in Emil Oberholzer, Jr., *Delinquent Saints: Disciplinary Action in the Early Congregational Churches of Massachusetts* (New York, 1956), and are used by permission of the Columbia University Press.

2. The most thorough exposition of the covenant theology is in Johannes Cocceius' *Summa Doctrinae de Foedure et Testamento Dei* (Leiden, 1648), although Robert Browne discussed the covenant as early as 1582 in his *Booke Which Sheweth the Life and Manners of All True Christians* (Middleburg). On the covenant

was only a modification of Calvinism, rather than a distinct movement in Protestantism, it reduced the harshness of Calvin's emphasis on predestination and furnished a *via media* between Calvinism and Arminianism.[3]

It left God's sovereignty unimpaired: he could elect to salvation or damnation whomever he pleased. But God could not break his own promise, and once a person had entered into the covenant with God, any violation of the agreement must be on the part of man.[4] A breach was possible at any time. The contract implied more than it expressed about the obligations of man to God, and throughout the covenanter's life it remained executory; never was it executed. The covenant, therefore, gave the Congregational churches a basis for their disciplinary authority. Any violation of the standards of behavior accepted by the churches could be construed as a breach of contract. Typical of the early covenants was the one adopted by the saints at Salem in the year 1629.

We covenant with the Lord, and one with another and doe bynd ourselves in the presence of God to walke together in all his waies, according as he is pleased to reveale himself unto us in his Blessed word of truth.[5]

Once a group of the elect had constituted themselves a church by "owning" the covenant, they were the judges of other requests to enter into the contract with them and with God for salvation. Since members were to be "free from gross and open scandals . . . so that in charitable discretion they may be accounted saints by calling," no notorious sinner could be admitted until he had manifested his repentance.[6] If an individual desired to become a church member, he normally had an interview with the pastor, who then presented the applicant's name and a summary of the interview to the previous covenanters. If the members were satisfied that the applicant was qualified for membership, the prospective churchman was required to make a public confession of his faith; he was then permitted

---

theology in Anglo-American Puritanism, see Perry Miller, "The Marrow of Puritan Divinity," Col. Soc. of Mass., *Publications*, 32 (1937), 247-300, and Sidney A. Burrell, Kirk, Crown, and Covenant (unpublished Ph.D. dissertation, Columbia University, 1953), 208.

3. See P. Y. De Jong, *The Covenant Idea in New England* (Grand Rapids, Mich., 1945), 195, and G. D. Henderson's review of L. J. Trinterud, *The Forming of an American Tradition*, in Jour. of Ecclesiastical Hist., 2 (1951), 240-42, for an example of extreme disagreement. Also see J. T. McNeill, *The History and Character of Calvinism* (New York, 1954), 266.

4. Perry Miller, *The New England Mind: The Seventeenth Century* (New York, 1939), 389-400; Raymond P. Stearns, "Assessing the New England Mind," *Church History*, 10 (1941), 250-51.

5. Quoted in Ola E. Winslow, *Meetinghouse Hill* (New York, 1952), 22.

6. *A Platform of Church Discipline* (Cambridge, Mass., 1649), hereafter cited as *Cambridge Platform*, Chap. III, secs. 1-3.

to own the covenant by adding his name to the list of those who had previously agreed to the terms of the contract with God and with each other.[7]   Once admitted to the covenant relationship, he was entitled to partake of the Lord's Supper and to have his children baptized.   These children were in turn expected to make a confession of their faith upon attaining the years of discretion.[8]   With rare exceptions this method of acquiring church membership continued throughout the seventeenth century and often well into the eighteenth.

The new member was now subject to the discipline of the church. Inevitably some members violated their obligations, as John Cotton well knew when he observed that what church members "ought to be *de jure* ... [was not] what they are, or are want to be *de facto*."[9]   The problem of the Christian who falls from the standard expected of him is as old as the Church itself; Biblical and patristic references furnished ample guidance on the treatment of delinquent saints.   Cotton Mather, for example, expressly cited Tertullian's description of the exomologesis practiced in the medieval church,[10] although he varied the requirements somewhat, insisting upon "Humility, Modesty, Patience, Petition, Tears, with Reformation" as the signs of true repentance, instead of sackcloth, ashes, fasting, and groaning. If an offender was truly penitent, Mather wrote, he must be restored, no matter how grievous his offense, even if he had been excommunicated at the time of his transgression.   Unless the sinner was at the point of death, his repentance must be judged by the church as a whole and his restoration approved by majority vote.[11]

In the administration of ecclesiastical discipline, a careful distinction was made between public offenses—those committed in the presence of more than one or two witnesses—and offenses committed privately. The former required public action by the church; the latter were to be dealt with secretly, unless the offender was obstinate and refused to give satisfaction.   Because of the Puritans' aversion to ecclesiastical tribunals, each church functioned as a court when occasion arose, and disciplinary cases dominated the agendas of church meetings unless some other weighty

7. Cotton Mather, *Ratio Disciplinae Fratrum Nov-Anglorum* (Boston, 1726), 90-91.

8. *Ibid.*, 81; Thomas Hooker, *A Survey of the Summe of Church Discipline* (London, 1658; first pub. 1648), 60.

9. John Cotton, *A Defense of Mr. John Cotton from the Imputation of Self-Contradiction* (1658), quoted in Perry Miller, *Orthodoxy in Massachusetts* (Cambridge, Mass., 1933), 197.

10. Mather, *Ratio Disciplinae*, 144. See Tertullian, *On Repentance*, Chap. IX, in A. Cleveland Coxe, ed., *The Ante-Nicean Fathers*, American edn. (Grand Rapids, Mich., 1951), III, 664.

11. Mather, *Ratio Disciplinae*, 151-52, 157, 145; Hooker, *Summe of Church Discipline*, 36.

problem of church administration intervened. Although not generally marked by formalities of pleading and practice, church trials were usually conducted in a quasi-judicial manner. This was particularly true in the eighteenth and nineteenth centuries, when the accused was often accorded safeguards comparable to those which he would have received in the courts of law. In the seventeenth century, however, some church trials bore little resemblance to judicial trials.[12] In the case of the Salem witch trials, there is no indication that the accused persons had the slightest chance to be heard before they were excommunicated.[13] The trial of Anne Hutchinson is another notorious example of ecclesiastical injustice, but the majority of seventeenth-century hearings appear to have been fair.

One of the principal aims of any disciplinary action was to bring the offender to repent and thereby to restore him to communion with the church. If a member acknowledged his offense or if it was proved against him after a trial, he was expected to show his repentance. In public cases this was generally effected by reading to the congregation a confession which had been evaluated and approved by the church members in closed session and acknowledged by the penitent as his own. Such confessions were distasteful to even the most penitent of sinners, and especially in cases involving sexual acts, individuals were reluctant to air their transgressions before the public. The accused churchman who sought to escape judgment by failing to appear before the church for a hearing, or the convicted member who failed to offer a satisfactory confession, might receive a warning or two if he were fortunate. If he disobeyed the summons of the church too often, or if he persisted in refusing to acknowledge his violation, he was subject to the most severe penalty a church could inflict: excommunication.[14] But even an excommunicate was considered as a potential penitent and could restore himself to communion with the church by showing "an Exemplary Repentance . . . Satisfactory to the Sentiments of a Reasonable Piety."[15] He was therefore to be treated not as an enemy but as a brother in need of admonition. He was permitted—and expected—to at-

---

12. The record of the church trial is in Charles Francis Adams, ed., *Antinomianism in the Colony of Massachusetts Bay* (Boston, 1894), 285-336.

13. Records of the First Church of Salem (Mss. copy, Essex Institute, Salem; hereafter cited as Salem Records), 345, 347, 349; Records of the First Church of Danvers (Mss. in custody of First Congregational Church, Danvers; hereafter cited as Danvers Records), 12.

14. The power to excommunicate was in the church members as a whole. In some cases an accused person was suspended from active church membership pending the determination of the case, but this was regarded as an interlocutory measure only. See C. E. Park, "Excommunication in the Colonial Churches," Col. Soc. of Mass., *Transactions*, 12 (1911), 328; and Emil Oberholzer, Jr., *Delinquent Saints*, 279n.

15. Mather, *Ratio Disciplinae*, 156.

tend services in the hope that he might be moved to repent.[16] If he repented and offered an acceptable confession, he was restored to the
communion of the saints. He was not admitted anew, for he had never
ceased to be a member; he had temporarily forfeited the privileges of
membership.[17] Until he repented, however, the excommunicate was to be
avoided as much as possible by members of the congregation. Although his
civil rights were not affected by the censure as far as the churches were
concerned, the Cambridge Platform provided that the excommunicate was
to be deprived of "all familial communion . . . farther than the necessity
of natural, or domestical, or civil relations do require," and he was not to
eat with members in good standing.[18]

Congregational polity was incompatible with an appellate body which
could reverse the decision of a church. Intercommunion, however, enabled
the churches to consult and, if necessary, admonish each other.[19] An aggrieved member could request his church to join him in convening a council
of churches to review the judgment against him. If the church refused
to call a mutual council, he could request other churches to meet in an
ex parte council. In either case, the council, consisting usually of both
clerical and lay delegates from various neighboring churches, heard the
parties in open session and, like a court of law, retired for private deliberation to draw up a "result," which was roughly analogous to the opinion
of an appellate court. In this document the council stated its findings of
fact and conclusions of law and furnished advice to the church which had
jurisdiction in the case. The advice was often heavily supported by ju-
diciously selected prooftexts. No church was required to accept the result
and advice of a council, but if it refused to concur, the council could
recommend that other churches withdraw from fellowship and intercommunion with the recalcitrant body. If a church failed to comply with a
request that a member be restored, the council could ask another church to
admit him to membership, waiving the normal requirement of a formal
dismissal.[20] Although these occasions were rare, councils did not hesitate
to recommend such action when the circumstances justified it.

The offenses of which the church took cognizance ran the gamut from
adultery to a curious case of quasi Zoroastrianism. They included acts
which today would be considered "secular" rather than "religious": dis-

16. *Ibid.*, 151-52; *Cambridge Platform*, Chap. XIV, sec. 6.
17. William Ames, *The Marrow of Sacred Divinity* (London, 1642), 191.
18. *Cambridge Platform*, Chap. XIV, secs. 5-6; Mather, *Ratio Disciplinae*, 155-56.
19. John Cotton, *A Defense from the Imputation of Self-Contradiction*, 44-48;
Cambridge Platform, Chap. XXV.
20. Mather, *Ratio Disciplinae*, 155-61, 175.

orderly conduct, larceny, arson, assault, fraud, and murder. The Puritan's view of the world was Biblical and sacramental, and to him all aspects of life had religious significance. The Decalogue prohibits theft and murder no less than it prohibits idolatry or enjoins the worship of God. Massachusetts, however, was not a church-state. The saints controlled the government by excluding the non-members from the polls, and the clergy had considerable influence on their flocks, but they enjoyed no special status in the body politic. The distinction between church and state was carefully maintained, although amicable relations advantageous to both powers resulted in a system of close but informal cooperation between the religious and civil authorities.

The alliance grew spontaneously and had no basis in constitutional or legal enactment. To speak of the churches as state-churches is misleading; the very polity of Congregationalism was incompatible with a state-church. We may properly call Massachusetts a theocracy only if we use that term to designate a state which considers itself to be under the rule of God, whether that rule be exercised through political or religious agencies.[21] The distinction between the churches and the state, as well as the belief that both were divinely ordained, was clearly affirmed by John Cotton:

It is very suitable to Gods all-sufficient wisdome . . . [to] avoide both the churches usurpation upon civill institutions . . . and the commonwealths invasion upon ecclesiasticall administrations. . . . Gods institutions (such as the government of church and commonwealth be) may be close and compact, and co-ordinate one to another, and yet not confounded.[22]

This principle was officially recognized in the platform adopted by the Cambridge Synod of 1649:

Church-government stands in no opposition to civil government . . . nor any way intrencheth upon the authority of Civil Magistrates in their jurisdiction . . . . both stand together and flourish the one being helpful unto the other, in their distinct administrations.[23]

21. See H. R. Niebuhr, *The Kingdom of God in America* (Chicago and New York, 1927), 70; A. P. Stokes, *Church and State in the United States* (New York, 1950), I, 158; Thomas J. Wertenbaker, *The Puritan Oligarchy* (New York and London, 1947), 62; C. E. Merriam, *A History of American Political Theories* (New York, 1903), 5; W. A. Visser't Hooft, *The Background of the Social Gospel in America* (Haarlem, 1928), 74; Oberholzer, *Delinquent Saints*, 10-12. Also see Thomas Lechford, *Plain Dealing or Newes From New England*, ed. by J. H. Trumbull (Boston, 1867; first pub. 1642), 29-36.

22. Letter to Lord Say and Seal, in Thomas Hutchinson, *History of the Colony and Province of the Massachusetts Bay*, ed. by L. S. Mayo (Cambridge, Mass., 1936), I, 414-15.

23. *Cambridge Platform*, Chap. XVII, sec. 2. See also secs. 3, 5, 7.

The state recognized this principle in the Body of Liberties, which provided that no person should be tried twice for the same crime "by Civill Justice," implicitly permitting churches to try persons previously acquitted by the courts.   The civil courts could fine criminals, send them to the pillory or jail, or impose the death penalty for their illegal acts; but no civil court could excommunicate a person.[24]   The churches, on the other hand, had the power to censure their members for whatever actions they considered improper; but they could not trespass upon the right of the civil authorities to impose temporal punishments.   Thus we find churches censuring embezzlers and thieves, while the courts fined those persons who failed to go to church and in at least one case banished a woman whose opinions were considered heretical by the church.

An examination of the actual cases in the church records discloses the vast scope of the deeds with which the churches concerned themselves. In the area encompassed by the first table of the Decalogue, absence from church services and breach of the Sabbath are frequently mentioned. Censures of absentees were abundant in the eighteenth century, but relatively few cases have been found in the seventeenth-century records.[25] Like God and the Sabbath, the churches and the clergy were entitled to be treated with due respect; a contemptuous remark made in the heat of an ecclesiastical trial might be overlooked if the offender acknowledged his primary transgression, but the churchman who deliberately insulted the church might be severely treated.[26]   Understandably enough, the churches felt no further responsibility toward those members who converted to other

24. The term "civil court" was generally used in the seventeenth and eighteenth centuries to designate a court other than ecclesiastical, whether of civil or criminal jurisdiction.

25. A minute in the records of the Bradford church is of considerable interest because it clearly indicates that by the end of the seventeenth century the ecclesiastical sanctions, supplementing those of the civil authority, had failed to secure the ideal of perfect attendance. A Church Book (Mss. in custody of the First Church, Bradford), page number obscured; date probably about 1694.

26. *Records of the First Church of Charlestown, Massachusetts, 1632-1724* (Boston, 1880; hereafter cited as *Charlestown Records*), xi (1670-72); "Plymouth Church Records, 1620-1859," Col. Soc. of Mass., *Publications*, 22 and 23 (Boston, 1920; hereafter cited as *Plymouth Records*), I, 257 (1685), 258 (1686), 269 (1690); portions of the Quincy Church Records (hereafter cited as *Quincy Records*), in C. F. Adams, "Some Phases of Sexual Morality and Church Discipline in Colonial New England," Mass. Hist. Soc., *Proceedings*, 2nd ser., 6 (1891), 477-516; extracts from the "Scituate and Barnstable Church Records," *New Eng. Hist. and Genealogical Register*, 10 (1856), 41 (1649); J. B. Felt, *The Ecclesiastical History of New England* (Boston, 1855), I, 151-52 (1631). For other cases, taken from unpublished records, see Oberholzer, *Delinquent Saints*, Chap. IV *passim*; but compare C. K. Shipton's review in *Wm. and Mary Qtly.*, 3rd ser., 13 (1956), 410.

denominations. In the seventeenth century, excommunication was the rule for former Congregationalists who affiliated with the Baptists or Quakers.[27]

Christianity's traditional concern for the sanctity of marriage and the family is also revealed in the early records. The colonial church served the Puritan families in many capacities: as pastor, marital relations consultant, child psychologist, and domestic relations court. Members who abused their spouses were admonished and sometimes excommunicated. Family quarrels were aired before the church, and, if a confession were in order, the entire congregation heard it.[28] Children who behaved disrespectfully to their parents were censured, but the obligations inherent in the parental relationship were reciprocal, and parents who neglected or abused their children were similarly disciplined.[29] In their efforts to uphold the integrity of domestic relations, the churches relied largely on the Seventh Commandment, which was interpreted to prohibit fornication as well as adultery. More persons were censured for sexual offenses than for any others, and the evidence clearly indicates the prevalence of premarital relations in colonial Massachusetts. The embarrassment involved in public confessions of sexual misconduct undoubtedly accounts for the inclination of some offenders to deny their guilt or even flee from the colony.[30] In fact the main incentive to a public confession by sexual offenders may have been the parents' desire to have their children baptized, for in early American Puritanism, baptism was not regarded as the right of a child born of Christian parents but as a privilege granted to the parents.[31]

27. *Charlestown Records*, i-vii (1658-65); Records of the Second Church, Boston (Mss. on deposit at the Mass. Hist. Soc.; hereafter cited as Boston Second Church Records), III, 19-24, 43 (1665, 1683); Felt, *Ecclesiastical History of New England*, I, 486 (1643).

28. "The Rev. John Eliot's Record" of the Roxbury Church, Boston, *Report of the Record Commissioners* (Boston, 1884; hereafter cited as *Roxbury Records*), VI, 85 (1644); Records of the First Church of Boston (Mss. copies in office of the City Register, Boston; hereafter cited as Boston First Church Records), I, 124 (1668), 140 (1672); Salem Records, 317 (1679); *Records of the First Church at Dorchester . . . 1636-1734* (Boston, 1891; hereafter cited as *Dorchester Records*), 88 (1682); Records of the West Parish at Barnstable (Photostats at New York Hist. Soc. and Boston Public Library; hereafter cited as Barnstable Records), 31-32 (1683); *Plymouth Records*, I, 258, 269 (1686).

29. Boston First Church Records, III, 8 (date uncertain but before 1635), 9 (1638), and I, 116 (1664); *Plymouth Records*, I, 251 (1683); The Publick Records of the Church at Westfield (Mss., Westfield Athenaeum; hereafter cited as Westfield Records), 129 (1697).

30. Boston First Church Records, I, 103 (1655), 114-15 (1664); Boston Second Church Records, III, 37-38 (1678); *Plymouth Records*, I, 251 (1683); terminology and classification are discussed in Oberholzer, *Delinquent Saints*, 127-29, 254-58.

31. C. F. Adams, "Some Phases of Sexual Morality," Mass. Hist. Soc., *Proceedings*, 2nd ser., 6 (1891), 493; A. W. Calhoun, *A Social History of the American*

In dealing with intoxicated or intemperate persons, the churches assisted the civil authorities in their efforts to suppress the abuse of alcoholic beverages. Recognizing that alcoholism is a condition rather than an act, one church experimented with a system of probation, but the experiment failed to accomplish the desired end. Recidivism was frequent, and the proportion of alcoholics who remained unrepentant or unreformed was high. Somewhat more than a third of all fully recorded cases resulted in excommunication.[32]

Crimes against the person appear only rarely in the seventeenth-century church records, but the existing examples seem dramatic: Nathaniel Eaton, the erstwhile Harvard educator, assaulted his usher and almost caused the drowning of a peace officer; William Franklin, of Roxbury, was condemned to die for his fatal assault on a servant and remained unrepentant to the end; and Isack Heath, also of Roxbury, attempted suicide but lived to make his confession to the church.[33]

An area of law enforcement traditionally in the hands of ecclesiastical authorities was the punishment of perjurers. Although this crime was punishable by law, the churches also dealt severely with members who committed perjury while testifying in courts of law.[34]

Puritan moral theology had no quarrel with the enjoyment of worldly goods; indeed, material riches, though useless as a means of obtaining grace, were evidence of grace already received. But wealth was neither an end in itself nor conclusive evidence that its possessor was in a state of grace. If acquired unjustly, it was evil and its acquisition was a breach of the covenant. Common thieves were arraigned before the churches throughout the colonial period, but in the seventeenth century, offenses involving business ethics were also treated by the churches. The business practices of Robert Keayne induced John Cotton to preach a vigorous

---

Family (Cleveland, 1917-19), I, 132; First Book Containing the Records of the First Congregational Church in Marblehead (Mss. in custody of the church), unnumbered page (1702). See *Plymouth Records*, I, 212 (1712), for a reversal of this position. Of the thirty-one women who confessed fornication in Salem between 1670 and 1740, thirteen had children baptized soon thereafter (Salem Records, 453-574 *passim*).

32. For the probation experiment, see *Dorchester Records*, 75, 80-83 (1677-79). On alcoholism generally, see Oberholzer, *Delinquent Saints*, 152-59.

33. John Winthrop, *History of New England*, ed. by James K. Hosmer (New York, 1908-9), I, 310-15 (1639); *Roxbury Records*, 85-87, 95 (1669, 1682).

34. For the practice in England, see T. P. Oakley, *English Penitential Discipline and Anglo-Saxon Law in Their Joint Influence* (New York, 1923), 141-42, 159, 199. For church action against perjurers in Massachusetts, see *Roxbury Records*, 203-5 (1665-66); "The First Church Records of the Church in Beverly," *Essex Institute Historical Collections* (hereafter cited as *Beverly Records*), 35 (1899), 197-200 (1677-80); *Dorchester Records*, 112 (1696).

sermon on commercial ethics, and Keayne's censure was followed by other
rebukes for fraud or embezzlement.[35]

The Puritans' abhorrence of ostentation, their restraints on amusements, their emphasis on industry and piety, all are reflected in the records
of the churches' disciplinary action. Outward manifestation of pride was
censured from an early date. In Dedham, a man's application for admission to the church was deferred because of his self-confidence, and elsewhere
members were censured for pride of "inordinate walking."[36] Unfortunately the details are missing in these cases, although we know of
one Boston woman who was excommunicated for persisting in her assertion
that Christ had commanded her to remain idle.[37]

These moral restraints do not justify Weeden's remark that training
day and the gallows furnished the New England Puritan with his principal
amusements. Music, games of skill, and sports were never banned by the
churches, and dancing probably was permissible in the early part of the
seventeenth century. Games of chance, however, were condemned by
Increase Mather as a sinful waste of time. John Cotton had earlier
banned card games, but for a far different reason; the distribution of cards
among players was in the hands of God, and "to appeal to him and his
providence for dispensing these ludicra, seemeth . . . a taking of God's
name in vain." Curiously, only one case of gaming has been found by
this writer in the seventeenth-century church records and the case is
dominated by a charge of adultery.[38]

Records of the private cases adjudicated by the churches prove that the
censoriousness of the Puritans was matched by their litigiousness. Early
opposition to civil litigation among church members seems to have de-

35. Winthrop, *History of New England*, I, 315-18, II, 4; Boston First Church
Records, III, 12-14 (1640), and *Roxbury Records*, 83, 187 (1642) (cheating on
weights and measures); Boston First Church Records, I, 69, 78 (1644-46) and 78
(1645-46) (misleading advertising); *ibid.*, 89-90 (1648) (fraudulent workman-
ship); Church Records of the Old Town of Reading (Typescript copy, Reading
Public Library; hereafter cited as Reading Records), 7-8 (1663) (forgery); Boston
Second Church Records, III, 25-28 (1675), Westfield Records, 127 (1685), and
Boston First Church Records, II, 65 (1698) (fraud). See also Bernard Bailyn,
"The *Apologia* of Robert Keayne," *Wm. and Mary Qtly.*, 3rd ser., 7 (1950), 568-87.

36. "The Record of Baptisms, Marriages, and Deaths, and Admissions to the
Church and Dismissions Therefrom," *Dedham Historical Records Series*, 2 (1888),
6-7, 24-28; *Roxbury Records*, 95-98 (1683); Boston First Church Records, II, 45
(1691).

37. Boston First Church Records, I, 105 (1657).

38. W. B. Weeden, *Economic and Social History of New England* (Boston and
New York, 1890), I, 423, II, 696; Increase Mather, *A Testimony Against Several
Prophane and Superstitious Customs* (Boston, 1688); Cotton, Letter to R. Levett,
quoted in E. D. Hanscom, ed., *The Heart of the Puritan* (New York, 1917), 177;
Boston Second Church Records, IV (1669). See also Oberholzer, *Delinquent Saints*,
227-32.

terred few persons from going to law, and by providing popular tribunals in which aggrieved members could press their cases without the risks and costs incident to lawsuits, the churches actually encouraged members to air their disputes.[39] In addition to settling a number of private disagreements of an unspecified nature the churches tried defamation cases. Frequently the complainant accused the respondent of telling a lie. One case involved a printed libel; in another an incensed almshousekeeper brought charges against an inmate who had complained about the food and had accused the keeper of attempting to have sexual relations with her. Similar slander cases were tried in the eighteenth century, but most of the later private disputes involved other torts or commercial issues.[40] For the seventeenth century the church records examined disclose only one non-tortious private case: a member alleged that a deacon of his church owed his son the sum of five shillings and six pence. The deacon was acquitted.[41]

The extent to which the churches were responsible for the enforcement of moral standards cannot be determined from an analysis of the church records alone. Both the churches and the civil authorities were concerned with the conduct of the people. There was no division of power regarding the nature of offenses, each body censuring persons under its jurisdiction for whatever acts violated the accepted norms.

The church records show that in a number of cases the ecclesiastical censure was preceded by a conviction in court. Save for the obviously atypical case of Anne Hutchinson, the earliest known case of this nature concerns a Boston woman who was convicted of cheating on weights and measures. The church records state that her guilt was proved by four witnesses, but it fails to indicate whether they testified before the church or whether the record of their testimony in court was used at the church hearing.[42] In deciding the fate of a man convicted of drunkenness, the Salem church utilized the court records, which included a summary of the

39. Felt, *Ecclesiastical History of New England*, I, 238; Boston First Church Records, I, 93; Zechariah Chafee, Jr., ed., *Records of the Suffolk County Court, 1671-1680* (Col. Soc. of Mass., *Publications*, 29 and 30 [1953]), xxvi.

40. Reading Records, 13 (between 1670 and 1685); *Plymouth Records*, I, 156-57 (1681); Salem Records, 325 (1683); Salisbury Church Records (Mss. at Massachusetts Historical Society; hereafter cited as Salisbury Records), 45-47 (1698); Barnstable Records, 41 (1649); Boston Second Church Records, III, 39 (1682); *Dorchester Records*, 112 (1696); Reading Records, 3-4 (1653?-58); Boston Second Church Records, IV (pages not numbered, 1697); Oberholzer, *Delinquent Saints*, 201-5, 208-15.

41. Salisbury Records, 296-97 (1688).

42. *Roxbury Records*, 83 (1642). The records of the church clearly allude to the prior conviction in court of the respondent, Mrs. Webb. Cf. the *Records of the Court of Assistants of the Colony of the Massachusetts Bay, 1630-1692* (Boston, 1901-28), II, 127, which mention the conviction of William Webb.

testimony of seven witnesses. The church record gives the impression that while the members would not automatically accept the court's judgment, they were ready to consider the court's summary of the evidence and to evaluate it themselves.[43]   In some instances it is not clear whether the church based its verdict on that of the court, or whether it merely initiated proceedings because of a prior conviction.[44]

In at least three cases, however, the church took judicial notice, as it were, of the respondent's conviction in court.   Joseph Belcher, whose bond for twenty pounds had been forfeited because he violated a court order not to keep company with a certain woman, was convicted by the church before he had even been summoned to appear, "the matter of scandal [being] so notoriously infamous both in Court and Country."   In dealing with a convicted horse thief the church followed the court's verdict on faith, "the fact being so notorious and evident."   A puzzling variant is found in the case of another convicted horse thief, who, according to the church record, acknowledged his guilt before the church.   Then follows a curious sentence: "The matter of fact being notorious it needed no further proof." What proof could the church have desired in view of the offender's acknowledgment?   The implication is that the church was reluctant to convict a member on the strength of his own statement but would do so by taking judicial notice of his conviction in court.[45]

In these cases the ecclesiastical sanctions supplemented the penalties of the law.   In hearing private disputes, on the other hand, the churches in effect exercised concurrent jurisdiction with the courts, thus partially replacing their functions.   Sometimes the meetinghouse was used by the courts in connection with temporal punishments.   In 1646, for example, the Essex Quarterly Court required an Antipaedobaptist to acknowledge his error before the congregation in the meetinghouse, and later in the century two slanderers were ordered by a court to make public confessions on a Sunday morning.[46]   It must be remembered that these sentences were not imposed by the churches, but by courts of law.

The famous cases of Anne Hutchinson and the victims of the Salem witchcraft hysteria are outstanding examples of cooperation between the churches and the government.   In the former, a theological disputation

43. Salem Records, 250 (1664).   The summary of the testimony appears in *Records and Files of the Quarterly Courts of Essex County* (Salem, Mass., 1911), III, 179-80.

44. Salem Records, 254 (1665), 305 (1676), 340 (1688); *Dorchester Records*, 88-89 (1682).

45. Quincy Records, 482 (1677); *Beverly Records*, 189 (1668-69); Salem Records, 258 (1665).

46. Felt, *Ecclesiastical History of New England*, I, 568 (1646); *Records and Files of the Quarterly Courts of Essex County*, III, 24, 29-30.

arranged by the civil authorities at the request of the clergy preceded the civil trial, and in the related case of the Reverend John Wheelwright the court asked the advice of the clergy on certain theological questions. Precisely what doctrinal errors led to the convictions by court and church cannot be ascertained, but since the outcome of the case was predetermined, it was hardly necessary to specify the exact reasons. The civil authorities were unable to try Mrs. Hutchinson for heresy, which was not a crime at the time, so they convicted her of sedition. The church could properly condemn its members for doctrinal errors, and it excommunicated her for heresy.[47]

The records of the Salem witchcraft trials indicate no more regard for orderly legal procedure than do those of the Hutchinson trial. At first the clergy appear to have acted with a degree of responsibility, but once the defendants had been condemned by the courts, the churches readily sanctioned the judgments by excommunicating the victims.[48] Even the case of Giles Corey, who by refusing to plead was subjected to the *peine forte et dure,* presented but a momentary problem. The church artfully concluded that Corey was "undoubtedly either guilty of the sin of witchcraft or of throwing himselfe upon sudden and certain death, if he were otherwise innocent." For the sin of either suicide or witchcraft, Corey was excommunicated without further trouble.[49]

An interesting illustration of close cooperation between a town and the church is found in the Westfield Records for 1682. The case arose from the efforts of John Mosely, a resident of Westfield, to prevent the construction of a lane adjacent to his property. Unable to effect a change in the plans by pressing an apparently untenable claim against the town, he addressed a preposterous petition to the General Court. When the church heard of his petition, it charged Mosely with violations of three commandments: of the Eighth, by attempting to obtain a gift from the town instead of enriching himself by his own labors; of the Ninth, by pressing a false claim against the town; and of the Tenth, by seeking to keep the lane away from his estate.[50]

The cooperation of the civil and ecclesiastical authorities is clearly apparent in this case. The leaders of the town were the rulers of the church.

47. Boston First Church Records, III, 9 (1638); C. F. Adams, ed., *Antinomianism in the Colony of Massachusetts Bay,* 321, 330-32; Oberholzer, *Delinquent Saints,* 79-85.

48. Salem Records, 345, 347 (1691-92); Danvers Records, 12 (1691).

49. Salem Records, 349 (1692). Subsequently, when the churches repealed the censures for witchcraft, Corey's excommunication was posthumously repealed on the strength of what the church construed as a proleptic confession. *Ibid.,* 212-13 (1712).

50. Westfield Records, 125-26 (1682).

A civil trial would have involved considerable costs and nuisance; if the town lost its case, it would suffer even greater damage. What could have been safer than to refer the issue to the church? Ecclesiastical litigation could, if necessary, be swift, and there were neither fees nor the danger of an award for costs. Had Mosely pressed his claim, which certainly appears unfounded, he would have been excommunicated. By acting in the church, the leaders of the town won their case without troublesome recourse to law. Mosely confessed his error; the town lost no property and, presumably, proceeded to construct its lane.[51]

These examples of cooperation should not obscure the fact that the churches and the state were sometimes in conflict. If the case of Anne Hutchinson illustrates cooperation from beginning to end, the more important case of Roger Williams exemplifies extreme antagonism between a church and the General Court. Not until the government virtually bribed the churchmen of Salem with the land on Marblehead Neck did the church excommunicate the man it had twice called to be its pastor.[52]

For an illustration of disagreement between a church and the state in a case devoid of political implications, we may turn to the morass of law suits and church actions which occurred in Lynn in 1663. Proceedings began when William Langley brought suit against Henry Collins and John Hathorne, who represented the town of Lynn; Langley alleged that he had not been allotted the land to which he was entitled. The court gave judgment for Langley, but evidently the title to the land was not conveyed to him by Hathorne and Collins, because the marshal, armed with a writ, soon attached Hathorne's property and took execution on the body of Collins. Both Hathorne and Collins then sued the officer for misconduct. At the ensuing trials, Langley and Andrew Mansfield testified. Hathorne then went before the church, accusing Langley and Mansfield of perjury in court. The respondents in the ecclesiastical trial in turn brought a civil action against Hathorne, charging that he had slandered them before the church. In this case the jury required the defendant, Hathorne, to acknowledge his tort in the meetinghouse. In the meanwhile, however, the church seems to have decided the perjury complaint in favor of Hathorne, and the court, hoping to avoid an open conflict with the church, did not consent to the verdict of the jury. Instead it sent a letter to the church at Lynn, asking it to reconsider its decision in the case pressed by Hathorne:

Now because it is much to be desired that contrary judgement in one and the same case may be prevented if possibly it may . . . and one power not

51. *Ibid.*, 126.
52. Oberholzer, *Delinquent Saints*, 216-19. The excommunication is found in *Plymouth Records*, I, 65 (1638).

clash against the other [,] wee thought it expedient before we give judgment in the case to comend the same to the serious consideration and further examination . . . of the church . . . soe as to give the Church op[por]tunity and cause to change their mynd and reverse sensures. . . .

The reply of the church has been lost, but judging from a second letter by the court, the church stood its ground and refused to reopen the case. Since the church had been offended by the request to reconsider its decision, the court apologized to the church and affirmed its acceptance of the traditional relationship of the civil and ecclesiastical powers:

Wee are very sorry our endeavors . . . seemes to have been interpreted contrary to our intentions. . . . We have been taught and do verily beleeve the civil and ecclesiastical power may very wel[l] consist, and that no cause is so purely ecclesiastical but the civil power may in its way deale therein, wee are farr from thinking the churches have no power but what is derived from the christian magistrate, or that the civil magistrate hath ecclesiastical power.

Judgment was apparently entered in favor of Langley and Mansfield, and the Court of Assistants, affirming the judgment below in one of these cases, held that Hathorne must pay damages of £22 10s and make a public acknowledgment.[53]

Just as the study of legal records can contribute toward our knowledge of the function of the churches in relation to the state and society, so the study of the church records can help us toward a fuller understanding of certain aspects of seventeenth-century jurisprudence. Some legal historians have asserted that the Puritans rejected equity and idealized the common law. "The Puritan has always been a thoroughgoing opponent of equity," wrote Roscoe Pound, in the spirit of a similar statement by Sir Frederick Pollock.[54] Administered by the Court of Chancery, equity had its origin in the prerogative of the sovereign to administer justice in situations which did not admit of an adequate remedy at common law. Like the latter, it developed independent of legislation, but unlike the common law it lacked certainty and depended largely on the wisdom of the chancellor, although by the seventeenth century, case law had influenced equity as well as the

53. The cases, conveniently summarized in M. D. Howe, ed., *Readings in American Legal History* (Cambridge, Mass., 1949), 133-37, are found in *Records and Files of the Quarterly Courts of Essex County*, II, 268-71, 350-53, 431-32, and III, 24, 29-32, 74, and in *Records of the Court of Assistants*, III, 137. A case in which a church excommunicated a member in spite of the fact that the grand jury repeatedly had refused to find a true bill is found in *Dorchester Records*, 112 (1696).

54. Pound, *The Spirit of the Common Law* (Boston, 1921), 53; cf. Pollock, "The Transformation of Equity," in Paul Vinogradoff, ed., *Essays in Legal History* (London, 1913), 295.

common law. Common law had gradually become a method of injustice in cases where unusual circumstances existed which the justices could not recognize because the legal principles did not meet the requirements of the situation. Hence equity was introduced, its object being "to . . . do full, adequate, and complete justice . . . in accordance with the dictates of natural justice and good conscience unfettered by the formalism and inflexibility which in varying measure limits the power of the [common] law courts."[55]

While the Puritans disliked the Court of Chancery, they willingly incorporated many of the other features of equity into their legal system. Nor did their aversion to Chancery have the extreme results described by Pound, who noted, for example, that the Barebone Parliament "abolished" the Chancery.[56] This statement is an exaggeration. Parliament did indeed regard the Chancery as "a great grievance, one of the greatest in the nation,"[57] but its sternest action against it was reform, not abolition. Influenced by attacks on the abuses, delays, and costs incident to equity litigation, the Barebone Parliament at one time voted "that the Court of Chancery should be taken away."[58] But the committee which was to prepare the bill to eliminate this court was plainly instructed to provide for pending actions and for future relief in equity. The first bill presented by the committee made no provision for future causes in equity and was rejected by the moderates. The second was unacceptable to the radicals. Still another was turned down; finally the committee drafted a bill which might possibly have been enacted had not Parliament been preoccupied with other business. The Nominated Parliament was dissolved by Cromwell before it could again give its attention to the Chancery.[59]

A year later an ordinance of the Lord Protector reformed the administration of equity. The greater part of the ordinance was concerned with the regulation of fees and technicalities of court process, although it affirmed the recognized principles that the Chancery could not issue decrees

55. *Webster* v. *Archer*, 176 Maryland 245, 251 (1939), quoted in 30 Corpus Juris Secondum, 319.

56. *Spirit of the Common Law*, 53. The subject is thoroughly treated in W. S. Holdsworth, *A History of English Law* (London, 1903—), I, 431-34, and in two monographs on the Interregnum: H. A. Glass, *The Barebone Parliament* (London, 1899), 97, and F. A. Inderwick, *The Interregnum* (London, 1891), 223-24. Also see F. W. Maitland, *The Constitutional History of England* (Cambridge, Eng., 1908), 312, who comments that "even Cromwell found that the Chancery lawyers were too much for him."

57. Walter Scott, ed., *Somers Tracts*, 2nd edn. (London, 1811; first published in 1748-52), VI, 275.

58. Whitelocke's *Memorials* (London, 1682), 543.

59. *Ibid.*, 549; *Somers Tracts*, VI, 275-76; *The Old Parliamentary History*, 2nd edn. (London, 1763), XX, 198-206, 239, 311-13.

contrary to statute law and that its power was limited to situations which could not be adequately remedied at common law.[60] It did not abolish the Chancery, and no action was taken on a resolution for further reform which was introduced a year before the Restoration. These facts strongly suggest that Parliament realized that equity was not expendable.[61]

Colonial legal practice also repudiates the suggestion that the Puritans loved the common law and hated equity. Although the United States Supreme Court recognized as early as 1798 that not all of the English common law had been adopted in the colonies, it remained for the legal historians to show that the influence of common law was relatively slight.[62] Pointing out the influence of customary, rather than common, law, Goebel concluded that Plymouth law was "a curious melange of religious ideas and remnants of English customs and practices," and Reinsch noted the "continued, conscious, and determined departure from the lines of the common law" in Massachusetts.[63]

While equity did suffer an eclipse in the eighteenth century, it is false to assume that, because there was no Chancery Court in colonial Massachusetts, equity was never administered in that colony.[64] "If there be matter of apparent equity, as the forfeiture of an obligation, breach of

60. C. H. Firth and R. S. Raith, eds., *Acts and Ordinances of the Interregnum, 1643-1660* (London, 1911), II, 949-67. The ordinance of 1654 was confirmed by Parliament, for its duration, in 1657; *ibid.*, II, 1140. The alleged act abolishing the Chancery is conspicuous by its absence from these volumes.

61. Holdsworth, *History of English Law*, I, 434, V, 237. Complaints concerning the administration of justice during the Commonwealth period were not limited to equity; they extended to the intricacies of common law pleading. In a sermon before Parliament in 1646, for example, Hugh Peter attacked the common law courts as well as the Chancery. Goldwin Smith, "The Reforms of the Laws of England, 1640-1660," *Univ. of Toronto Qtly.*, 10 (1941), 471-73, 477-78.

62. For representative cases, see *United States v. Worrall*, 2 Dallas 384, 394 (1798); *Van Ness v. Packard*, 2 Peters 137, 144 (1829); *United States v. Reid et al.*, 12 Howard 361, 362 (1851); *Olmstead v. United States*, 277 U. S. 438, 466 (1929). For the views of historians, see Pollock, "The Transformation of Equity," in Vinogradoff, ed., *Essays in Legal History*, 295; R. B. Morris, review in 83 *Penn. Law Rev.* 102; T. F. T. Plucknett, review in *New Eng. Qtly.*, 3 (1930), 157-58.

63. Julius Goebel, Jr., "King's Law and Local Custom in Seventeenth Century New England," 31 *Columbia Law Rev.* 416; Paul S. Reinsch, "The English Common Law in the Early American Colonies," *Select Essays in Anglo-American Legal History* (Boston, 1907-9; hereafter cited as *Select Essays*), I, 367-415. The quotation is from 385.

64. The Puritans attempted to create a court of equity in Massachusetts in 1692, but the statute was disallowed, as *ultra vires*, by the Queen in Council. Thus the responsibility for the absence of a court with equity jurisdiction in the eighteenth century does not rest with the Puritans. Private legislation did much of what equity might have done. S. D. Wilson, "Courts of Chancery in the American Colonies," *Select Essays*, II, 780, 784. See the opinion of Edward Northey, Attorney General, dated April 21, 1703/4, in George Chalmers, *Opinions of Eminent Lawyers*, 1st Amer. edn. (Burlington, 1858), I, 194-95.

Covenant without damage, or the like," the seventeenth-century statutes of Massachusetts read, "the Bench shall determine such matter of equity."[65] In neighboring Plymouth a similar statute in force by 1671 provided that the court was to "have power to determine all such matters of equity, as cannot be relieved by the Common Law."[66]

The published records of the Suffolk County Court for the years 1670-79 show that no less than forty-five bonds were processed according to the principles applied by the English Chancery Court. Thirty-two of these cases were brought as actions for trespass on the case, a form of action used quite indiscriminately in colonial New England. This in itself was a departure from the precision of common law pleading then in force in England.[67] The records also show two sequestrations; an order for possession or writ of assistance; and the granting of injunctions to abate a nuisance, to remove an obstruction, and to maintain the status quo in the case of an estate in the process of settlement. All of these were equitable decrees designed to secure the respondent's obedience to the court. The records also reveal such commonplace aspects of equity litigation as the administration of trusts, and in one case we find the application of equitable principles in a common law action in which the common law procedure rendered the plaintiff helpless.[68]

Contrary to Pound's characterization of Puritan law as stubbornly retributive, in the tradition of the common law we find that the courts of seventeenth-century Massachusetts gave equitable relief which probably would not have been available in England.[69] Indeed, in some Massachusetts cases it is difficult to justify the granting of equitable remedies even under English Chancery practices. A decree for specific performance, for

65. *The Colonial Laws of Massachusetts* (Boston, 1887), 86.
66. *The Compact, with the Charter and Laws of the Colony of New Plymouth* (Boston, 1863), 260.
67. Chafee, ed., *Records of the Suffolk County Court, 1671-80, passim.* See also Daniel J. Boorstin, *The Americans: The Colonial Experience* (New York, 1958), 20-28, especially 27.
68. *Ibid.,* liii; 103 (1672); 294-99 (1673); 338, 392 (1673/74); 442 (1674); 429 (1675); 726-27 (1676); 881 (1677/78); 885 (1677/78); 890-94 (1677/78); and 981 (1678/79).
69. Chafee, ed., *Records of the Suffolk County Court, 1671-80,* li, lii-lvi. It has been suggested that the absence of any mention of equity in the indexes to the *Records and Files of the Quarterly Courts of Essex County* suggests the absence of equity in that county. In reply, one might observe that an index to legal records which lists "Utensils, household" from "andirons" to "winnowing sheets," and "Tools" from "adze" to "yokes," but which does not mention assumpsit, covenant, or case, and which can do no better than the wholly inaccurate reference, "Trespass, *see* Crimes," suggests that a legal mind was not at work when the indexer compiled his references. To prove the presence or absence of equity in Essex County, one would have to examine every case in the volumes; for legal research the index is next to useless.

example, is an equitable remedy which compels the performance of a contract rather than awards damages for its breach; it may be obtained in situations in which the damages available at common law are inadequate. The three decrees for specific performance in real estate transactions found in the Suffolk Records are not unusual, for specific performance is commonly granted in such transactions because every piece of land is unique.[70] While such orders are not unknown in cases involving chattels which are unique or of unascertainable value,[71] the historian may view with curiosity the use of this remedy in cases concerning 5,000 feet of pine boards or what seems to have been the draft of a Mercator map.[72]

No less interesting than the award of equitable relief in cases of dubious merit is the use of special verdicts in straightforward cases at law. Such verdicts were authorized by the Massachusetts statutes in cases in which the law was obscure or the jury was unable to reach a verdict on the issue.[73] Thus, in the case of *Crisp* v. *Joanes* (1674), the jury in the Court of Assistants returned a most unusual verdict: if the word of the defendant was sufficient to prove a promise, the judgment should be upheld; if not, the former verdict should be reversed.[74]

According to Pound, equity was objectionable because it conflicted with the Puritans' desire to control behavior absolutely—where the common law prevailed, a person who chose to break it knew what the consequences would be. The Puritans further objected to equity, Pound continues, because it acted *in personam*, against the person, rather than *in rem*, against the thing, and because it permitted the magistrate to apply a standard suitable to the particular case rather than an inflexible rule.[75]

That equity was not as objectionable to the Puritans as Pound maintains is evident from the records of the ecclesiastical trials of seven-

70. *Thayer* v. *Paine* (1675), *Billing* v. *Rawson* (1677), *Baker* v. *Johnson* (1673/74); Chafee, ed., *Records of the Suffolk County Court, 1671-80*, 563, 819, 392. In the first two cases the defendant was given the curious option of paying damages.

71. Apart from items which have sentimental value, the following may serve as illustrations of chattels involved in recent actions in which specific performance was awarded: twenty reindeer and their issue (*Ottoson* v. *Widstead*, 6 Alaska 319 [1920]), and a half interest in a mare with the potentiality of a racehorse (*Elliott* v. *Jones*, 11 Del. Ch. 343 [1917]).

72. *Davie* v. *Hall* (1677/78), and *Atherton* v. *Lockwood* (1674); Chafee, ed., *Records of the Suffolk County Court, 1671-80*, 875-86, 512-13.

73. *The Colonial Laws of Massachusetts*, 87.

74. Chafee, ed., *Records of the Suffolk County Court, 1671-80*, 457-59. Another special verdict is found in *Hutchinson* v. *Paine*, ibid., 530-36 (with discussion on pp. lii-liii); the fact that such verdicts were returned is mentioned in *Williams* v. *Woodbridge*, ibid., 767-70 (1676/77), and *Broughton* v. *Chickly, Records of the Court of Assistants*, II, 132-34 (1662/63).

75. Pound, *Spirit of the Common Law*, 53-56.

teenth-century Massachusetts. These records are perhaps more significant than judicial practices, for, unfettered by restraints from Westminster and Whitehall, the Puritans in America could fashion religious institutions according to their own desires. Many of the characteristics of the church trials, which indeed can be expected to reflect the Puritan ideal, are typical of equity.

A maxim descriptive of equity applies equally well to the theory underlying the Puritan ecclesiastical trials: "It will not permit a wrong without a remedy." The churches, in their quasi-judicial actions, displayed the same effort to achieve justice without the hindrance of the technicalities of common law procedure. There was no distinction between judge and jury; the entire church served in both capacities, deciding issues of fact and law, and the parson was but the foreman of the jury and the presiding member of an enormous bench of judges. No pleadings were exchanged between the litigants to focus their dispute on one matter on which the issue could be joined; the church considered the case as a whole and supervised every step in the proceedings. Complainants and respondents were subjected to examinations which could be searching and even inquisitorial.[76] If a case was appealed to a Council, that body considered the entire case and gave a judgment analogous to a final decree which the church concerned was expected to accept. As in the case of medieval ecclesiastical law, the proceedings were strictly *in personam*.[77] If a church member failed to respond to his church's summons or if he remained impenitent once the church had decreed that he must make a confession, he was excommunicated for contempt of the church.[78] All of these features of church procedure had their counterparts in equity pleading and practice; none resembled common law procedure.

That the Puritans disliked the Court of Chancery cannot be denied. But their dislike was not simply an abhorrence of the principles of equity: this is indicated by the chancery-like procedure of the churches, the inability of the English Puritans during the Interregnum to do without equity, and the practices of the courts of colonial Massachusetts. The abuses, delays, and costs incident to equity litigation may have been a factor in the

76. The church trial of Anne Hutchinson is a good example. See Adams, *Antinomianism*, 285-336. See also *Charlestown Records*, i-vii.

77. See Holdsworth, *History of English Law*, IV, 275; C. C. Langdell, "The Development of Equity Pleading from Canon Law Procedure," *Select Essays*, II, 773-74; Maitland, *Equity*, 5; F. W. Maitland and F. C. Montague, *A Sketch of English Legal History* (New York and London, 1915), 125.

78. Mather, *Ratio Disciplinae*, 145-50. For the application of the principle, see Boston First Church Records, III, 9 (1638); Barnstable Records, 31-32 (1683); *Dorchester Records*, 51-52 (1666); *Quincy Records*, 483-84 (1683); Records of the First Church of Northampton (hereafter cited as Northampton Records), 25 (1697).

Puritan distrust of Chancery, but perhaps more significant was the fact that Chancery had a "twin sister," the dreaded Court of the Star Chamber. The procedure of the two courts was largely similar, and few Puritans could have any affinity for the Star Chamber.[79] Having forsaken its legitimate functions to become a political agency, it was the delight of this grisly court, with its Addamsesque sense of humor, to torture Nonconformists. It had punished Prynne for the publication of his *News from Ipswich* by ordering the executioner to cut off his ears, which had already been cropped for his *Histriomastix*, and it later inflicted the same penalty on Bastwick and Burton. On the eve of the Civil War the Star Chamber had thoroughly merited the hatred of the Puritans, although they later set up courts of their own which could be as demonic as the Star Chamber.[80] Much of the Puritans' alleged hatred of equity was caused by the intense distrust of a prerogative court under whose authority they had suffered. It hardly seems to have been a dislike of the principles of equity.

It is a gross simplification to identify the Puritans with Parliament and the common law, the Anglicans with the Crown and Chancery. Not all champions of the common law were Puritans: Coke was a nominal Anglican, Selden an Erastian. In no part of the British Isles were the Puritans in as strong a position as in Scotland; but the Scots jealously followed their own law, rather than the common law. Nor did the lawyers among the continental Puritans obtain their training at the Inns of the Court, where the common law was taught; they attended the continental universities, where the Roman law tradition prevailed. There is no obvious inherent connection between Puritanism and the common law. What at first sight appears to have been a marriage for love may actually have been no more than a union of convenience.[81]

To summarize, the churches' disciplinary functions had considerable effect on the behavior of the saints and may have exerted a powerful influence on the general society. The alliance between the churches and the state was informal and spontaneous in origin; each entity carefully guarded its own rights, yet each recognized the need for cooperation with the other. The procedure of church trials in Massachusetts corroborates the evidence of the court records that the Puritans incorporated many aspects of equity into their judicial and religious practices.

The possibilities for future study in this field are enormous, for the full truth of the churches' influence in Puritan society remains to be de-

79. For a concise comparison of Chancery and Star Chamber procedure, see Edward Jenks, *A Short History of English Law*, 6th edn. (London, 1949), 166-67.
80. See Maitland and Montague, *Sketch of English Legal History*, 118-20.
81. I am greatly indebted to Dr. Sidney A. Burrell of Barnard College for his helpful suggestions on the subject. Professor Burrell's own work should go far in helping us to see some of these problems in a clearer light.

termined. It lies partly in a careful study of the surviving records of Puritan communities in America. A comparative analysis of church and court records for a particular period and jurisdiction is, for example, the key to the relationship between the influence exerted by the courts and that of the churches. On this subject alone many questions remain to be answered. Did the churches follow the example of the courts and try the same cases, is the reverse true, or did the two bodies act independently of each other? Were the courts inclined to be less severe in sentencing persons who had been disciplined by the churches, or the churches in censuring members who had been subjected to temporal punishments? Such a study presupposes that members and non-members would be clearly distinguished. The laborious compilation of membership lists is necessary; the names must be extracted from the minutes of admissions and dismissions scattered throughout voluminous church records, many of which contain no systematic communicant rolls.

Prosecution for fornication is a subject which could be further studied with some profit. Charles Francis Adams' study of the Quincy court and church records suggests that the incidence of civil and ecclesiastical prosecutions for fornication varied in an inverse ratio. Henry Bamford Parkes has observed that the last known civil prosecution for fornication in Suffolk County occurred in 1707 and in the other eastern counties of Massachusetts in 1737 or 1739.[82] The records of the Suffolk County churches show a marked increase in fornication cases from the beginning of the eighteenth century; church records in the remaining eastern counties show a similar increase after the first quarter of the century.[83] Was this change merely a coincidence or was it the effect of the Great Awakening? Or did the churches intensify their disciplinary efforts precisely because the civil government had ceased to punish fornication, applying the suggestion of John Knox that offenses neglected by the law should be dealt with by the church?[84]

Another question which remains unanswered by factual evidence concerns the morality of the saints. Did church membership have any appreciable effect on their behavior or were the saints no better than the strangers? It must be determined whether the names of non-members appear proportionately more often in the records of the criminal cases, and both church and court records must be examined. In this connection, the use of the Halfway Covenant requires further investigation. To what extent was it a part of the ecclesiastical life of Massachusetts? Some church

82. Adams, "Some Aspects of Sexual Morality," Mass. Hist. Soc., *Proceedings*, 2nd ser., 6 (1891), 497-503; Parkes, "Morals and Law Enforcement in Colonial New England," *New Eng. Qtly.*, 5 (1932), 442.

83. Oberholzer, *Delinquent Saints*, 254-55, Table IV.

84. Knox, "The Buke of Discipline," *Works*, ed. by David Laing (Edinburgh, 1864), II, 227.

records identify certain persons as members under the provisions of that compromise; others never allude to it. Was there a difference in the treatment meted out to communicants and that accorded to halfway members? These are questions for the social historian who is willing to explore not only the church records but also those of the courts, too few of which are published in book form.[85] The study of these records and the background research necessary to interpret the resulting statistics constitute an exhaustive task. Yet these records are important, for through them we may come to know more concerning such subjects of perennial controversy as Puritan sexual morality or the interaction of church and state in the area of social control.

The word "Puritanism" itself is in need of definition, and the very essence of Puritanism remains to be determined. Certainly Puritanism was not limited to America, and the historian must distinguish between the various forms in which the movement manifested itself as it transcended national boundaries. Characteristics of the American Puritan of the seventeenth century may be no more than characteristics of the environment and may differ from those of the Scottish or English Puritan of the same time, or from those of the American Puritan of the eighteenth century. Accidents of polity must also be distinguished from characteristics which apply to Puritanism generally.

The student of any aspect of American Puritanism would be greatly aided by a comprehensive study of American Puritan doctrinal thought. Nothing written on the subject even approximates the great work on English Puritanism by William Haller.[86] There are notable and important studies on the intellectual development of New England, but the comprehensive history of American Puritan theology remains to be written. Where, for example, in any of the standard secondary works on the American Puritans can one find a discussion of their doctrines of the ministry, of matrimony, or even of the sacraments? Scholars of Puritanism are either fascinated by particular doctrines, notably the doctrine of man in his relation to God, or they tend to attempt the neat arrangement of all New England thought into an all-embracing pattern. In order to write a satisfactory history of Puritan theology the scholar must have some understanding of historical and systematic theology and a willingness to catalogue theological minutiae. Such an approach on the part of a competent scholar may lead us closer to an understanding of the nature of Puritanism.

85. See R. B. Morris, "Early American Court Records: A Publication Program," *Anglo-American Legal History Series*, 1st ser., 4 (1941), 9-12.
86. *The Rise of Puritanism* (New York, 1938).

VIII.

THE ANGLICAN CHURCH IN
RESTORATION COLONIAL POLICY

Philip S. Haffenden
UNIVERSITY OF ABERDEEN

THE FRAMERS OF THE Canada Act of 1791 believed that the failure to re-create in the New World the relationship between church and state that prevailed in the Old had helped pave the way toward the American Revolution. The entrenched position of the Church of England in the new province of Upper Canada reflected this view and the desire to avoid repetition of error. It reflected also the deep-rooted belief of the English that political stability derived in good measure from the support of the Establishment. Superficially, it would seem that conditions under the Restoration were favorable for the crown to use the church for its own purpose. State and church were closely united in the mother country during most of the period, and some reflection of this might be expected in the policy pursued toward the colonies.

Restoration colonial policy pivoted on the economic orientation of the empire; it derived from mercantilist principles expressed in the parliamentary legislation of 1660, 1663, and 1673. The resulting system possessed one explicit aim: the creation of a self-sufficient imperial superstate. However, the high degree of political centralization necessary to the control of a colonial network was never achieved and political directives to the colonies were only sporadically obeyed. A number of bold steps toward some measure of centralization were indeed taken during the Restoration, but it has become almost traditional for the historian to regard them as mere expediences. Yet there are many hints that they may instead have been signs of a completed plan that was hindered from full expression

by domestic upheaval and the circumspection of royal power. It is doubtful that at any other time in the history of British imperialism was there a
greater desire to run the empire on doctrinaire lines. This was true in
1660, as Restoration statesmen surveyed the anarchy into which intra-
imperial relations had degenerated; and it was also true in 1686, when
the Dominion of New England was established.

The political role of religion needs to be assessed within this framework.
How aggressively, in fact, were the overseas pulpits used to conjure
obedience? How far were they consciously employed as an instrument for
bolstering the authority of royal representatives? What exactly was the
function assigned to religion in these early years of the old colonial system?
The evidence to answer these questions is meager, for governmental decisions covering all the western plantations were the exception rather than
the rule. One rarely finds council committee or select council sufficiently
free from pressing domestic issues to adopt a colonial course of action
designed to direct events. Ordinarily such bodies could attempt no more
than a modification of what had already taken place. This was true in all
spheres of colonial policy, but especially in that of religion. Decisions from
the court at Whitehall were qualified by delay between the adoption of a
course of action and its translation into terms suitable for the settlements;
administrative inefficiency and poor communications added further distor-
tion; a change of minister or of royal will might well cancel a decision
before it could be made effective. Even though there occasionally was a
striking parallel between events at home and overseas, this was not the
case as frequently as might otherwise have been expected. Because of the
sudden shifts and changes which took place in England, for example, there
was no counterpart in North America to the substitution of Catholic for
Protestant officials, though James in exile was to boast that the conversion
of the empire to Rome had been his intention. It was in fact a period when
major resolutions were rarely committed to paper. Even if we do not find
explicit approbation of the conscious harnessing of religion to serve an
imperial purpose, we cannot dismiss the possibility of such a course. And
there is enough evidence available to justify a considerable degree of freedom for speculation.

Would Restoration religious policy favor toleration or Anglican
domination? Before the convening of the Long Parliament the Church of
England had been a persecuting church; in the overseas plantations, whatever its intentions, it had not been able to persecute. Now the opportunity
had come again after twenty years of Presbyterian and Independent abuse.
The failure of the Savoy Conference and the development of the Clarendon
Code restored Anglicanism in 1661 to a position of unassailable superiority

over the sects. Yet during the archiepiscopate of Sheldon the colonies were as free from the worst excesses of Anglican arbitrariness as they had been during the archiepiscopate of Laud. Was the practical toleration enjoyed during both decades derived from identical or from different causes? That of the 1630's was clearly the result of ineffectual political control; but it is generally held that by the time of the Restoration, Whitehall had shrewdly realized that toleration could be beneficial to imperial development. From the modern viewpoint this awareness, if awareness it was, seems both realistic and farsighted; but it contrasts strangely with much of what is known of the theory and practice of the era.

The founders of any such policy of toleration almost certainly knew that their ideas could only lead to further racial and religious diversification. To an age which looked on centralization and uniformity as a means to prosperity, the concept of "unity in diversity" could only be regarded with suspicion—especially in a country which had just suffered the agony of civil war and the Interregnum. Where would the doctrinaire mercantilist stand? Would he not desire to plant the impress of the mother country not merely on the political and economic but on the social sphere as well? If, in denying this, we accept the unqualified endorsement of "toleration," we are presented with the paradox of crown ministers pursuing a policy of rigid control of form and practice for England, while permitting a latitude of worship far in advance of the age for her colonies. Is it not conceivable that toleration was adopted initially as no more than a temporary expedient?

Given more favorable circumstances and greater material resources, men such as the Earls of Clarendon and Danby might well have planted the Church of England where it had failed to grow and have promoted its growth where it had languished. There were numerous advantages which could accrue to England from a thriving Erastian Church within the context of the colonial system, and few administrators were seemingly wedded to toleration for sheer love of it. In short, many of the politicians of the Restoration, it is suggested, viewed the development of the Anglican Church overseas with far greater favor than historians usually attribute to them. This paper will seek to examine this question of development and to inquire into contemporary evaluation of the political usefulness of the church.

To understand Restoration colonial policy it is necessary to review briefly the progress of church policy during the reign of Charles I. The Laudian Church had failed in England, but in the colonies its policy was never really put to the test. However, William Laud had been exceptionally confident in his approach to the problem of regulating the religious affairs of the colonies. The policy of Thorough, it has been said, broke under its own weight; but not before the English Church had shown that it construed its power as coincident—at the least—with the political bounds of the English state. In 1634 Laud, backed by the Arminian Bishop Neile, headed both the Commission for New England and the Commission for Foreign Plantations. These two bodies, composed of identical personnel, were authorized to legislate for the colonies, punish and imprison ecclesiastical offenders, set up courts ecclesiastical and civil, and regulate colonial charters. The previous year the archbishop had proposed to the Privy Council that the English congregations in a number of Dutch towns should hear only ministers approved and licensed by the bishop of London, and read only the English Prayer Book. Similar restrictions were subsequently proposed for factories in Hamburg, Turkey and India, as well as for the colonies of Virginia and Barbados.[1]

Although their manifest aim was religious uniformity, Laud and his commission did little to bring transatlantic Englishmen under the control of the metropolitan church. Some of his measures were ludicrously feeble in application. Laud, for example, tried to restrict the emigration of Puritans by granting licenses for departure from the country. In 1634 a few ships were detained at East Anglian ports, although even these were ultimately permitted to depart on condition of engaging to use the Prayer Book on voyage. A more vigorous approach to the problem looked to the sending of a bishop to America, backed, if need be, by military force. But these schemes were not realized. While Charles became embroiled, first with his Scottish subjects, then with the full force of the English Parliamentarians, Laud's cherished designs were curtailed, and the archbishop was humiliated, imprisoned, and finally executed.

Laud was defeated by the inadequacy of his own resources. He failed to achieve his objective not from lack of political support but because that support lacked the means to render it effective. If men of the Restoration sought instruction from the experience of the hapless archbishop, they must have been aware of the error of condemning a policy which had never been properly tested.

The dependence of the church upon the king, its political protector, was a factor of consummate importance for the entire Restoration period, but never more so than during the closing years of the reign of Charles II. In a spirit of gratitude for the assured continuance of royal support, the University of Oxford on July 23, 1683, unanimously condemned a number of propositions justifying resistance to authority. These were drawn from the works of such dissenters as John Knox, Milton, Thomas Hobbes, and

1. Hugh Trevor Roper, *Archbishop Laud, 1575-1645* (London, 1940), 253.

George Buchanan. Copies of their writings were later burnt in the quadrangle of the schools. The university also decreed that all teachers should instruct their scholars

in that most necessary doctrine, which, in a manner, is the badge and character of the Church of England, to submitting to every ordinance of man for the Lord's sake, . . . teaching that this submission . . . is to be cleare, absolute, and without exception of any state or order of men.[2]

The doctrine of passive obedience was closely related to the theory of the divine right of kings; both were designed to serve the state by binding the community more closely together. It held kings accountable for their stewardship to the Almighty only. He in turn demanded that subjects should not resist a divinely appointed ruler. These beliefs had proved their value in statecraft during the Middle Ages, but after the sixteenth century, when the development of nationalism added to the power of the monarchy in Europe, they gained a new usefulness. Kings asserted that the divine character of their office entitled them to establish whatever religion they pleased within the state. The interdependence of church and crown could hardly have been expressed in clearer terms than those used by Bishop Richard Montague to Charles I: "Domine Imperator, defende me gladio, et ego te defendam calamo."[3]

As Puritan opposition to Charles I developed, both the church's loyalty to the throne and its sense of attachment to the monarch's person seemed to increase. While Sibthorpe preached that subjects were bound in conscience to submit even to immoderate or unjust taxes, Manwaring taught that all significations of royal pleasure were in the nature and force of a command, even when kings flatly commanded against the law of God. Thus the Oxford declaration of 1683 had strong and well-nourished roots.

Because of the close liaison between church and state, Laud had been able to aim high; but the feebleness of the state explains why his shots had been so few and so short of the mark. During the Restoration years, conditions were qualitatively changed. Charles I had been a conscientious church-goer and a staunch and unfaltering upholder of the principles of the Anglican Church; his son was a man without serious religious faith. Before the Restoration the church had persecuted in accordance with the king's wishes, but despite the opposition of Parliament; now the church

2. Andrew Clark, *The Life and Times of Anthony Wood, Antiquary of Oxford* (Oxford, 1900), III, 62-64; "Decree . . . of Oxford," *Hist. Mss. Comm., Fourteenth Report, Appendix: The Manuscripts of Lord Kenyon* (London, 1894), Part IV, 165.

3. "Protect me with the sword, O my Lord and Master, and I will defend you with the pen." Richard Montague, *Appello Caesarem* (London, 1625), 321-22.

persecuted in accordance with Parliament and in spite of the indifference of the king.

Historians no longer believe that the Clarendon Code was passed and accepted by the royal government for other than political reasons.[4] The king's speech of May 3, 1660, had urged that the "old principles" be uprooted.[5] To this end Presbyterians and Independents were denied the spiritual and academic foundations of their religion: never again should they control England as they had during the Commonwealth. It was hoped that with the ruin of the sects the Anglican Church would expand to embrace the vast majority of the nation. Manifestly, such backing was motivated by considerations which were largely non-religious. In view of these factors, the future for the Established Church in the colonies seemed vastly improved.

However, the colonial system in 1660 could scarcely have presented greater lack of political uniformity. So limited was the degree of contact between the various colonies, it is even questionable whether the term "system" can justifiably be applied. Separated from the homeland by thousands of miles of ocean and nurtured in the wilderness, many of the colonists found political obedience to England unnatural. Many of the colonial governments had enjoyed virtual independence for more than twenty years. Yet discipline was an urgent requirement if the mercantile empire was ever to become more than a dream. The issue focused upon the new navigation laws imposed from London.

The new legislation presented an opportunity, however limited, for the church to play a role similar to that which it exercised in England. At this time the power of the pulpit as a means for airing grievances was considerable; as a vehicle for urging the acceptance of unpopular laws or moderation in civil strife its influence was somewhat less. But ably handled and applied with caution this influence could act as a gentle leaven to aid the work of the state. Many an astute colonial governor recognized this, but much hinged upon the caliber of the church leaders at home and their assessment of the relative importance of the plantations.

The first fifteen years of the Restoration were hardly a period of spiritual vigor. Unfortunately for centralization, church leadership was singularly lacking in spirituality. The failings and virtues of two men— Gilbert Sheldon and Humphrey Henchman—were especially important to overseas communicants. Sheldon was bishop of London and became archbishop of Canterbury on the death of Juxon in June, 1663. In the

4. Keith Feiling, "Clarendon and the Act of Uniformity (1662-3)," *Eng. Hist. Rev.*, 44 (1929), 290.
5. *Parliamentary History*, IV, 179.

History of His Own Time, Samuel Parker, bishop of Oxford, described him as "transacting everything with a peculiar strength and penetration of judgement—a man of eminent piety." Parker, however, may have been prejudiced in Sheldon's favor, for at one time he had acted as his chaplain.[6] To Bishop Burnet, historian of the Reformation in England, Sheldon was a man who seemed lacking in any deep sense of religion, who spoke of it most commonly as "an engine of government and matter of policy." But he judged him "keen, clever, polite and politic . . . fitted to grace a drawing room and to take part in State affairs."[7] Henchman was moved from Lincoln to London after the death of Juxon and the promotion of Sheldon. The Presbyterian Baxter who had met him at the Savoy Conference, not in the friendliest of circumstances, described him as "of grave, comely, reverend aspect" and "possessed of good insight in the Fathers and Councils." It was known that he had a pronounced hatred of Roman Catholicism.[8]

Although both men lacked sufficient interest in the church overseas to develop its spiritual welfare on their own initiative, they could have been valuable political servants under able direction. For most of the Restoration, however, consistent direction in any sphere of administration could not be counted upon; until the translation of Henry Compton to the bishopric of London in 1675, there is little indication of the Established Church's taking the lead in colonial matters.

Because of the king's religious indifference and his indolent approach to state affairs, the political impetus to use religion as an instrument of colonial policy had to come either from the crown's ministers or from members of a select council concerned with trade and plantations. With the exception of the Lord Chancellor it is difficult to discover in the 1660's many government officials who placed excessive emphasis on its use as a binding force of empire. The Earl of Clarendon, it is true, was prepared to hazard a tentative step, but his zeal was moderated by an awareness of the immense task which confronted the king's government on the purely political plane.

During the first decade of the Restoration, the inability of the king to give a strong lead was largely responsible for the piecemeal approach to the problem of imperial government. Numerous factors hampered the development of sound policy and prejudiced England's colonial military ventures: the weakness of Charles's financial position, the refusal of Parliament to grant him an adequate revenue, and the general distrust of his

6. W. H. Hutton, *History of the English Church* (London, 1913), VI, 197-98.
7. John Stoughton, *History of Religion in England* (London, 1901), III, 458-60.
8. *Ibid.,* 480.

motives. Responsibility for the severe limitations imposed on the king rested ultimately on Parliament. But Charles deserves a full measure of blame for many of the colonial decisions, and particularly for the introduction of fresh forms of proprietary government into the imperial framework. Although the charter terms granted to Rhode Island and Connecticut after 1660 may have been unavoidable, the addition of the proprietaries of New York, New Jersey, and the Carolinas served only to swell the already numerous non-royal colonies. This inevitably delayed the attempt at greater centralization. With aims in the political sphere so divergently pursued and achievements so modest, it is not surprising that little was done to develop the church overseas—much less use it for political purposes.

Although no complete picture of the Anglican Church in the plantations is available for the first decade of the Restoration, a fair indication of its nature and growth is gained from gubernatorial reports and letters, and other correspondence. The problems of the colonies differed widely. The infant church in Jamaica, fretting over lack of suitable places of worship and insufficient ministers, sought various expedients to encourage growth. Barbados was absorbed less with problems of expansion than with those of regulation. Virginia, more mature, was primarily concerned with the quality of its incumbents and with episcopal supervision.

The Leeward Islands, which, like Jamaica, were later to become vigorous Anglican communities, were still struggling to achieve order out of ecclesiastical chaos. The islands were described in 1666 as being in a "sad and desperate condition,"[9] in urgent need of "pious and learned divines."[10] The government of Clarendon, its attention concentrated on the more pressing problems of New England, demonstrated scant interest in the plight of these communities, which had been severely aggravated by the second Dutch War. This contrasts noticeably with the care shown by Danby and later royal officials. The Leewards undoubtedly suffered from neglect while they were under proprietary control and largely governed from Barbados, but little positive information is available about them.

Of all the provincial churches, that of Jamaica probably attracted the most attention in the 1660's. In 1661 the Council of Foreign Plantations recommended that the archbishop of Canterbury and the bishop of London should choose five able ministers to be maintained at royal charge for twelve months. The king was induced to grant the necessary financial aid in order to encourage development.[11] Suitable clergy were sent out

9. W. N. Sainsbury *et al.*, eds., *Calendar of State Papers, Colonial Series, America and West Indies, 1661-68* (London, 1880), no. 1257.

10. Gov. Lord Willoughby to Lords of Council, July 9, 1668, *ibid.*, no. 1788.

11. Minutes of Council for Foreign Plantations, June 27, 1661, *ibid.*, no. 118.

the following year in company with eighty planters, and payment for their upkeep at the rate of £100 per annum was continued for some time.[12] Only two of these were properly ordained; the third—an old army preacher —was reported as "not yet in orders," and two more were Germans. By 1664 the island boasted seven parishes: St. Catherine's, St. John, Port Royal, Clarendon, St. David, St. Andrew, and St. Thomas. However, only one of these possessed a church—an old Spanish edifice which had been brought back into use after extensive repairs.[13]

Religious liberty was granted to all Christians by the Proclamation of 1662,[14] these rights being confirmed in the Instructions issued to Sir Thomas Modyford two years later.[15] The governor was permitted to dispense with the oath of allegiance and supremacy and to allow free exercise of religion. But he was obliged to profess the Protestant religion and to recommend it to all others. From such beginnings the Anglican Church in Jamaica flourished. Before the fall of Shaftesbury and the Cabal it could compare favorably with its sisters in Virginia and Barbados.

If the limited references to Barbados' ecclesiastical affairs in surviving government correspondence are any criteria, it is doubtful whether Whitehall at this early period possessed very detailed knowledge of the composition and character of the church there. It was known, however, that the Barbadian Church was divided into eleven parishes and served by an adequate number of incumbents. The island thus escaped a problem which vexed most other territories. Of the moral character of the clergy, one description pithily remarks that their "lives run counter to their doctrines."[16] But even if this judgment be accepted, it is more than probable that the church was reasonably well regulated in comparison with the scandalous laxity which characterized many of the overseas communities.

Virginia, the oldest settlement, attempted to induce the home government to set the regulation of the plantation churches on firmer foundations. Such agitation, however, was no sign that the province had solved the problems which beset her neighbors; rather it was indicative that she recognized how seriously these problems affected her spiritual growth. The first move of the home government was the drafting of formal instructions for Sir William Berkeley in 1662. By these the governor was ordered to take especial care for the devout service of God and to ensure that the Book of Common Prayer was read and the sacrament administered according to the rites of the Church of England. More churches were to be built, and each was to be assigned 100 acres as a glebe. Finally,

12. *Ibid.*, nos. 264, 401.   13. *Ibid.*, no. 810.
14. October 10, 1662, *ibid.*, no. 374.
15. February 18, 1664, *ibid.*, no. 664.
16. *Ibid.*, nos. 1788, 1860.

yearly reports on the state of the Anglican faith in the colony were to be sent to the Council of Plantations.[17]

Advice and precept were one thing; help was another. In 1661 the Assembly of Virginia petitioned the king that the universities of Oxford and Cambridge might "furnish the church here with ministers." The plea went unnoticed, and it was not until the 1680's that any endeavor was made to meet the request. Proposals for a Virginia bishop were made before the Restoration was one year old, but their reception was no more enthusiastic than had been accorded the call for more ministers. Not until the next decade was the appeal properly considered and action taken to develop a colonial episcopate such as Laud had envisaged.[18]

It is difficult to justify the indifference of the higher English clergy toward the spiritual welfare of the overseas communities. One fundamental difficulty, of course, was the provision of financial inducements sufficiently attractive for ministers to undertake the hazardous voyage across the Atlantic. The cost of transportation was one problem, but the poverty of colonial parishes, with their extensive boundaries, was an even greater one. Only men of great spiritual fire, or whose standards had failed to meet the requirements of an English living, would be willing to commit themselves to voluntary exile. There were few of the former, and the latter were not aided to emigrate even were they inclined to do so.

The total activity of the English government during the 1660's was nowhere very marked. But there are indications that given more favorable circumstances, greater efforts would have been made. Despite the multitudinous sins accredited to their account by the mother country, the New England colonies were for many years rebuked with the velvet glove. Indeed, English administrators took great pains to assure the various political entities that the Puritan way of life would be disrupted as little as possible. Such restraint on the part of the home government, whatever its motives, could not be pursued without certain limitations. For the government, it was imperative, for example, that the New Englanders come gradually to realize the determination of the imperial power to supervise them. For political and economic reasons, nothing could be allowed to interfere with this. The Puritans' suppression of Anglicanism and their intolerance of other denominations was opposed because of such considerations, but not because of them alone. For personal reasons Charles found a policy of toleration attractive, but he loved it not so well as his life, and he was ready to abandon it if expediency so demanded. Before long he withdrew his

17. September 12, 1662, *ibid.*, no. 368.

18. S. E. Baldwin, "American Jurisdiction of the Bishop of London in Colonial Times," Amer. Antiq. Soc., *Proceedings*, N.S., 13 (1899-1900), 201.

support from the Quakers, so that the liberty of conscience earlier urged upon New England was henceforth no longer to be extended to this sect: "It having been necessary by advice of parliament to make a sharp law against them, we are well content that you do the like. . . ."[19]

When an expedition sailed from England in 1664 for the conquest of the New Netherlands, it included government representatives who were instructed to accept the formal submission of the New England colonies to the restored Stuart monarch. If Clarendon's intention was merely to impress the Puritan colonists that the religious situation in England had undergone a drastic change since the days of Cromwell, then he could hardly have pursued his aim in a more emphatic manner, for Sir Robert Carr, Richard Nicholls, and Samuel Maverick were all enthusiastic royalists and two of the three were strict Episcopalians.

Although Clarendon's policy toward Massachusetts had frequently been criticized as excessively cautious,[20] he may have been attracted at one time by the chimera of Puritan subjugation and the forceful imposition of the Anglican Church. So the Dutch seem to have believed. In the spring of 1664 the governor and Chamber in Amsterdam wrote to the governor and Council of the New Netherlands to advise of English intentions in the New World. Amsterdam had received news from London that Charles II, "being inclined to reduce all his kingdom under one form of government in Church and State, hath taken care that Commissioners are ready to repair to New England to install bishops there as in Old England."[21] The Dutch had intelligence as early as April of an impending attack, but it is not necessarily true that the religious information dispatched to New Amsterdam was correct. If Boston had heard that bishops were being sent to the colonies, the New Englanders probably would have broken with the Englishmen and thus split the forces opposed to the Dutch. The least the Dutch could have hoped for would have been a Puritan refusal to support Nicholls, and perhaps even active aid against him. If the news was fabricated, however, it seems odd that the governor of New Amsterdam was not privy to the plot. Most probably the Dutch sincerely believed that religious revision was the aim of the English.

Upon what grounds did the Dutch base their knowledge? Two possibilities present themselves. First, details of a discussion held by the king with his ministers, either in the Privy Council or in private, may have leaked to the outside. Although the minutes of a discussion have not

19. P. L. Kaye, *English Colonial Administration under Lord Clarendon* (Baltimore, 1905), 51.

20. *Ibid.*, 47-51.

21. Baldwin, "American Jurisdiction of the Bishop of London," Amer. Antiq. Soc., *Proceedings*, N.S., 13 (1899-1900), 202.

survived, the enterprise against the New Netherlands was obviously well debated. It would be singularly surprising if the feasibility of a more vigorous approach to the religious separatism of New England was not discussed. The Dutch may well have received a garbled version of what had taken place and drawn the wrong conclusions.

The second possibility is that the Dutch saw and misinterpreted the private instructions to Colonel Richard Nicholls. These instructions were issued on April 23, 1664. The fifth article reads in part:

You shall let them [the New Englanders] know that you have no orders from us . . . to make the least attempt to encourage alteration in the way they professe their religion: for though nobody can doubt but that we could look upon as the greatest blessing God Almighty can confer upon us in this world that He would reduce all our subjects in all dominions to one faith and one worship with us; yet we could not imagine it probable that a confederate number of persons, who separated themselves from their own country and religion established, principally (if not only) that they might enjoy another way of worship . . . could in so short a time be willing to return to that form of worship they had forsake; and therefore that we had been so far from giving you any direction to promote and countenance any alteration in the religion practiced there, that you have express order to the contrary.[22]

Read out of context, the observation on the value of religious conformity may well have been misleading. But the essence of the policy, outlined in the above extract and confirmed by the text of the complete fifth article, is clearly moderation: strict recognition is given to the possible, not the desirable.

The parenthetical endorsement of "one faith and one worship" could have been permitted by Charles in deference to the wishes of his ministers. It may indicate the course of debate in the Council chamber when these instructions were determined upon, for it shows the obvious reluctance with which Clarendon's administration accepted the Puritan regime in New England. But its acceptance was wise and virtually inevitable. It is unlikely that any informed advisor to the king imagined England strong enough to exercise rigid ecclesiastical supervision at a distance of 3,000 miles when such control was not wanted and had, in fact, not been fully achieved at home. Force could have succeeded only in rousing the most spirited opposition. Although the instructions imply that proposals for a sterner policy were rejected, it can be hazarded that they were more likely shelved until the time was opportune.

22. E. B. O'Callaghan, ed., *Documents Relative to the Colonial History of the State of New York* (Albany, N. Y., 1856-87), III, 59.

In spite of growing dissatisfaction with the Puritan regime in New England, the attitude of the home government remained unchanged on these issues even after the fall of Clarendon. The draft patent prepared in 1672 for the proposed bishopric of Virginia stated explicitly that episcopal authority should in no manner be enforced over New England:

We declare that the said—and his successors, bishops of Virginia, shall in no manner enforce their episcopal jurisdiction and authority [over] New England: but we desire that our subjects dwelling below in New England shall be void, free, and wholly exempt from all episcopal rule and authority, until by us it shall be otherwise ordained.[23]

The final clause, "until by us it shall be otherwise ordained," could signify no more than a formal safeguarding of the prerogative. It probably indicates that the freedom of New England from episcopal control was a temporary measure which it might be possible to withdraw in the near future. But a decade and a half was to pass before the home government dared send even a single minister of the Established Church to weaken the theocratic structure of the northern colonies.

The policy of toleration for religious dissidents was applied in some manner to all the colonies during the Restoration. It was especially desirable in New York and New Jersey, the acquisitions which England had gained under the Treaty of Breda. Apart from the personal inclinations of the proprietors, political expediency made it advisable to weld the populace to the conqueror as firmly as possible. Common sense dictated that existing practices should not be interfered with. Even by the 1680's the Anglican Church had achieved little strength in these plantations.

In Carolina, however, where there was no civilized settlement before the English came, considerable provision was made for the growth of Anglicanism. The vowed purpose of the charter granted in 1662-63 was "the propagation of the Christian faith, and the enlargement of the King's empire." Those settlers who would not conform to the public exercise of religion according to the liturgy and ceremony of the Church of England were given liberty of worship according to the dictates of their conscience. This admittedly prevented such extreme forms of repression as the church was able to exercise in England; but among the proprietors were such ardent Anglicans as George Monck, Duke of Albemarle, William, Lord Craven, Sir William Berkeley, and the Earl of Clarendon himself—a factor which was to weigh heavily when the balance was set. These men were given the right of patronage and advowsons of all churches, chapels,

23. H. W. Foote, *Annals of King's Chapel* (New York, 1900), II, 229-30; Protestant Episcopal Society, *Collections* (New York, 1851), I, 136-57.

and oratories within the province. They had an additional power to erect whatever buildings for the Established religion they deemed necessary.

By the end of the 1660's the Anglican Church had gained even firmer ground with a recognized position in the new colony. The constitution drawn up by John Locke in 1669 contained in its ninety-sixth clause the stipulation that Parliament should provide for the building of churches and the public maintenance of divines, who were "to be employed in the exercise of religion according to the Church of England." This, it was said, being "the only true and orthodox and the national religion of all the king's domains, is also of Carolina: and therefore it alone shall be allowed to receive public maintenance by grant of parliament." Locke claimed this provision was inserted by some of the chief proprietors against his better judgment.[24] By this time Clarendon had fallen from power, and it is hardly to be supposed that Shaftesbury, with his known political affiliations, would have supported such a course, or acquiesced in its adoption, had he not been convinced of the benefit to over-all colonial policy.

In the second decade of the Restoration the interest manifested in promoting the Anglican faith was applied more purposefully. In part this was due to the renewed alliance between church and state which followed the fall of the Cabal in 1672. Of equal influence was the translation of Henry Compton to the See of London in 1675, and the vigorous supervisory work begun by the Lords of Trade in the same year. But a limit upon possible achievement had already been set by the failure to erect a bishopric in Virginia several years earlier. Dr. Alexander Murray, the man nominated, had been a companion of the king during his "travels." By the terms of the draft patent all the churches on the mainland and its adjacent islands from Virginia northward were to be united under the diocese of Virginia, thus providing uniformity of doctrine, discipline, authority, and jurisdiction.[25] Beyond this point the project failed to develop, in spite of the influence of Murray at court. Had it not been halted, religious centralization would have antedated political centralization by over ten years.

Failure, with the project relatively close to success, seemed to inhibit further consideration of the subject during the seventeenth century. The fact that the bishopric was even considered in 1672 is indicative of the Anglican Church's increased awareness of its responsibilities; the fact of its failure reveals the administration's inability to understand the value of such a step. Its demise has been attributed to several possible causes: the fall of Clarendon and the consequent dismissal of Sir Charles Bridgman,

24. J. S. M. Anderson, *History of the Church of England in the Colonies* (London, 1848), II, 523-24.
25. Foote, *Annals of King's Chapel*, 229-30.

to whose care the matter had been entrusted; the opposition aroused because the endowment was payable out of the customs;[26] the character of Murray. Other difficulties may have been raised by the Cabal, which was only too pleased to discredit the schemes of Clarendon.[27] Moreover, the proposed bishop is believed to have died in London shortly after 1675.[28] Whatever the cause, it is clear that the support of those who mattered was not forthcoming.

Thus a principal difficulty continued to exist. Without a bishop in the plantations there was no one authoritative individual to act as spokesman for the welfare of the church overseas. The proposals of the colonists, without superior direction, were in fact to play little part in influencing major decisions. Under these circumstances it is not surprising that the condition of the church reflected little more than the wishes of those men who directed its policy from Whitehall. There is no evidence to suggest that the Earl of Danby participated actively in supervising the spiritual care of the plantations, but it is fairly certain that the work of Compton and Sir Leoline Jenkins met with his cordial approval. From the beginning Compton showed keen interest in the activities of the newly instituted committee of the Privy Council and made good use of his right to attend its meetings.

In the first years of their sessions the Lords of Trade commenced a survey of the plantations upon a more searching and comprehensive scale than had hitherto been attempted. The resulting inventories reflected one problem common to all the plantations: lack of an adequate number of incumbents. Governors often enough complained of the churches over which, in the absence of direct pastoral supervision, they were expected to exercise paternal care. But such shortcomings were inevitable when many parishes held no more than a lay reader, and available ministers were not of the highest character.

Efforts to deal with the ministerial shortage were now speedily undertaken. The pamphlet entitled "Virginia's Cure" had urged the establishment of fellowships in both Oxford and Cambridge for the benefit of the province. These were to be held for seven years, at the expiration of which the fellows would go to Virginia and serve the church in that colony for another period of seven years. During this time they were to be

26. A. L. Cross, *The Anglican Episcopate and the American Church* (New York, 1902), 90.

27. Anderson, *Church of England in the Colonies*, II, 569.

28. G. M. Brydon, *Virginia's Mother Church and the Political Conditions Under Which It Grew* (Richmond, Va., 1947), I, 184; Mary F. Goodwin, "The Reverend Alexander Moray [Murray], M.A., D.D., The First Bishop-Designate of Virginia, 1672-3," *Hist. Mag. of the Protestant Episcopal Church*, 12 (1943), 59-68.

maintained from colonial resources, but afterwards they should be free to return to England or stay in Virginia as they pleased.[29] Some such provision was urgently needed for all the plantations, although it was futile to expect a seventeenth-century Parliament to undertake the financial burden that this would entail. Neither Henchman nor Sheldon showed willingness to promote the scheme, and it was not until Compton joined the Council that steps in this direction were taken.

It was Compton who encouraged Sir Leoline Jenkins, a former Secretary of State, to provide in his will for the establishment of two fellowships at Jesus College, Oxford. The conditions of tenure obliged the holders either to take holy orders and go to sea, or at the direction of the bishop of London to settle in one of the plantations, "there to take upon them the Cure of Souls, and exercise their ministerial functions." Although Jenkins' will did not become operative until 1685, the situation in the meantime had been considerably improved by the institution of a royal bounty for clergymen going overseas. The bounty was a payment of £20 transportation money doled out to incumbents taking up a colonial benefice. The initiation of this also was primarily the work of Compton.[30]

From these measures, provision for the spiritual needs of Anglican colonists improved steadily. In 1679 the scarcity of clergymen was extreme: outside of Virginia and Maryland there were thought to be only four Church of England ministers in the whole of North America. The southern plantations claimed between them no less than thirty, of which Maryland was said to have thirteen.[31] But between 1680 and 1688 at least forty-five clergy left England for parishes in the West Indies and on the mainland. By far the largest number went to the Leewards—twenty-one in all—while five were directed to Jamaica, three to Barbados, and one to the West Indies, island unspecified. Of this large migration Maryland received only two, though Virginia with nine was more fortunate.[32]

The greatly increased volume of correspondence relating to church welfare in the early 1680's is evidence of the progress made since the early years of the Restoration. The comments on those matters which appeared before the Plantations Committee indicates that many of the

29. Foote, *Annals of King's Chapel*, II, 230.

30. White Kennett, *Account of the Society for Propagating the Gospel in Foreign Parts* (1706); William Wynne, *Life of Sir Leoline Jenkins* (London, 1724), I, lxv.

31. David Humphreys, *An Historical Account of the Society for Propagating the Gospel in Foreign Parts . . . to 1728* (London, 1730), 8, 9.

32. N. W. Rightmyer, "List of Anglican Clergy Receiving a Bounty for Overseas Service, 1680-1688," *Hist. Mag. of the Protestant Episcopal Church*, 17 (1948), 174. Rightmyer's list is almost complete, but omits Charles Shau, who went out to the Leeward Islands. See J. Y. Akerman, ed., *Moneys Received and Paid for Secret Service of Charles II and James II* (London, 1851), 141.

Lords of Trade had read the detailed colonial reports and were less ignorant of the problems which faced governor and clergy than had been their predecessors.

Of all the plantations it was the Leeward Islands where the Anglican Church developed most rapidly. Although complete religious uniformity was not achieved, the Anglican faith was in a position of unquestioned strength by the end of the reign of Charles II. Most of the dissenters in the islands appeared willing to frequent its churches and to listen to Anglican sermons, providing they were "lively." Only in Montserrat, with its Irish population, was the Church of England not predominant. Of the ten churches, two were in St. Kitts, four in Nevis, two in Montserrat, and two in Antigua. The ministers were maintained by a levy of ten pounds of sugar per head, black and white, besides what was given at marriages and funerals. But the need for more ministers was great. Five of the ten churches in 1676 were without regularly ordained clergymen; and if the number of parishes be considered, an additional fifteen were required, besides one for each of the smaller islands of Statia, Saba, and Anguilla.[33] Awakened to this need by the governor's request for help, the Lords of Trade toward the end of 1677 supervised the sending of six clergy, each of whom was guaranteed £100 per annum or 16,000 pounds of sugar, and marriage and funeral perquisites.[34] Apparently the offer was not unattractive; a flood of ministers toward the close of the Restoration ensured that some of the worst difficulties of the islands were past.

Yet despite the very real advances, the effect was limited by lack of pastoral supervision, the one element necessary to the smooth functioning and unity of the islands' parochial system. The immediate regulation of the church devolved on the governors and, good as they often were, their duties were too numerous for them to perform adequately the role of "lay bishop." Most were well aware of this, and sought the obvious remedy. One of them, Sir Charles Wheeler, in 1671, petitioned the king to send Dr. Turner, the master of St. Johns, Cambridge, to take charge of an episcopal See designed to embrace the seven Leeward Islands. The bishopric was to be guaranteed £400 per annum "with an house that may deserve the name of bishop's palace." The bishop was requested to bring eight fellows of colleges, who were to have £800 per annum among them. It was not proposed that Dr. Turner should spend more than a few years in the West Indies—merely sufficient time to "settle the islands." After this, it was agreed, he could more profitably direct affairs from England.[35]

33. Answers to Inquiries sent to Colonel Stapleton, 1676, British Public Records Office, CO 1/38, no. 65, Answers 29, 30.

34. PRO/CO 153/2, 252, 253; CO 1/42, no. 16; CO 154/4, 45-46.

35. Sainsbury et al., eds., Cal. State Papers, Col., 1669-74, no. 592.

Turner may not have been attracted by the idea of exile, however temporary. Moreover, Wheeler does not appear to have consulted him first. At any rate, no further consideration was given to the proposal. Failure to send a bishop to the West Indies crippled the church there, as it did on the mainland, and severely curtailed its political usefulness to the imperial system.

In Jamaica, in spite of the early aid granted by the king, the church was still beset by basic difficulties. To these the bishop of London drew attention in 1677 by a memorandum addressed to the Plantations Committee, showing that of the fifteen parishes in the island, only six had churches, and of these only five possessed ministers.[36] It was also evident that Jamaican legislation had placed the clergy in too great subjection to the vestries. Prompted by Compton, the Lords now decreed that ministers should be made part of the vestry in all matters save the settlement of their maintenance.[37] But there were other officials, outside of England, impatient with the unimaginative pace of reform. Governor Sir Thomas Lynch, a man of some intelligence, perceived more clearly than most colonial officials the kind of aid which the Established Church could lend to the civil administration. He realized the value of such care and surveillance which his office allowed him to exercise, but this very realization gave him an acute awareness of the weakness of the ecclesiastical organization in which he played a prominent part. In a communication addressed to Henry Compton, Lynch discussed the dangers that might befall an infant church from negligent or irreligious governors. He asked particularly to be sent good churchmen, "sober and learned," to ease the unnatural burden of supervision resting on lay shoulders. Governor Lynch hoped that some cure or prebendship would be set apart and provided for by the Treasury; but to this even the Lords of Trade failed to give their support.[38]

Throughout the Restoration the Anglican Church clearly dominated the religious life of the island of Barbados, although a considerable number of Quakers did migrate there. But supremacy caused the weaknesses to be more critically observed. In particular, the manner in which the sacraments were administered laid the church open to a charge of irregularity. The bishop of London, informed of this and similar failings by two successive governors, Sir Richard Atkins and Sir Richard Dutton, drew the attention of the Lords to the need for reform measures.[39]

36. November 10, 1677, PRO/CO 1/41, no. 103.
37. Lords of Trade Journal, July 19, 1677, PRO/CO 391/2, 87-89, 92-93.
38. Sir Thomas Lynch to Bishop of London, October 23, 1682, PRO/CO 1/50, no. 87.
39. Memo. of the Bishop of London concerning the Church in Barbados, PRO/CO 1/45, no. 77.

Barbados set higher store than did most colonies on the value of the Anglican pulpit in inculcating civil obedience and counteracting the influence of dissenting sects. In 1673 a Barbadian grand jury inveighed against the increasing number of Quakers "who under pretence of piety, seduce many ignorant persons from due obedience to authority, and the true worship of God, which opens a gap to all heresies and schisms in Government." To meet such a danger many remedies were proposed, chief of which was that "orthodox ministers be countenance against the insolent tongues and pens of ungodly heretics" and that all dissenters who "speak evil of dignities and are disobedient to authority . . . be restrained by good and wholesome laws."[40] Ten years later Lieutenant Governor Stede made inquiries about Barbadian schools to learn how far they were qualified in learning, loyalty, and manners. His intention was the suppression of any whose disaffection to the king was such as to cause them to instil "eveil and dangerous principles in the giddy and unwary."[41] For the remainder of the Restoration the island continued to be well supplied with clergy who were provided for by one pound of muscovado sugar for every acre of maintenance. Stede observed in 1685 that all eleven parishes were filled with men of good lives and conversation, most of whom were excellent preachers.[42]

Bermuda was brought under royal governance in 1684, when its charter was annulled. Previously the Bermuda Company had provided means of worship according to the Church of England. Nine churches and five Anglican ministers had been supported, and this was probably sufficient for a population two-thirds of which was Quaker, Independent, or Anabaptist.[43] Moreover, the scandalous behavior of the Anglican clergy on the island harmed rather than enhanced the prestige of the church.

Requests for clergy from the Ashley River plantation followed the pattern of petitions arriving in London from other parts of the empire: they emphasized the need for financial aid to help establish the colonial church on firm foundations. Carolina, in spite of the terms of her charter, possessed only one Anglican minister by the 1680's, the Reverend Atkin Williamson. Of the several schemes put forward to gain the necessary clergy, one proposed that young men from the universities be sent to the plantations for five years, the expense of their voyage defrayed, £100 per annum allowed them, and "his Majesty's countenance [given] at their return." This plan was justified on the grounds that it was no

40. Sainsbury *et al.*, eds., *Cal. State Papers, Col., 1669-74,* July 8, 1673, no. 1116.
41. Lt. Gov. Stede to Lords of Trade, April 27, 1686, PRO/CO 1/59, no. 62.
42. Stede to Earl of Sunderland, August 20, 1685, PRO/CO 29/3, 329.
43. Answers of the Somers Island Company to Inquiries, July 15, 1679, PRO/CO 1/43, no. 89.

greater infringement of a subject's liberty to be sent abroad by the king to preach than to suffer impressment as a soldier or sailor. Both occupations, religious and military, were considered "warfares," and the former "fifty times the consequence for the Crown" on the grounds that no good Christian was ever a bad subject.[44]

Since the Lords of Trade encountered such difficulties in supplying the royal plantations with incumbents, it is no surprise they were of little assistance to the proprietaryships. In Virginia, for example, only thirty of the fifty parishes had ministers, and twelve of these clergy were shared with one or even two other communities.[45] In three parishes there were lay readers only. Most livings were nominally valued at an average of £80 per annum, but general poverty and the low price of tobacco had diminished this to scarcely one-half of the sum. As far as they were able, the parishioners made up the stipends of the clergy, and in so doing they often gained control of the right of presentation.

Unlike Maryland, Virginia was little troubled by dissenters; but the difficulty of attracting good clergymen and the need of a bishop continued to vex the growth of both plantations. The situation in Maryland was brought to the notice of the Plantations Committee by the Reverend Mr. Yeo as well as through lay supplication.[46] Lord Baltimore was asked why there were no more than three Anglican clergy resident to serve some five thousand communicants and was sharply rebuked for failing to introduce others. Four ministers were subsequently sent to Maryland after 1680, two of these with the royal bounty, but the numbers were still insufficient to meet the demands of the inhabitants.

The Church of England figured little in the life of the settlements north of Maryland. At Fort James in New York, there were a chapel and chaplain for the soldiers of the Duke of York, which also served the governor's household and a number of Anglicans in New Jersey. There were a few Scottish Episcopalians at Perth Amboy and Elizabeth Town, and a minister was to be found at Brookhaven on Long Island.[47] In New England an Anglican minister was unknown until the close of the Restoration. Edward Randolph had petitioned the Lords of Trade to send a divine, but the Lords were unwilling to take any active steps until the charter of Massachusetts had been annulled. During the 1670's the bishop of London was ordered to send only such clergy to Boston as the

44. Sainsbury *et al.*, eds., *Cal. State Papers, Col., 1669-74*, no. 473.

45. List of parishes and ministers in Virginia, June 30, 1680, PRO/CO 1/45, no. 27.

46. "Request for a Church," *Maryland Hist. Mag.*, 3 (1908), 179-80.

47. E. C. Chorley, "The Beginnings of the Church in the Province of New York," *Hist. Mag. of the Protestant Episcopal Church*, 13 (1944), 7.

people were willing to maintain, a provision which effectively hindered the sending of anyone. There was no formal representative of the Established Church in the Bay colony until the time of the provisional government. New Hampshire, under the influence of the town of Boston and the college of Harvard, was also largely Puritan. After a cautious beginning, Edward Cranfield, the first royal governor, urged the establishment of the Anglican Church, with the regulation of both officers and ministers to depend wholly upon the king. Cranfield, however, was removed when New Hampshire was placed under the Dominion of New England, and the colony subsequently became dependent upon Sir Edmund Andros for its religious policy.

In 1681 began the alliance between the Duke of York and the two sons of the former Lord Chancellor, the second Earl of Clarendon and Laurence Hyde. In face of this novel alignment of power, Charles II abandoned his attempt to obtain relief for dissenters. This action won the enthusiastic support of an Anglican Church fully committed to the doctrine of passive obedience. The new combination between state and church, assured of the support of Sir Edward Seymour and Sir Leoline Jenkins, was a potent force, and in the first flood of optimism Hyde endeavored to induce the Duke of York to rejoin the Church of England. His failure defined the limits within which a new policy might expect to operate.

In spite of this setback, however, the political situation in England had never been more favorable to the Anglican Church. Charles was no more fervent a son of the church than he had ever been, but having suffered from the excesses of Whig and Dissenter, he was ready with fewer reservations than ever before to allow the church to dominate and its adherents to rule. For four years the political complexion of the administration remained largely static, a Tory pudding spiced with a Trimmer's sauce. In part this carried over into the first eighteen months of the reign of James II, until the new king's lack of moderation destroyed the short-lived tranquillity. Moreover, although Parliamentary help did not seem possible, royal income from other sources was rising steadily, and England was as free as she had ever been from the direct threat of any continental power. Added to this, Laurence Hyde, Clarendon, Sir Edward Seymour, and Sir Leoline Jenkins were all fervent sons of the church, and all four, knowledgeable in the ways of governing the transatlantic possessions, held a sustained interest in their development.

It may be allowed that the first twenty years of the Restoration saw a religious policy pursued by England which was recognized as second best— a policy pursued because of the need to attract settlers; because of fear of arousing a conquered colony; or merely because stronger endorsement of the Established Church would further expose the mother country's inability to impose her will.   One might expect, however, in view of the favorable concurrence of events in the later Restoration, that the closing years of the reign of Charles II would uncover a plan for change.   One might expect talk—there would be little time for more than this—of a thoroughgoing scheme on the part of the English government to increase the Anglican parishes throughout the empire and fill them all with incumbents steeped in the positive teachings of the universities.   The failure of such a policy to develop in the 1660's and 1670's can fairly readily be understood, but by the end of 1684 the absence of discussion of a well-ordered ecclesiastical system to pair with the political reorganization of the empire calls for some explanation.

First, how much responsibility must be attributed to the king's resolution, or lack of it?   Tory historians hold that Charles underwent a great change of character as a result of the strain imposed by the national hysteria of the Popish Plot.   Certainly in the last four years of his life he diverted his energies toward administering the state with a diligence he had never before shown.   He had reason to feel grateful toward a church that had displayed such steadiness during the years of peril.   He knew enough about the colonies to subscribe to the plan for political revision in New England. It is also true, however, that in colonial affairs one looks in vain for evidence of purposeful royal initiative.   But if the king was unlikely to initiate designs involving complex planning, it is not to be expected that at this stage he would oppose any feasible scheme put forward by his ministers. But there is no mention in official records of the use of the Anglican pulpit as an instrument of colonial policy or of its value relating to any one plantation specifically.   This does not necessarily preclude the existence of a policy, since the form of government to be imposed upon New England was determined in November, 1684, with only the most cursory record of discussion surviving.   Restoration statesmen were singularly loath to commit to paper the general principles which governed their actions.

What then were the real achievements of the closing years of the Restoration?   They were plainly unspectacular.   They can be partially seen in the instructions issued to royal governors, in the modest increase in the powers of the bishop of London, in the modification of the Pennsylvania patent, and in the policy eventually developed for New England.

The instructions to governors, prepared under the guidance of Compton, show the care which the Anglican Lords were ultimately prepared to spend on the details of overseas worship.   They relate to the use of the Book of Common Prayer, the hanging of tables of marriage within the church, the licensing of ministers and regulation of their maintenance, the administration of the sacrament, and the inclusion of all ministers as members of the vestries. If financial support was given in little else, it was generously applied for the purchase of religious books for use in the colonies. In December, 1684, £215 10s was paid for church Bibles, prayer books, and other works delivered to Barbados and elsewhere in the West Indies. In 1685, almost £200 was spent for the delivery of similar works to Virginia and New England. A further sum of £137 procured books for the Duke of Albemarle, going as governor to Jamaica.[48] The Book of Canons, the Homilies of the Church, the Book of the Thirty-Nine Articles, and the tables of marriage, as well as the Bible and prayer books, were supplied to all the colonies in considerable numbers during the closing years of the Restoration.[49]

The influence of the bishop of London over the plantations was only moderately effected by his formal increase in powers. No minister was to be preferred to any ecclesiastical benefice without a certificate from London that he was conformable to the doctrine and discipline of the Church of England. Jamaica received notification in 1678, Virginia in 1679, and Barbados in 1680, but the Leewards were not informed until a new governor arrived in 1686. Bermuda and New York, both recently brought under royal control, were affected by this new ruling the same year. In 1685, however, Compton's supervision of clergy and laity alike was considerably strengthened when he received ecclesiastical jurisdiction in the West Indies over all matters save the disposal of parishes, licenses for marriage, and probate of wills.[50]

Compton demonstrated his interest in colonial affairs when he effected the alteration of William Penn's patent and made provision for the admission of an Anglican chaplain to the new colony upon the request of any number of planters. In his intervention he was supported by the Lords of Trade, who had objected to the issue of a new proprietary charter and were eager to restrict its privileges as severely as possible.[51]

Some of the measures proposed for New England, in the latter part of the Restoration, smacked of thoroughgoing absolutism. They came not from Compton nor indeed from officials in England at all, but from men on the spot. Edward Cranfield, who as governor of New Hampshire observed the sources of Puritan power which centered at Cambridge, began

48. Akerman, *Secret Services*, 98, 122, 161.
49. Privy Council register of Charles II, PRO/CO 2/69, 250, 333, 367, 419, 437, 460; Register of James II, PC 2/71, 143, 147, 415.
50. Report of Rt. Rev. Dr. Sherlock on the Church in the Colonies, 1759, O'Callaghan, ed., *New York Col. Docs.*, VII, 363.
51. Lords of Trade Journal, January 22, 1681, PRO/CO 391/3, 249-50; February 24, PRO/CO 391/3, 253; *Pennsylvania Council Minutes, 1683-1700* (Harrisburg, 1838), I, xvii.

to consider the possible advantages of Harvard's being taken over by the Church of England and used for the propagation of Anglicanism. In New England more than anywhere else in the empire, education was the well-spring of religion. By a rigid control of schools and schoolmasters, the Puritans had virtually ensured the perpetuity of the theocratic state. It seemed easier to destroy the educational system and erect another under Anglican supervision than to attempt conversion by force. There was, perhaps, less difficulty to be expected in guiding young minds than in seeking to re-direct mature ones. Edward Randolph, who thought far more of plans than of people, was another like Cranfield, attracted by the vision of New England reborn.[52]

At the opening of James II's reign, the bishop of London was granted the right of supervision over all schoolmasters leaving England for the plantations, and no one was permitted to teach in a royal colony without his license. This power was applied to Bermuda, Jamaica, the Leewards, New York, and Virginia but only partially extended to New England.[53] Had it been vigorously used and additional control developed over those teachers already overseas, the education of youth throughout the king's possessions would for a time have been conducted in a style that exalted the king's name. In actual fact few positive controls were accomplished during the two and a half years in which New England was under a general governor. The laws which provided taxes for educational purposes were allowed to lapse, so that teachers whose salaries had previously been supported by the rates were no longer maintained. In addition, no person could teach in the Dominion of New England without license from the governor. These conditions in large measure broke the Puritan hold on education, but if a substitute had been prepared, it was not used.

Although Randolph may have been wrongheaded in the methods he proposed, he deserves credit for having comprehended the need for direct state action to ensure the future loyalty of New England. He suggested to the archbishop of Canterbury that funds reserved for evangelizing the Indians should be used to build a free school "that our youth might no longer be poisoned with the seditious principles of this country." His aim, of course, was political. "We want good schoolmasters, none being here allowed but of ill principle, and until there be provision made to rectify the youth of the country, there is no hope that this people will prove loyal."[54]

52. R. N. Toppan, ed., *Edward Randolph* (Boston, 1899), IV, 109; A. T. S. Goodrick, ed., *ibid.*, VI, 245-46; "Edward Randolph," *New Eng. Hist. and Genealogical Register*, 37 (1883), 157.

53. PRO/CO 1/57, no. 91; CO 391/5, 138; O'Callaghan, ed., *New York Col. Docs.*, VII, 362.

54. Toppan, ed., *Randolph*, IV, 90, 104.

But despite the numerous appeals of Cranfield and Randolph, nothing was done to bring Harvard under royal control; and Increase Mather took advantage of the king's increasing reliance upon Non-conformist support in England to gain verbal assurance that the Puritan integrity of the college would be maintained.

With Massachusetts, Rhode Island, and Connecticut under royal government, it was inevitable that an Anglican minister should be introduced into New England, if only to provide for the spiritual needs of the governor general, his officials, and the two companies of soldiers. After the favorable reception of the petition of Edward Wanton of Scituate, the financial basis of the Puritan Church was undermined.[55] It was now possible for the Anglican Church to compete on equal terms, although financial aid was necessary to counteract initial weakness. This was not forthcoming. Archbishop Sancroft had instructed Randolph to investigate the resources of the corporation formed to evangelize the Indians, hoping that its funds might be applied to the construction of a new church. Sancroft later had second thoughts upon this and, in spite of Randolph's pleas, the Anglican congregation was left to support its minister and provide for a church building as best it could.

The interest shown by New Englanders both in Anglican ceremonial and the preaching of Robert Ratcliffe was promising, but hardly more than that. Although James II was committed to maintaining his vast new dominion that stretched north from the Delaware, he shifted his alliance from Church to Dissent after 1686. He was therefore not prepared to afford Sir Edmund Andros more than nominal aid in the immense task that confronted him. Since his ultimate if rather confused aim had become the Catholicization of the empire, James was not willing to spend money overseas for a faith he had deserted at home. Lacking such support, the Anglican Church entered the New England scene in the most humiliating circumstances. The prestige so necessary to its growth was denied from the very beginning.

The Restoration closed with the painful comedy of an Erastian Church supporting with almost unquestioning devotion a monarch whose confessed aim was its overthrow. But the deposition of James ended the divine reverence in which the reigning monarch was generally held by the church. Henceforth, loyalty to the throne was bereft of much of its mystical significance. In many respects the Restoration had revealed the limitations of colonial policy: 1688 was thus a real dividing line in church-state relations. For almost a hundred years after the Glorious Revolution, interest in the plantations was rarely greater, statesmen never more knowledgeable, than in the quarter century preceding. Generally speaking, those measures that survived the overthrow of the Stuarts were destined to endure, while those that failed to prosper under Charles and James were never to prosper.

The fervor that burned so brightly at Oxford in 1681 failed to express itself in systematized Anglicanism. To have done so successfully would have required—at the least—an efficient administrative organization such as then did not exist. All else being unchanged, had England possessed the political stability of the Victorian era, the story might have been different. Instead, the mother country was convulsed by turmoil as religious and constitutional principles of major importance were determined. The years 1681-86 seem a peaceful interlude in contrast to what had preceded and what was to follow; but the peace was more apparent than real. Even if this lull had been utilized for the Anglican Church, a Catholic king determined to rule would have prevented lasting results. In any case, the Revolution must inevitably have robbed Anglicanism of much of its driving force.

Was then the marriage of church and state under the Restoration a fruitless union? Far from it; for the gains were very real. The church had secured its position in Barbados, Jamaica, and the Leewards; it had gained an opportunity in the Carolinas and Pennsylvania; it had been defended in Maryland, and had insinuated itself into New England. It is true that the opportunity of creating a colonial bishop had been rejected for relatively feeble reasons, and this loss in terms of both immediate and potential value should not be underestimated. But if the progress made was of a pedestrian and uninspired nature, it did yield solid achievement. The pace was, in some degree, a virtue; for what was begun with slow deliberation and without much sense of planning was able to endure the Glorious Revolution and outlive the transient Dominion of New England.

The idea of a political church, which the Restoration had neglected, not repudiated, was revived after 1783 when the American colonies were gone. It was finally abandoned half a century later as having aggravated rather than stilled colonial discontent. The context, of course, was different, but such stability as was achieved in Upper Canada had clearly been bought at a price. We cannot estimate what price may have been demanded had the Anglican Church under the Restoration been similarly supported abroad. In this earlier age, it is arguable that it may not have been excessive when weighed against the administrative gains which the empire could have reaped.

PART FIVE

History and Historians

I wonder no Body has ever presented the World, with a tolerable Account of our *Plantations*. Nothing of that kind has yet appear'd, except some few General Descriptions, that have been calculated more for the Benefit of the Bookseller, than for the Information of Mankind.

ROBERT BEVERLEY

IX.

SEVENTEENTH-CENTURY ENGLISH
HISTORIANS OF AMERICA

Richard S. Dunn

UNIVERSITY OF PENNSYLVANIA

DURING THE COURSE of the seventeenth century, Englishmen on both sides of the Atlantic widely discussed the unfolding story of English settlement in America. A significant number of formal histories of the English plantations, individual or collective, were published. Hundreds of less ambitious, less systematic narratives of colonization may be found in contemporary promotional pamphlets, polemical tracts, official reports, private letters, and journals.[1] Taken collectively, these historical and pseudo-historical writings document a most subtle and important phenomenon: the initial development of an American consciousness and a growing sense of distinction between the colonial and his fellow Englishman at home. If we trace the changing character of historical writings on English America during the seventeenth century, we may observe the beginnings of two views of America as seen from the two sides of the Atlantic. The seventeenth-century histories are, in fact, our best guide to the emerging awareness by Englishmen at home that they held a large empire, and contrariwise, to the colonials' increasingly self-conscious identification with their new land.

Several preliminary qualifications should be made concerning the character of this body of historical writing. In the first place, while there

---

1. The fullest survey of this miscellaneous body of narrative writing is Jarvis M. Morse's *American Beginnings: Highlights and Sidelights of the Birth of the New World* (Washington, D. C., 1952). Mr. Morse has supplied a very useful guide through hundreds of seventeenth- and eighteenth-century narratives on British America, although he has been content to describe rather than analyze this literature.

were chroniclers of America on both sides of the Atlantic, the majority and the best were colonials. When a person in England undertook to write about the plantations, he necessarily borrowed most of his materials from colonial writers, merely refashioning them according to his own point of view. Secondly, among the colonists in the seventeenth century the local sense of history varied tremendously from one plantation to another. The New Englanders were far and away the most interested in recording their own story. The Virginians came next. Elsewhere, attempts at chronicle writing were fugitive, piecemeal, and unmethodical. Thus New York, the Jerseys, the Carolinas, and to a lesser extent Maryland and Pennsylvania had no real written history by 1700. Most of these colonies were founded in the second half of the century, when the work of combating the wilderness appeared both less novel and less heroic than it had the generation before. With the exception of Pennsylvania, most of them also were founded by men who lacked the thumping ideological purpose of the Pilgrims and Puritans. So their story was patently less susceptible to dramatic treatment than the origins of Virginia and New England. The relative paucity of contemporary narratives goes far to explain why we today have a less vivid image of the middle colonies in the seventeenth century than of New England or Virginia.

The New Englanders, alone among the seventeenth-century planters, found a moral purpose in their colonization of America, and this allowed them to see their own history as an idea in action. They were trying to establish a godly community in the midst of a "howling Wilderness" and "Desert Land": here was the proper framework for a story of pathos, drama, nobility, and grandeur. Here was the reason why future generations of Americans, looking back for heroic national origins, could readily identify themselves with the Pilgrims and Puritans. Yet the New England Puritan conception of history was only partly usable for future generations. Seeing history as the revelation of God's providential dealings with His people, the seventeenth-century New Englanders were much more concerned with analyzing the changes in their communal state of soul than in recording their reaction to the unique American environment. It is hard for the modern reader of these New England narratives to visualize the physical setting, because it did not often excite or even particularly interest the narrators. We hear often of Indians, and sometimes of wild animals, forests, swamps, rocks, summer's heat, and winter's cold as tests of Puritan fortitude. Always the focus is on the people, not the place, and specifically on the relation between the people and their God. Thus the seventeenth-century New Englanders wrote histories of Puritanism rather than histories of America.

Seventeenth-century historians of Virginia had a theme also, but it lacked the same nobility and grandeur. In effect their story was a reworking of the second and third chapters of the Book of Genesis; Virginia was a natural paradise, the Garden of Eden. But the Virginia planters immediately established their descent from Adam and Eve. They chased after gold, engaged in petty disputes, mishandled the Indians, and in their general improvidence failed to exploit a great opportunity. Here was the inversion of the New England theme. The contrast dramatizes the difference in character between the northern and southern colonies in the seventeenth century. The self-righteousness of the New England chroniclers and the self-criticism of the Virginia chroniclers also help explain why most Americans ever since have found it easier to respond emotionally to Plymouth Rock than to Jamestown, despite the latter's priority.

Striking as this contrast was between the New England and Virginia chroniclers, it was secondary to the transatlantic contrast between colonists writing the story of their plantations and Englishmen at home writing the story of their empire. In order to examine the formulation of these rival historical perspectives, let us take two dozen prominent seventeenth-century narratives on English America. As it happens, these narratives were all written either by Englishmen at home, by New England colonists, or by Virginia colonists. In date of composition they range from 1588 to 1708, and may be distributed into four chronological periods: (1) the opening of the seventeenth century; (2) the first generation of settlement in America, 1607-60; (3) the second generation of settlement, 1660-89; and (4) the close of the century.

At the opening of the seventeenth century, before they had made any permanent American settlements, the English viewed America as a place without history. Richard Hakluyt's great compilation, *The Principal Navigations, Voyages, Traffiques and Discoveries of the English Nation*, published in its final form between 1598 and 1600, illustrates this attitude. Hakluyt's purpose in gathering hundreds of narratives of English overseas exploration in a single collection was clear. He was proclaiming England's maritime prowess. Other nations, he claimed, have been extolled for their enterprises by sea while the English have been condemned for their sluggishness. But actually the Elizabethan sailors "in searching the most opposite corners and quarters of the world . . . have excelled all the nations and people of the earth."[2] Patriotism spurred Hakluyt's labors: "The honour and benefit of this Common weale wherein I live and breathe, hath

2. Richard Hakluyt, *The Principal Navigations, Voyages, Traffiques and Discoveries of the English Nation* (8 vols., Everyman's Library; London, n.d.), I, 2-3.

made all difficulties seeme easie, all paines and industrie pleasant, and all expenses of light value and moment unto me."[3]

He admired the heroic Elizabethan seamen who passed through dangers as great as those of Columbus, and he scrupulously printed each sailor's narrative separately in order to give credit to the individual—as well as to hold him accountable for his statements. Travel literature is naturally biographical in form, and each of Hakluyt's narratives, in detailing the travels of an individual or group, is necessarily organized around the actions of the traveler. Although we are led on a gigantic excursion through unknown parts of the world, Hakluyt's focus is always on the gallant English explorer.

Hakluyt devoted the final third of his collection to narratives of America, moving from north to south, from Frobisher's and Davis' voyages to the narratives by Lane, Hariot, and White on Roanoke colony, and from there to accounts of the Spanish colonies. To Hakluyt's voyagers, America was the New World in the sense that it had been unused by European society; it had no records, no traditions, no previous history. The picturesque and barbarous behavior of the Indians was eagerly described, but it was not supposed that these savages had established a social tradition. They were merely part of the natural environment, to be manipulated by the Europeans. History, it was clear, began with the arrival of the white men. Yet the Hakluyt narrators on the New World, aside from their personal, biographical focus, were too isolated from the American scene to be labelled as American historians. The juxtaposition between civilization and wilderness was too sharp. Thomas Hariot, for example, whose *Briefe and true report of the new found land of Virginia* (1588) was reprinted by Hakluyt in his collection, described Virginia's natural resources in enthusiastic detail to encourage further colonization. But mingled with his excitement at Virginia's fruitful and exotic qualities was an essential ignorance and loneliness in the midst of a strange land. Hariot and his fellows described what they saw, but they did so as alien observers, and ended by telling us more about themselves than about America. Their experience is European history, not American history, because they had not assimilated themselves into the American environment. A certain remoteness hangs over the pages of the Roanoke narratives and gives their sad story its peculiarly poignant quality.

During the first generation of permanent English settlement in America, broadly defined from 1607 to 1660, there were four colonists

3. *Ibid.*, 19-20.

in Virginia and New England who wrote notable large-scale narratives describing the establishment of their particular plantations: Captain John Smith, William Bradford, John Winthrop, and Edward Johnson. Englishmen who stayed at home during these years produced no histories of the plantations in any way comparable to these four narratives. The colonial chroniclers, however, differed from their brethren in England not merely in the quantity and quality of their writings, but in their whole attitude toward America.

The founding of England's first successful colony will always be indelibly associated with Captain John Smith. A number of other early Virginia planters wrote chronicles, and thanks to the Virginia Company's strenuous efforts to build good public relations there was ample promotional literature about the colony. But because Captain John Smith wrote at far greater length on Virginia than anyone else, and because his writings were infused with an extraordinary individuality, his report of the events at Jamestown made a far more lasting impression than all the other accounts.

Smith's report on Virginia was based on three assertions, at least two of which were corroborated by other contemporary observers. First, he claimed that the land itself was extremely attractive: "Heaven and earth never agreed better to frame a place for mans habitation."[4] Many others shared his enthusiasm, notably William Strachey, whose *Historie of travell into Virginia Britannia* gave a favorable picture of the Virginia countryside comparable to that in Smith's *Map of Virginia*. Second, Smith claimed that most of his fellow colonists were extremely unattractive. "Many in *Virginia*," he complained, were "meerely proiecting, verball, and idle contemplators." During the starving time in 1609-10, "the labour of twentie or thirtie of the best onely preserved . . . the idle livers of neare two hundred of the rest."[5] Here also, many others echoed his complaint. Even the clergyman Alexander Whitaker admitted in his *Good newes from Virginia* that "many of the men sent hither haue bin Murtherers, Theeues, Adulterers, idle persons, and what not besides. . . ."[6] Lastly, Smith claimed that he had personally saved the colony in its early days, and that his leadership had ever since been badly needed. In 1624, one of his reasons for publishing his major work, *The General History of Virginia, New England and the Summer Isles,* was to persuade the government to give him 1,500 men so that he could return to Virginia and rebuild the

4. Edward Arber and A. G. Bradley, eds., *Travels and Works of Captain John Smith* (2 vols.; Edinburgh, 1910), I, 48.
5. *Ibid.,* 379-80.
6. Alexander Whitaker, *Good newes from Virginia* (London, 1613), 11.

plantation.[7] Smith's egocentricity annoyed his critics at the time and ever since, but it is the prime ingredient in his robust storytelling.

Smith's literary style resembled that in the Hakluyt narratives. The *General History* was largely autobiographical, the author presenting himself to his audience as a rude soldier with an interesting tale, but no pretense at eloquence. "I know," he confided, that "I shall bee taxed for writing so much of my selfe: but I care not much." And in a later passage he burst out, "Ah! were these my accusers but to change cases and places with me but 2 yeeres, or till they had done but so much as I, it may be they would iudge more charitably of my imperfections."[8] We are face to face with another heroic English adventurer.

Smith's sturdy patriotism also resembles Hakluyt's. "I cannot chuse but grieue," he wrote, "that . . . the command of *England* should not be as great as any Monarchy that euer was since the world began. . . ."[9] This patriotism helps explain the breadth of his interest in America. He was chiefly concerned with Virginia, to be sure, but his *General History* treated all parts of America planted by the English at the time he wrote. Although Smith was the only significant seventeenth-century colonist to write about more than one region of America, he was never more than a temporary colonist, and he retained the home Englishman's collective view of the plantations. In sum, his task in the *General History* was to demonstrate that his own actions had been far from inferior, and to publicize America (and chiefly Virginia) as a field for England's greatness.

Both the strength and the weakness of Smith's handling of the Virginia story can be attributed to his personal approach. His theme was vigorous and dramatic: a strong man struggling against a negative environment. Manfully he coped with the barbarous Indians and gold-crazed white men, keeping the colony alive almost singlehandedly. There has been too much controversy over Smith's highly charged personal adventures, such as the Pocahontas episode. The chief weakness of his autobiographical approach is that his stay in Virginia was too brief to supply the framework for a historical narrative. Although he purported to present the history of Virginia from 1584 to 1624, his personal connection with the colony extended only from 1607 to 1609, and he treated this phase out of all proportion to the rest of the story. During the long years when the hero was off stage, Smith did not attempt any connected historical narrative; instead he gave a series of extracts from other planters' accounts or from public records. Consequently the *General History* is uneven, unsystematic, and shapeless. Its only over-all conclusion is that Virginia's single period of

7. Arber and Bradley, eds., *Travels and Works of Captain John Smith,* II, 614.
8. *Ibid.,* 602, 622.
9. *Ibid.,* 603.

success coincided with Smith's presence in the colony. Raleigh's abortive efforts in the 1580's and the Virginia Company's inability to develop the plantation which Smith initiated both demonstrate the need for the captain's leadership. Once again, as in the case of Hakluyt's heroes, the focus is on the man, not the place.

Turning from Virginia to New England, we find that the early Pilgrim and Puritan chroniclers developed a radically different set of values from Captain John Smith's, but in some ways a rather similar attitude toward America. As Smith's *General History* established the standard picture of early Virginia, so William Bradford's *Of Plymouth Plantation* established the popular image of the Plymouth Pilgrims. The Pilgrim legend, with its distinctive emotional appeal, was fashioned in three stages by three successive chronicles. The first version was presented by a pamphlet known as *Mourt's Relation,* anonymously published in London in 1622, which described the opening year of the Plymouth colony. This charming tract tells modestly and cheerfully how a small band of people landed at a strange country in midwinter, built their town despite cold and sickness, and made friends with the Indians. The religious character of the undertaking was not stressed. The new home in America was agreeably pictured as "so goodly a Land, and woodded to the brinke of the sea."[10] Two years later the second version of the Pilgrim story appeared when Edward Winslow published *Good Newes From New-England,* covering the second and third years of the colony. Despite its title, Winslow's story is less cheerful than *Mourt's Relation.* He tells of the fickleness of the Indians and the sufferings of the colonists in the starving time of 1623. Winslow liked the New England countryside, but he was more impressed by God's unique favor to the Plymouth colonists: "If euer any people in these later ages were vpheld by the providence of God after a more speciall manner then others, then wee."[11] The final version of the Pilgrim story, more somberly dramatic and more deeply infused with religious zeal than Winslow's tract, was Governor Bradford's extensive and unpublished narrative, *Of Plymouth Plantation.*

The contrast between Smith's *General History* and Bradford's *Of Plymouth Plantation* is extraordinary. Whereas Smith dramatized his personal prowess, Bradford submerged his own identity in the sufferings of an entire community. Smith pictured Virginia as a natural paradise and criticized his fellow-planters for corruptly abusing its resources, but Bradford pictured New England as "a hideous and desolate wilderness, full of

10. *A Relation or Iournall of the beginning and proceedings of the English Plantation setled at Plimoth in New England* (London, 1622), 1.

11. Edward Winslow, *Good Newes From New-England* (London, 1624), 49-51.

wild beasts and wild men," and thanked God for sustaining the Pilgrims.[12] An exposition of how God's people could surmount great physical ordeals in a state of spiritual grace, Bradford's book is directly descended from Foxe's *Book of Martyrs.* "What was it then that upheld them? It was God's visitation that preserved their spirits."[13]   Bradford is the most famous seventeenth-century historian of America and deservedly so, for he is the best.   He tells with simple dignity and fierce conviction an unforgettable story of human courage and idealism.

Yet was Bradford really a historian of America?   He was concerned with a band of men, not the place they settled in.   When he and his fellows withdrew from civilization and headed across the Atlantic, says Bradford in a famous passage, "they knew they were pilgrims, and looked not much on those things, but lift up their eyes to the heavens, their dearest country, and quieted their spirits."[14]   Certainly Bradford never pictured America as an earthly paradise, nor even as an intrinsically interesting place, although after the bitter shock of the first winter had dimmed, he came to feel that New England was as good as any other land.   Bradford began his history with the Marian and Elizabethan persecution of radical Protestants, and then proceeded to a lengthy discussion of the Separatists' removal to Holland and their tribulations there.   His focus was always on the Pilgrim community; his story followed them from place to place.   Thus there is some similarity between Captain John Smith's theme and Bradford's.   Smith dramatized the exploits of a single individual in conflict with a negative environment; Bradford dramatized the exploits of a small band of people in the same situation.   In both cases, America provided the background rather than the foreground of the story.

Even so, Bradford made a much sharper differentiation between his American plantation and the mother country.   Although he opened his history with "the first breaking out of the light of the gospel in our honourable nation of England," it is obvious that the gospel was more precious than England.[15]   Unlike Smith, Bradford and his fellows had deliberately separated themselves from the home community, and again unlike Smith, they lived out their days in America, where they proceeded to create a new community much more to their taste.   They took the first step toward creating a distinct American society.

As Bradford chronicled the Pilgrims' exodus to Plymouth, so John Winthrop chronicled the far larger transatlantic migration of the Puritans

12. William Bradford, *Of Plymouth Plantation, 1620-1647,* ed. by Samuel Eliot Morison (New York, 1953), 62, 66.

13. *Ibid.,* 329.   14. *Ibid.,* 47.   15. *Ibid.,* 3.

to the Massachusetts Bay colony. Winthrop's *Journal,* the prime source for New England history from 1630 to 1649, lacks the dramatic unity and emotional appeal of Bradford. Recording data day by day, instead of collecting it year by year, Winthrop achieved no narrative flow. Furthermore, the very qualities which make his *Journal* a rich source for modern scholars of Puritan New England impair his effectiveness as a storyteller. Far from writing in the Foxe tradition of God's persecuted saints, Winthrop wrote of the worldly triumph of Puritanism in Massachusetts. He justified the colony's staunch orthodoxy and narrow political structure, insubordination to Charles I and Parliament, and intolerance toward any internal criticism of the established order. Through the pages of his *Journal* Winthrop did battle with such diversified critics of the Massachusetts status quo as Thomas Morton, Roger Williams, Sir Ferdinando Gorges, Anne Hutchinson, John Wheelwright, Samuel Gorton, Samuel Maverick, and Robert Child. Winthrop's *Journal* is a much more personal narrative than Bradford's: as governor of Massachusetts Winthrop consciously plays the role of founding father. Although he refers to himself in the third person, his own achievements are conspicuous. Winthrop's approach is thus a fusion of Smith's and Bradford's, being autobiographical and simultaneously detailing the principles and progress of a whole community.

John Winthrop has more valid claim to the title of American historian than either Captain John Smith or William Bradford. He did not venture across the Atlantic in the spirit of an Elizabethan blade, nor did he wish to retreat to a remote land in order to establish the true church. Winthrop and his fellow Massachusetts Puritans went to America to challenge the home Stuart government. They erected a model of the kind of godly state they hoped to see some day in England—a society superior to the one they were leaving. "Wee shall be as a Citty vpon a Hill, the eies of all people are vppon us."[16] Winthrop's famous Biblical evocation may seem close to the Pilgrim motif, but the essential difference is that Winthrop was more positive about his place of settlement. He did not share Bradford's image of a hideous wilderness, but rather saw his new home as happily distinct from corrupt England and dignified by the godly community rising upon its shores. By belligerently insisting that his Massachusetts city upon the American hill was a beacon for all people, he became proud of both city and hill.

Winthrop's *Journal* is more squarely set in America than is Bradford's *Of Plymouth Plantation.* There is no English background. Winthrop chose to begin his diary record on Easter Monday, 1630, as his ship stood

16. Allyn B. Forbes, ed., *Winthrop Papers, 1498-1649* (5 vols.; Boston, 1929-47), II, 295.

off the Isle of Wight preparing to sail west. His initial impression of the New England scene was favorable, but his attitude was not determined by romantic affection. The only important question was whether God intended His people to settle in New England or somewhere else; and once Winthrop convinced himself that New England was the favored place, he had no patience with people who complained about hardships or yearned for a balmy climate. In 1631, as the ranks of the inadequately provisioned colonists were being decimated by the rigors of the first winter, he noted grimly: "It hath been always observed here, that such as fell into discontent, and lingered after their former condition in England, fell into the scurvy and died."[17]

Southern plantations he darkly suspected of lasciviousness. When the first master of Harvard College moved to Virginia, Winthrop heard that he had become "given up of God to extreme pride and sensuality, being usually drunken, as the custom is there."[18] In 1640 the Puritan migration to New England dried up, and Winthrop was disturbed because some planters wanted to return home or move further south. He had become more loyal to his plantation than to the general Puritan cause. He feared that "the Lord was not with them in this way," for to leave New England will "bring up an ill report upon this good land, which God had found out and given to his people. . . ."[19] By the time of his death in 1649 it was painfully apparent to Winthrop that though the Puritans at home had indeed overthrown king and church, they had refused to reform England in the image of Massachusetts. Only in orthodox New England was God's law properly obeyed. The closing years of his *Journal* are thus set in an atmosphere of intellectual isolation, accentuating the emergence of a community quite distinct from the mother country.

In 1653, a few years after Winthrop's death, there appeared in London bookstalls the first large-scale New England history to be published by a colonist: Edward Johnson's *Wonder-Working Providence of Sions Saviour in New England*. Johnson's book is a militant propaganda tract for the Massachusetts Bay colony, cast in the form of history. He enunciates Winthrop's central conviction that the Massachusetts Puritans, through God's grace, have erected a model community for the regeneration of the rest of the world. At the outset the reader is promised, "Here thou shalt find, the time when, the manner how, the cause why, and the great successe which it hath pleased the Lord to give, to this handfull of his

17. John Winthrop, *The History of New England from 1630 to 1649*, ed. by James Savage (2 vols.; Boston, 1853), I, 54.
18. *Ibid.*, II, 26.
19. *Ibid.*, I, 400.

praysing Saints in N. Engl."[20]   Infinitely more verbose and turgid than Winthrop's and correspondingly less accurate and precise, Johnson's style is sustained only by his energy and zeal.   The *Wonder-Working Providence* does, however, demonstrate more plainly and systematically than Winthrop's *Journal* the difference between the Puritan and Pilgrim conceptions of the settlement of America.

To Johnson, the history of Massachusetts was a series of pitched battles between the soldiers of Christ and Antichrist.   The tone of his story is established by the opening scene—England in 1628, where "the multitude of irreligious lascivious and popish affected persons spred the whole land like Grashoppers."   Christ's heralds trumpet a twelve-page proclamation calling on the oppressed godly to volunteer for service in New England as soldiers of Christ.[21]   The rest of his history tells how the army of God fights and conquers Satan in the New World.   In allegiance with Satan are not merely Papists, but all the religious critics of the Massachusetts Bay colony: Gortonists, Familists, Seekers, Antinomians, Anabaptists, and Episcopalians.   At last all these enemies are suppressed, and thirty orthodox churches founded in Massachusetts.   "Thus," he concludes, "hath the Lord been pleased to turn one of the most hideous, boundless, and unknown Wildernesses in the world in an instant . . . to a well-ordered Commonwealth, and all to serve his Churches. . . ."[22]   This picture of Puritanism, military and triumphant, is far removed from Bradford's persecuted Pilgrims.   Johnson did, however, share Bradford's conception of America as a hideous wilderness, or at least he used it as a dramatic technique.   But if he lacked Winthrop's positive attitude toward the New World, he asserted more enthusiastically than any other first generation colonial the self-conscious freedom of Puritan New England from old England.

In the historical narratives of Smith, Bradford, Winthrop, and Johnson we can therefore observe the evolution of the America colonials' sense of distinction from the mother country.   Smith felt no such distinction, for he wrote as an Englishman and not as a colonial.   Bradford felt that Plymouth Plantation was distinct from and superior to the home society, but his distinction rested solely on ideological grounds.   He found no intrinsic value in any physical region.   Plymouth was simply the setting for Bradford's church; the three thousand miles of open water between Plymouth and Whitehall conveniently permitted freedom from the corruption of England.   With Winthrop and Johnson the distinction between Massa-

---

20. Edward Johnson, *Wonder-Working Providence of Sions Saviour in New England, 1628-1651*, ed. by J. Franklin Jameson (New York, 1910), 21.
21. *Ibid.*, 23-24.   22. *Ibid.*, 248.

chusetts and England had something of a geographical as well as ideological basis. Initially, as with Bradford, America was valuable to them chiefly for its distance from home. They could safely construct a model state for the future reformation of England—indeed a rival state to the Stuart monarchy. But as the people at home blindly refused to imitate the New England model, and as Satan continued to inspire disgruntled colonists to rebel against Massachusetts orthodoxy, Winthrop and Johnson were stung into a local loyalty. Isolated and maligned, they insisted upon the superiority of their society to any other. Here were the materials for the development of a native historical tradition, distinct from England.

It is not easy to generalize about the home attitude toward America during the first generation of colonial settlement. The two most conspicuous kinds of writing on America displayed in the London bookstalls were promotional pamphlets sponsored by the several colonizing projects and vituperative pamphlets issued by disenchanted colonists. Writers of both categories may be deliberately ignored for our purposes, since they were too obviously engaged in special pleading. The average Englishman with no personal investment or experience in the plantations was probably little interested in these pamphlets. In any case, the miscellaneous group of detached observers in England between 1607 and 1660 who wrote on the American plantations were usually dubious or openly unfavorable in their appraisal of America.

Symptomatic of this doubtful attitude is the difference in tone between Hakluyt's *Principal Navigations* and its successor, Samuel Purchas' *Hakluytus Posthumus, or Purchas His Pilgrimes* (1625). Purchas' mammoth work devoted much space to the American plantations, more space in fact than any other English writer on the subject during the seventeenth century. Purchas attempted to follow Hakluyt's method of collecting voyages, but the very title of his work suggests how he altered the formula. In place of Hakluyt's emphatic English patriotism we find a windy religiosity and a sycophantic adoration of James I. Purchas begins with the navigations of the ancient Jews under King Solomon, eventually working around to the wanderings of modern English pilgrims under the guidance of the English Solomon. "I meane to travell no more," says Purchas, understandably footsore at the close of his twentieth volume; "here I hang up my Pilgrims weeds; here I fixe my Tabernacle, it is good to bee here: wee have brought all the World to England, England it selfe to the greatest of her Soveraignes, King James."[23] Obviously we are further than ever from an emphasis on the American scene itself.

23. Samuel Purchas, *Hakluytus Posthumus, or Purchas His Pilgrimes* (20 vols.; Glasgow, 1905-7), XX, 132.

Purchas demonstrates that once permanent English settlements were begun in America, the travelogue compilation was an inadequate method of describing colonial developments. He industriously assembled and printed nearly two dozen narratives and other documents illuminating the history of the Virginia colony, as well as all available accounts of New England. Individually the documents are of prime value and interest, but collectively they are indigestible, partly because Purchas was a much inferior editor to Hakluyt. There is no clear distinction between his sources and his verbose running commentary. Either he ruthlessly abridged and paraphrased his documents, or he threw them at the reader with no prefatory explanation. Furthermore, he lacked Hakluyt's clear sense of mission. There is no particular emphasis on the heroism of the English explorers or planters. Purchas' mass of Virginia documents, for instance, fully describes the squabbling mismanagement which plagued the early Jamestown settlement: "Povertie, sicknesse, deaths, in so rich a Soyle, and healthfull a Climate; what should I say? I can deplore, I doe not much admire, that we have had so much in Virginia, and have so little."[24] The only remedy was to turn over the problem to benevolent King Solomon, and Purchas concluded by happily thanking James I for rescuing the colony from its original undertakers.

With religion a chief motivating force in England, writers who hoped to Christianize the Indians echoed Purchas' disappointment at the slow progress of the American plantations. In 1644, a bellicose Puritan named William Castell issued *A Short Discoverie Of the Coasts and Continent of America*, a tract which largely served to publicize the need for gospel work. In the first half of his treatise, a rapid survey of North America, Castell was unenthusiastic about New England and Virginia. He knew very little about either colony save that scant effort had been expended on converting the heathen. The second part, on South America, stressed the barbarous Spanish treatment of the Indians. Castell, like Purchas, looked to the English government to remedy this problem: he wanted Parliament to send over an expedition to drive the Spaniards from the New World.[25]

A clergyman of a very different stripe, Peter Heylyn, also criticized the lack of missionary zeal in the plantations, although he did not trust Parliament to remedy the situation. Heylyn was a Laudian churchman, forced into retirement during the Interregnum, who busied himself by writing a *Cosmographie*, or description of the world, which was published in 1652. The proportions of this ambitious work are revealing. Out of a thousand pages, Heylyn devoted ninety to the Americas, and merely six

24. *Ibid.*, XIX, 171.
25. William Castell, *A Short Discoverie Of the Coasts and Continent of America* (London, 1644), [3]; Bk. II, 1.

of these to the English plantations. Like Castell, he terminated his account of New England with the arrival of the Pilgrims, those notorious Separatists, at Plymouth. Virginia, according to Heylyn, was planted by "such as *were in distress, or debt,* or some way or other *discontented,*" commendable only in their unswerving adherence to the established Church of England.[26]

There was also criticism of the plantations as economically unsound. George Gardyner's *Description of the New World* (1651) sought to demonstrate in mercantilist terms that Spanish America was extremely valuable, and the English plantations were worse than useless. Starting with the bullionist premise that foreign trade is only beneficial when more precious metals are brought in than carried out, Gardyner proceeded to survey all the American plantations. The Spanish silver mines and Caribbean islands he found "golden and fruitfull Regions"; New England was barren rock, and Virginia full of swamps and rattlesnakes. The English investment in America, draining manpower to no good purpose, was "prejudiciall, very dishonest, and highly dishonourable to our Nation." Gardyner concluded that English bonded servants might better "serve fourteen years with the Turks, then four in the Plantations . . . especially in *Virginia.*"[27]

The most conspicuous bond between such diverse writers as Purchas, Castell, Heylyn, and Gardyner was their disappointment in the American plantations. Although colonies were now firmly established, the protracted early hardships in Virginia and the use of New England and Maryland as asylums for highly controversial religious factions had dissipated the fresh and simple pride in English overseas exploits which had characterized Hakluyt. Far from sharing the Massachusetts chroniclers' pride in their colony's superiority over any other society, writers in England were complaining in the 1640's and 1650's that their nation was still shamefully outdistanced by the hated Spaniards.

Another common bond between Purchas, Castell, Heylyn, and Gardyner was the fact that they discussed all of America, not just English America. Their interests were cosmopolitan, embracing the whole world, or at least the whole New World; they expressed no strong feeling of national identity with the specifically English plantations. Here they continued to see America in Hakluyt's terms, as external or foreign, in contradistinction to colonial writers like Winthrop and Johnson who were

26. Peter Heylyn, *Cosmographie in Foure Bookes, Containing the Chorographie and Historie Of the whole World, And all the principall Kingdomes, Provinces, Seas, and Isles thereof* (London, 1652), Bk. IV, Part 2, 113.

27. George Gardyner, *A Description of the New World. Or, American Islands and Continent* (London, 1651), 7-9.

identifying themselves with the American land. In short, there was beginning to be a susceptible difference, in the years before and during the Civil War, between home country and colonial attitudes toward America.

If we accept a bifurcated view of America as beginning between 1607 and 1660, we shall find that the bifurcation widened during what may be called the second generation of settlement, the years from 1660 to 1689. No really notable histories of English America were produced in these years, either by persons in England or in the colonies. But such as they are, the narratives illustrate a continuing process.

During the second generation of settlement no one in the colonies wrote a narrative as significant as those of Smith, Bradford, and Winthrop. There were several reasons. In the first place, while the founders of Virginia and New England had told a simple and dramatic story based on immediate experience, the second generation chroniclers had to be real historians, to coordinate a complex range of events extending beyond their own memories. Secondly, they were strongly tempted to borrow exhaustively from the writings of their predecessors, bringing the older narratives up to date by tacking on a few supplementary chapters at the end, in the fashion of the modern textbook reviser. Thus the more ambitious colonial narratives of the 1660-89 period were highly derivative and unoriginal. Finally, while the founders of New England in particular had been able to tell a tale of accomplishment, most of the second generation chronicles were filled with afflictions, defeats, and doubts. Although these years saw great expansion and prosperity in the colonies, the histories are filled with tales of Indian wars, internal disunity, and growing pressure from the home government. There was a new narrative tone, pleading and melancholy, which was altogether alien to the buoyant, assured sense of purpose voiced by Smith, Bradford, Winthrop, and Johnson.

In Virginia during these years little effort was made to record the development of the colony. No one attempted a large-scale history, and the accounts of current colony affairs which may be gleaned from scattered pamphlets, letters, reports, and journals are seldom polished in style or illuminating in content. Not even the great event of the time, Bacon's Rebellion, was adequately described or analyzed by contemporary observers. No colonist bothered to publish an account of the Rebellion, and the only contemporary published reports were two meager pamphlets, *Strange News From Virginia* and *More News From Virginia*, both compiled by an anonymous Londoner in 1677. Like most of the other contemporary commentators on the Rebellion, this writer found no deeper cause for it than Nathaniel Bacon's mercurial personality.[28]   Old Governor Berkeley, Bacon's target, gave a more intricate interpretation of the Rebellion in his report to the home government.   Anxious to absolve himself, yet shaken by the experience, Berkeley construed the early success of the Rebellion as God's way of punishing him for pride in his twenty-four-year governorship, and Bacon's sudden death as God's way of punishing the rebel leader for atheism.   According to Berkeley, Bacon's oath "which he swore at least a Thousand times a day was God damme my Blood and God so infected his blood that it bred Lice in an incredible number so that for twenty dayes he never washt his shirts but burned them."[29]   Yet Berkeley's interpretation was not entirely providential.   He upbraided the officers and troops he led against Bacon for cowardice and treachery, while in-sinuating his own skill in combating the crisis.   One is reminded of Captain John Smith.   Unfortunately, neither Berkeley nor any other second-generation Virginian inherited the captain's energetic interest in the writing of history.

In New England, on the other hand, there was a continuing school of Pilgrim and Puritan historians.   Nathaniel Morton, William Hubbard, and Increase Mather may be labelled the Bradford, Winthrop, and Johnson of the second generation.   The extent to which they copied and elaborated upon their predecessors shows how firmly a local New England historical tradition had already taken root, glorifying the achievements of the found-ing fathers.

Nathaniel Morton's *New Englands Memoriall* was the first historical work published in English America; it was printed at the Cambridge press in 1669.   Its purpose was to remind his readers of the first glories of Plymouth Plantation.   Bradford himself had complained in a number of passages that the Pilgrim community in the 1640's was degenerating from its early purity.   Nathaniel Morton, writing in the 1660's, consciously preferred the past to the present.   *New Englands Memoriall* was a sermon —one might almost say a funeral sermon—cast in historical form: "It is very expedient," the reader was told, "that (while sundry of the Eldest Planters are yet living) *Records* and *Memorials of Remarkable Providences* be preserved and published, that the true Originals of these Plantations

28. *Strange News From Virginia* (London, 1677), 6.   A much more full and cogent narrative was Thomas Mathew's "The Beginning, Progress, and Conclusion of Bacon's Rebellion," but Mathew wrote it in 1705 when he was an old man, as a private report at the instigation of the home government.   As he freely admitted, "in 30 Years, divers occurences are laps'd out of mind, and others Imperfectly retained."   Charles M. Andrews, ed., *Narratives of the Insurrections, 1675-1690* (New York, 1915), 15.

29. Wilcomb E. Washburn, ed., "Sir William Berkeley's 'A History of Our Miseries,'" *Wm. and Mary Qtly.*, 3rd ser., 14 (1957), 412.

may not be lost; that *New-England*, in all time to come, may remember the day of her smallest things. . . ."[30]

Morton was Bradford's nephew, and his book is largely a digest of Bradford's manuscript history. Although it is a completely derivative work, Morton significantly altered the emphasis in his uncle's story. He condensed Bradford's opening section on the adventures of the Pilgrims before their transatlantic migration from fifty pages to ten pages, thus effectively giving his story a consistent New England focus which it had lacked with Bradford. Furthermore, since Bradford's narrative stops in 1647, Morton appended his own discussion of the course of events down to 1668 in Plymouth. The gloom hangs heavy over these final pages, consisting as they do almost exclusively of obituaries of the colony founders, intermingled with evidences of the divine wrath. God has not yet punished New England with severe earthquakes, "but those we have been sensible of have been rather gentle Warnings unto us, to shake us out of our earthly-mindedness, spiritual security, and other sins. . . ."[31] Morton's book has a uniquely New England stamp; it is addressed exclusively to a New England audience. Whereas Bradford's theme of a godly community struggling against worldly adversity had abstract and universal qualities, Morton's theme of New England's falling away from early greatness was purely local and specific.

Six years after the publication of Morton's book, the New England colonists were struck by just such a calamitous earthquake as he had predicted: the agony of King Philip's War. The experience of this Indian war was so terrible that a number of colonists were moved to write narratives describing and explaining it. These accounts have the eyewitness immediacy of the founders' chronicles a generation earlier, but they carry a far grimmer message. The most notable of them were written by two rival Massachusetts clergymen, Increase Mather and William Hubbard. Mather's production consists of two complementary tracts with cumbrous titles: *A Brief History of the War with the Indians in New-England* (1676) and *A Relation Of The Troubles which have hapned in New-England, By reason of the Indians there* (1677); together they trace the Indian conflict from 1620 to Philip's death in 1676. Hastily written, with little or no attempt at over-all organization, both tracts are a bog of details. And Mather's tone and viewpoint are not altogether consistent. The *Brief History*, written amid the shock of the war crisis, is a day-by-day recital of blood and fire, which describes the colonists' blind struggles under

30. Nathaniel Morton, *New Englands Memoriall*, ed. by Howard J. Hall (New York, 1937), "To the Reader."
31. *Ibid.*, 163.

God's curse. The *Relation*, written after the crisis had been surmounted, reflects a reviving confidence in the sanctity of New England Puritanism. But in both tracts Mather is tackling the same question: Why were his people forced to undergo this savage Indian attack?

The answer, echoing Morton's lament, is that God is punishing New England for her degeneracy. In 1637, the founders had beaten the Pequot Indians rather easily, for there had been "a mighty Spirit of Prayer and Faith then stirring" among the English.[32] During the next forty years, says Mather, the Indians had given little trouble because the colonists' sins were not "ripe for so dreadful a Judgment, until *the Body of the first Generation* was removed, and another Generation risen up which hath not so pursued, as ought to have been, the blessed design of their Fathers. . . ." Despite such omens of divine displeasure as the great roar of a cannon shot heard in the Connecticut Valley in 1674, the people continued to indulge their carnal appetites for long hair, lace, ribbons, and tavern tippling. In recounting the colonists' conduct once the war broke out, Mather gave them no credit for having bled and starved the Indians into eventual surrender. To him, "it is God which hath thus saved us, and not we our selves." Mather's thesis, then, reads like Johnson's *Wonder-Working Providence* in reverse. Instead of working wonders for New England by flaying her enemies, God is flaying New England for her sins. Mather, like Morton, is reproving his own people, whereas Johnson had triumphantly boasted to the outside world. Yet the contrast must not be exaggerated. The climax of Mather's story, after all, was the hunting down of King Philip, a visible sign of God's repledged love for his fallible people. "It hath been observed by many," Mather concluded in a sentence strongly reminiscent of John Winthrop, "that never any (whether Indians or others) did set themselves to do hurt to *New-England*, but they have come to lamentable ends at last."[33]

Increase Mather's clerical competitor, William Hubbard, outdistanced him as a chronicler of King Philip's War. His *Narrative of the Troubles with the Indians in New-England* (1677) is the best historical effort published by a second-generation colonial. Combining considerable dramatic skill with an accomplished style and perceptive commentary, Hubbard sustains the reader's interest despite the length and detail of his narrative. His interpretation of the war is what chiefly distinguishes him from Mather. Hubbard rejected the notion that God is punishing New

32. Increase Mather, *A Relation Of the Troubles which have hapned in New-England, By reason of the Indians there*, ed. by Samuel G. Drake as *Early History of New England* (Boston, 1864), 184-85.

33. Increase Mather, *A Brief History of the War with the Indians in New-England* (London, 1676), 2, 11, 34, 50.

England for "some *notable Declension* from *former Principles and wayes*," for he pointed out that "this is not the *first time* that *Christian People* have been exposed to *many Outrages*, and *barbarous Calamities* from their *Pagan Neighbours*," as witness the Virginia massacre of 1622.[34] Hubbard believed in God's preordination of all events. But he supposed that God's method is naturalistic; as he said more than once, everything is beautiful in its season. He explains the cause-and-effect pattern of events by man's daily actions, rather than by omens and prodigies. This is why Hubbard's description of the war is strongly partisan, whereas Increase Mather sees both colonists and Indians as God's instruments. Hubbard repeatedly praises the colonial militia for bravery and repeatedly curses Philip's Indians as "faithless and ungrateful Monsters," "bloudy and deceitful Monsters," or "perfidious, cruel and hellish Monsters."[35]

When he asks why these hellish monsters had been able to score such awful success, Hubbard's answer is both more sophisticated and more buoyant than Mather's. Instead of fixing the blame on New England's worldliness and moral laxity, he traces the start of the trouble to "some *Irregularities and miscarriages* in our *Transactions* and *dealings* with the Indians themselves": selling them liquor and firearms. But he finds the French and Dutch traders even more culpable, not caring what use was made of the powder they sold the Indians, "no more than the Cutler did, to know (as the Tale goes) what the Cutpurse did with the knife he made him." Hubbard admits that the colonists' military strategy was sometimes poor, but he vehemently denies that they had been disunited or niggardly. And war had at least cleared the Narragansett country for English settlement. To be sure, it had also demonstrated how little progress had been made in Christianizing the heathen; but can one really expect to convert people who are utterly untouched by culture and civility? "It is not a *small thing*," Hubbard concludes, "that . . . the light of the Gospel should . . . cause any number of those *Vassals of Satan* . . . professedly to *owne* the Name of *the Lord Jesus Christ*."[36] Standing somewhat outside the orthodox New England providential school of history, Hubbard was nevertheless a stouter champion of his society than either Morton or Mather.

Evidently emboldened by his first essay into history, Hubbard began a much more ambitious project—*A General History of New England* from the beginnings to 1680. The bulky manuscript, which was unpublished for over a century after his death, illustrates how much more

34. William Hubbard, *A Narrative of the Troubles with the Indians in New-England* (Boston, 1677), Bk. II, 73-74.

35. *Ibid.*, Bk. I, 41-42.

36. *Ibid.*, Bk. II, 76-86.

difficult it is to recapture the past than to describe immediate experience. Hubbard's technique, like Morton's, was to borrow wholesale from the first generation chronicles. He began well, supported by the Pilgrim narratives, and then filled out nearly two-thirds of his space with a transcription of Winthrop's *Journal*. But the concluding chapters are extremely weak and disorganized. Lacking a structural framework, Hubbard imposed a pattern on history by dividing his story into five-year periods. Winthrop and Bradford had no organizational pattern either, but they both argued with vigor. Hubbard had lost his earlier assurance; writing in the 1680's when the Bay government faced the imminent loss of her chartered privileges, he was now much less certain about the meaning of the New England story. His borrowed chronicle has the ungainly quality of secondhand clothes.

Unlike Morton and Mather, Hubbard did not even attempt to recapture a sense of past greatness. In his *General History*, as in his Indian war narrative, he came much closer than any of the other seventeenth-century Puritan chroniclers to the attitude of dispassionate balance, which is often supposed to be the hallmark of the great historian. Unfortunately he was also dull. He felt it necessary to chide the Pilgrims for their extreme Separatism, to apologize for the Massachusetts Puritans' cleavage with the Church of England, to condemn the narrowness of the New Haven government, to equivocate about Massachusetts' persecution of the Quakers and about her behavior toward the government of Charles II.[37] He could no longer share Winthrop's and Johnson's conviction that New England was manifestly superior to the rest of the world. "The Church of God," he wrote, "is not now confined to a family or nation. . . . God hath so ordered . . . [the New Englanders] that they have found as comfortable a way of subsistence, by their diligence and industry, as their friends have done in other places."[38] If New England were a good land, there were also other good lands. Indeed, Hubbard's gift of critical detachment had by the 1680's degenerated into an intellectual paralysis. He knew that something had gone wrong in New England, but he was unable or unwilling to tell what it was. He side-stepped the issue by omitting most recent events, and his narrative trailed off unfinished.

Yet despite everything, Hubbard's *General History* expressed more fully than any previous colonial narrative the establishment of a native American historical tradition. Hubbard arrived in America when he was about fourteen years old, and he was a member of the first graduating class

37. William Hubbard, *A General History of New England from the Discovery to 1680* (Mass. Hist. Soc., *Collections*, 2nd ser., 5-6 [1848]), 42, 181, 333, 573, 575.
38. *Ibid.*, 385.

of Harvard College. Whereas Bradford and Winthrop came to America as adults, Hubbard was almost completely shaped by the colonial environment. His narrative does not begin with the English reformation, nor with the Puritan fleet setting sail for Massachusetts Bay in 1630, but with the land of New England itself: his opening six chapters deal with the discovery, topography, and aboriginal inhabitants of New England. Hubbard was also alone among seventeenth-century New England historians in attempting a general history of the region, embracing Connecticut, Maine, and even Rhode Island—though he was hardly appreciative of Roger Williams. Thus Hubbard, like Morton and Mather, had a more self-contained, isolated view of America than the first generation colonial narrators and, as we shall shortly see, a radically different view from contemporaneous observers in England.

By the Restoration era, Englishmen at home were being forced to alter their conception of the New World. No longer could the American coast be considered an exotic, half-mythical setting for the adventures of Elizabethan gallants. The plantations were becoming a significant national investment, and there were fewer disparaging remarks from such writers as Castell, Heylyn, and Gardyner. The English public was becoming more curious about the colonies. A new kind of book on America was needed, for the old travelogue compilation of Hakluyt and Purchas was outmoded. An answer was found in the topographical survey.

John Ogilby's *America*, a large and lavish volume published in 1671, demonstrates the trend. Ogilby's book is a guided tour through the New World, far more elaborate in scale than the efforts of Castell and Gardyner. He stole most of his material from continental writers, and consequently much of his volume is devoted to the Spanish empire. However, like earlier English writers, he treats America as a geographical unit and blurs the political distinction between rival European holdings. Completely contrary to the New England narrators, Ogilby was fascinated chiefly by America's great potentiality as a physical region and by the behavior of her aboriginal inhabitants. Although he emphasized topography, Ogilby introduced his tour through each colony with the history of its settlement. Here he emphasized the English background, colonizing companies, and royal charters; he ignored internal colonial issues. Ogilby's interpretation of colonial development was congenial to the government of Charles II. He clearly preferred the royal and proprietary colonies to the disaffected and insubordinate New Englanders. Thus, religious liberty was identified with Maryland, and the New England Pilgrims and Puritans were tiresome malcontents, who were indulged in their wish for an American asylum since they "could more conveniently be spar'd than the better affected part of the People."[39]   Ogilby's views, in short, illustrate the beginnings of an English feeling of imperial domain over America.

The topographical trend was carried further by two rival publicists, Richard Blome and Nathaniel Crouch, who each produced a handy guide-book to English America in the 1670's and 1680's.   In 1672, Blome issued a small volume entitled *A Description of the Island of Jamaica; With the other Isles and Territories in America, to which the English are Related*. His design was to advertise in concise and simple terms the physical advantages of England's various American possessions.   He devoted two-thirds of his space to Jamaica, which, he claimed, "is found to precede all the *English Plantations* in *America*, in the very *Commodities* that are proper to their several *Colonies*."[40]   Blome made only passing reference to historical development, but he clearly shared Ogilby's preference for those colonies which conformed to the mother country's mercantilist policies and administrative system.   He warmly praised the paternal governments established by the Carolina proprietors and Lord Baltimore.   And having equated luxuriant and well-governed Virginia with England, Blome compared New England to Scotland, emphasizing the cold climate and rigid Presbyterianism of both places.[41]

Nathaniel Crouch's writings on America are scarcely distinguishable from Blome's.   In 1685 Crouch published *The English Empire in America: Or a Prospect of His Majesties Dominions in the West-Indies*— a book chiefly significant for the firm imperial consciousness evidenced by its title.   Crouch wanted to describe "those Gallant Atchievements of our *English* Hero's in this *New World*, and to give my Countrymen a short view of those Territories now in possession of the *English* Monarchy in the *West Indies*. . . ."[42]   His book, like Blome's, was a series of brief sketches of the several English colonies, which touched on their discovery, topography, and principal products.   In several ways, however, Crouch was more old-fashioned than Blome.   He always sought the picturesque and the diverting; instead of quoting commercial statistics, he described Indian customs or exotic tropical fish and animals.   He reversed Blome's emphasis on the sugar islands, spending almost twice as many pages on the mainland colonies, largely because he had a larger stock of Indian anecdotes for the mainland.   Whenever his anecdotes were exhausted, he filled out

39. John Ogilby, *America: being the Latest, and Most Accurate Description of the New World* (London, 1671), 140, 185.

40. Richard Blome, *A Description of the Island of Jamaica; With the other Isles and Territories in America, to which the English are Related* (London, 1672), 56.

41. *Ibid.*, 138, 163, 174, 181.

42. Nathaniel Crouch, *The English Empire in America: Or a Prospect of His Majesties Dominions in the West-Indies* (London, 1685), ii.

the space with bald extracts from previously published travel books or promotional circulars. Crouch offered no opinions on the pattern of development in the American colonies.

Neither Ogilby, Blome, nor Crouch claimed to be writing histories; and certainly their presentation of chronology was cursory at best. Yet they were unmistakably moving toward a new style of historical writing in England: imperial history, in which the colonies would be seen as offshoots of the mother country. Ogilby, Blome, and Crouch focused more sharply on America than did Hakluyt. They more clearly established a tie between America and England, for English America was now taken for granted as a source of English raw materials, a field for English investment, and a market for English goods. If we compare Blome and Crouch with such prior critics of the English plantations as Castell, Heylyn, and Gardyner, it is obvious that Englishmen at home had recovered Hakluyt's buoyant confidence in the utility of English America. This extroverted, commanding viewpoint is far removed from the introspective, defensive attitude of the second generation New England chroniclers.

By the close of the seventeenth century, Englishmen on the two shores of the Atlantic had arrived at two distinct and reasonably mature historical conceptions of America. Let us compare three histories of the American plantations published shortly after 1700, two by colonials—Cotton Mather of Massachusetts and Robert Beverley of Virginia—and one by John Oldmixon in England. The measure of the development of historical consciousness toward English America during the seventeenth century is the difference between Hakluyt in 1600 and Mather, Beverley, and Oldmixon in 1700. The difference is considerable.

All the best and worst of Increase Mather's extraordinary son, Cotton, are to be found in his magnum opus, the *Magnalia Christi Americana*, published in 1702. It is perhaps easier to recognize the faults of this book than its virtues. A monstrous conglomeration of biographical sketches, didactic tracts, and sermons, the *Magnalia* appears to have no organization. Certainly it tells no connected narrative. The infinitely prolix style, the copious Biblical and classical allusions, the hectic italics, and the endless digressions—all swallow up Mather's story. And his factual content is generally thin and proverbially inaccurate. Yet the *Magnalia*'s segmented narrative and furious style are symptoms of Cotton Mather's overwhelming vigor, and as we make painful headway through the book, we sense that the reverend author did indeed have an over-all organization. Although Cotton Mather borrowed heavily from his predecessors, he was not a derivative writer in the fashion of Morton and Hubbard: he created an original work, which testified to the New Englanders' revived intellectual poise and sense of purpose after the Revolution of 1688-89. The bulk and energy of *Magnalia Christi Americana* demonstrate the fullness of the New England historical tradition which Mather was building upon.

In his introduction, Mather announced that he was writing about "the *Wonders* of the CHRISTIAN RELIGION, flying from the Depravations of *Europe,* to the *American Strand,*" but his chief interest centered on the rise and fall of New England Puritanism.[43] Like Edward Johnson, he divided his cast of characters into the perennial "generation of *Godly Men,* desirous to pursue the *Reformation of Religion*" and the perennial opposition trying to disturb the church. Like Nathaniel Morton, he looked back longingly to the godly founders of New England. Repeatedly he lamented the "visible *shrink* in all Orders of Men among us, from that *Greatness,* and that *Goodness*" which characterized the first generation. Even that fleshpot Virginia was outstripping New England, for "while those parts which were at first Peopled by the *Refuse* of the *English* Nation, do sensibly amend in the Regards of Sobriety and Education, those Parts which were *planted with a more noble Vine . . .* give *. . .* only the *degenerate Plants of a strange Vine.* What should be done for the stop, the turn of this *Degeneracy?*" Mather's solution to the problem was the same as Morton's: "I'll shew them, the *Graves* of their *dead Fathers.*"[44]

Mather began his tour of the graveyard by setting forth the various achievements of New England's past leaders and by presenting fifty biographical sketches of eminent clergymen. The middle sections of *Magnalia Christi Americana* described the finest fruits of this leadership: Harvard College and the system of church organization. Mather saw history as the visible record of God's favor and disfavor, and the final sections reveal God's increasing anger with New England, as demonstrated by the disruptive activities of Roger Williams, the Antinomians, the Quakers, and others, and especially by the growing menace of Indian massacres and wars. Thus the *Magnalia* may properly be called a gigantic pietistic tribute to the founding generation, but this phrase hardly suggests its distinction and sophistication as a piece of historical writing. For Mather had one great virtue over all earlier New England annalists: he had a sense of time. Far enough removed from the founders, he could portray New England in flux rather than as a static entity. However inaccurate his details and however specious his interpretations, Mather did succeed in

43. Cotton Mather, *Magnalia Christi Americana: or, the Ecclesiastical History of New-England from Its First Planting in the Year 1620. unto the Year of our Lord, 1698* (London, 1702), "A General Introduction," [i].

44. *Ibid.,* Bk. III, 11.

his essential task. He demonstrated that New England society had profoundly changed during the course of the seventeenth century.

In some respects Cotton Mather has less claim to the title of American
historian than William Hubbard. Mather had less interest in American
topography, and he did not attempt a comprehensive survey of New
England society; he was also much more thoroughly committed to a providential conception of historical causation. In other respects Mather was
more self-consciously a colonial than any of his predecessors, including
Hubbard. Despite his apparent despair at New England's degeneracy,
Mather's inspiration throughout the *Magnalia* was his lively sense of the
special qualities of his local society. Steadily directing his argument at back-
sliding neighbors, he never wavered from the exhortation to reform before it
was too late. But Cotton Mather's despondency was more synthetic than
the lamentations of his father or Nathaniel Morton thirty years before; his
exhortations were in part merely his technique as a preacher. It is revealing
that Mather incorporated into the *Magnalia* a dedicatory letter composed
in England by his uncle, Nathaniel Mather, and addressed to the royal
governor of Massachusetts, the Earl of Bellomont. Nathaniel Mather
boasted to Bellomont that New Englanders "are the best People under
Heaven; there being among them, not only less of open Profaneness, and
less of Lewdness, but also more of the serious Profession, Practice, and
Power of Christianity, in proportion to their number, than is among any
other People upon the Face of the whole Earth."[45] Here, surely, is good
evidence that by 1700 New England felt a sense of distinction from the
mother country. Cotton Mather in Massachusetts upbraids his neighbors
for deserting their local heritage, but Nathaniel Morton in England brags
to the outsider Bellomont that these are the best people on earth. Despite
superficial evidences to the contrary, the Mathers recaptured the buoyant
assurance of the first generation chroniclers, an attitude which was becoming a staple ingredient in the developing American temperament.

In turning from Cotton Mather's view of New England history to
Robert Beverley's view of Virginia history, we find an apparent amplifica-
tion of the earlier antithesis between Bradford and Smith. Beverley's *History and Present State of Virginia,* published in 1705 nearly a century
after the first settlement of the colony, is a completely secular analysis of
Virginia's past misuse of her resources and of her great potentiality for
the future. Rather than looking backward to the achievements of Virginia's
early planters, Beverly looked ahead. The chief lesson which he drew
from the past was that the Virginians had consistently been criminally lazy:
"Thus," he concluded, "they depend altogether upon the Liberality of

45. *Ibid.,* Bk. II, 35.

Nature, without endeavouring to improve its Gifts, by Art or Industry."[46]
Stylistically, also, the contrast between Mather and Beverley is severe.
The Virginian's prose is undecorated, succinct, and sometimes prosaic. "I
am an *Indian*," he announced in his preface, "and don't pretend to be
exact in my Language: But I hope the Plainness of my Dress, will give
the kinder Impressions of my Honesty, which is what I pretend to."[47] Thus
the heart of the difference between Beverley and Mather is that Beverley
identified himself with his native physical habitat; Mather identified himself with his native ideological tradition. The Puritan was not impressed
with the honesty of Indians.

The History and Present State of Virginia is a notable book. Beverley
was an analytical historian, and his view of causation was quite contrary to
the New England conception of God's controlling hand—indeed, he
shared the basic assumptions of the eighteenth-century Enlightenment.
He believed that man in a benevolent natural setting has the rational
capacity to achieve worldly progress. Beginning with the state of nature,
he devoted one of the four parts of his book to "the *Natural* Product and
Conveniencies of *Virginia;* in its Unimprov'd *State,* before the English
went thither"; another part was devoted to the idle and innocent Indians,
"happy, I think, in their simple State of Nature." The problem was that
Virginia is naturally too perfect: "Where God Almighty is so Merciful as
to work for People, they never work for themselves." To transform the
state of nature into a civilized society requires hard work, but the settlers
have succumbed to the Indians' laziness. "And indeed," Beverley argued,
"all that the *English* have done . . . has been only to make some of these
Native Pleasures more scarce, by an inordinate and unseasonable Use of
them; hardly making Improvements equivalent to that Damage."[48]

The intellectual framework of Beverley's history is more impressive
than his performance; his historical narrative is merely the prelude to a
survey of Virginia's natural resources and current social structure. His
narrative is too brief and uneven, lightly skipping over the poorly chronicled
middle fifty years of the seventeenth century. Since his theme was the
English failure to impose social progress upon the Virginian state of nature,
he had little room for heroism or epic adventures. Finding Captain John
Smith's criticism of the Jamestown settlers congenial, Beverley accepted
the interpretation of the founding of the colony in Smith's *General History.*
He credited the captain with being "the only Man among them that could

46. Robert Beverley, *The History and Present State of Virginia,* ed. by Louis B.
Wright (Chapel Hill, 1947), 319.
    47. *Ibid.,* 9.
    48. *Ibid.,* 115, 233, 297, 156.

manage the Discoveries with Success, and he was the only Man too that could keep the Settlement in Order."[49]

Worse than the colonists, according to Beverley, was the grasping Virginia Company. Although he accepted royal government in 1624 as a progressive step and sided with Governor Berkeley in Bacon's Rebellion, he criticized the English navigation laws and fixed most of Virginia's recent difficulties on a crew of wicked royal governors. The climax of his narrative is a ten-page harangue against the current governor, Nicholson, who was turning Virginia into "an *Ottoman* Province" and who allegedly pronounced that "he wou'd hang up those that should presume to oppose him, with *Magna Charta* about their Necks."[50] The closer the story gets to 1705, the more apparent it becomes that Beverley was converting his history into an indictment of Nicholson.

The contrast between Beverley and Mather seems to be complete. And yet are the two men entirely antithetical? Mather's chief distinction as a historian was his sense of process, and his strongest claim to the title of American historian lay in his suppressed belief that his fellow-colonists, for all their faults, were the best people on earth. Viewed from this standpoint, Robert Beverley's history complements Mather's. He too had a sense of process. Captain John Smith's view of Virginia had been no broader than the span of his personal adventures, but Beverley found a cause-and-effect pattern which he could superimpose upon the course of events during Virginia's first century. Furthermore, Beverley had a strong local patriotism; the self-professed Indian was also unlike Smith in identifying himself with his Virginia habitat and in distinguishing himself from Englishmen at home. He found that his fellow-colonists were an uncommonly generous and hospitable people, attempting to rid themselves of the "stiffness and formality" of English polite society. The whole purpose of Beverley's book was to stir them into throwing off their slothful indolence as well—to "rouse them out of their Lethargy, and excite them to make the most of all those happy Advantages which Nature has given them. . . ."[51] As with Mather, his critical approach to Virginia history stemmed from a conviction that his colony was really the best place on earth.

By the time Mather and Beverley published their histories, narrations of English overseas exploration had developed into two distinct genres in England: picturesque travelogue and imperial history. The travelogues need scarcely detain us. In 1700, multivolumed collections of voyages were still being published in London, but, unlike the earlier works of Hakluyt and Purchas, they rarely contained much material on British

America. The American plantations were now taken for granted by the home Englishman as a familiar, if somewhat distant, part of his landscape. Travel collections were designed to transport the reader to more improbable and exotic places. Thus, Awnsham and John Churchill's representative *Collection of Voyages and Travels* (1704) consists of trips to such distant lands as the Ukraine and the Congo, Chile, Formosa, and Ceylon. The lone traveller to English America included in this collection was Captain John Smith, and his adventures seem drab by comparison. It was characteristic of the Churchills' method that the piece by Smith which they chose to reprint was his *True Travels*, which is largely concerned with his youthful military service against the Turks in Hungary and his subsequent captivity in Tartary.[52] Here is a measure of the change which the century had accomplished. To Hakluyt's audience Virginia and Russia were equally remote and bizarre; to the Churchills' audience Virginia was commonplace and Russia more mysterious than ever.

In the genre of imperial history, John Oldmixon's *The British Empire in America,* first published in 1708, is an Englishman's grand tour of the colonial domain. In contrast to the Churchills, Oldmixon dealt exclusively with the British possessions in America, one volume for the continental colonies and a second for the West Indies. Adopting the topographical formula of Ogilby and Beverley, he gives a historical sketch of each colony, together with a description of its present state. More firmly than any earlier writer, he treats the colonies as a collective unit, with Whitehall the center of their unity. Although he was heavily indebted to both Mather and Beverley for factual details, Oldmixon's interpretation of colonial history was far removed from either the New Englander or the Virginian. More explicitly than Ogilby, Blome, or Crouch, he glorified the British empire. In his introduction he asked rhetorically: what value are the colonies to Britain? The answer was that they are an expression of Britain's economic and strategic power. Oldmixon rated the Sugar Islands especially high, but the mainland colonies were also "of great Use to *England,* for their Tobacco, Masts, Timber, breeding of Seamen, and Navigation." He argued, in sum, that "our Colonies in *America* are so far from being a Loss to us, that there are no Hands in the *British* Empire more usefully employ'd for the Profit and Glory of the Common-Wealth."[53]

52. Awnsham and John Churchill, eds., *A Collection of Voyages and Travels* (4 vols.; London, 1704), II, 371-412.

53. John Oldmixon, *The British Empire in America, Containing The History of the Discovery, Settlement, Progress and present State of all the British Colonies on the Continent and Islands of America* (2 vols.; London, 1708), I, xxxii, xxxvii.

Oldmixon was a young man when he wrote this book, and he had never visited America. But he was very cocksure. From his imperial vantage ground he chided the parochial colonials for their local chauvinism and their child-like neglect to record their own history. Beverley's work, however, he found judicious and eloquent, though marred by the Virginian's petty attack on Nicholson. But he was much less kind to Cotton Mather, claiming that he had sifted all the worthwhile matter out of the *Magnalia,* "leaving his *Puns, Anagrams, Acrosticks, Miracles, Prodigies, Witches, Speeches, Epistles,* and other Incumberances, to the Original Author, and his Admirers; among whom, as an Historian, this Writer is not so happy as to be rank'd."[54]

Oldmixon produced a more mediocre history of the British empire than his patronizing tone might lead one to expect. But he did a creditable job, considering that the task was too large for any man. His narrative was far fuller than Ogilby's, especially on the internal development of the several colonies, and incomparably fuller than Blome's or Crouch's. But he could not achieve a satisfactory over-all history of the empire, for he continued Ogilby's habit of treating the story of each colony independently. In addition, there are numerous factual errors and a disproportionate emphasis on recent events, although his lively, readable style largely compensates for these failings.

Oldmixon's politics and religion were Whig and Low Church. For instance, he generally followed Beverley's interpretation of Virginia history, criticizing the fumbling opening years of settlement, the high tobacco tax, and Bacon's Rebellion; but he had less sympathy than Beverley for the Tory Governor Berkeley. In the case of New England, he accepted Cotton Mather's picture of tyrannous bishops harrying the Puritans into leaving England in the 1630's and again in the 1660's. He accepted the parallel between the Boston revolt against Andros in 1689 and the Glorious Revolution at home. But he would not accept the essence of Mather's argument, the special sanctity of New England Puritan orthodoxy. Oldmixon found the colonial Puritans too formal, too morose, and, above all, too superstitious. In the 1690's, he observed tartly, the New Englanders were "got into such a Humour of Witch-hunting, that there was a Society of them at *Boston,* as there is of Reformation in *London;* and that Society engag'd themselves to find out and prosecute all Witches, as the Society in *London* seeks after and punishes all Whores."[55]

The most revealing defect in Oldmixon's history is that he said almost nothing about many of the colonies. His fullest discussions were of Barbados, Virginia, New England, Jamaica, and Carolina. For the other

54. *Ibid.,* viii-ix, 270.   55. *Ibid.,* 68.

plantations, particularly the middle colonies, he had few or no chronicles to draw upon. "We have met with very few Events relating to this Colony" he said of Pennsylvania, adding that "they have had no Wars either with the *Indians* or *French*, and consequently little Action has happen'd here."[56] Judged as a record of events in British America, Oldmixon's history cannot begin to compare with the best seventeenth-century colonial narratives. The importance of the book lies in its purpose and tone. As we move from Hakluyt's world-embracing collection of English voyages to Blome's topographical guidebook on English overseas plantations, and then to Oldmixon's display of the growth and potentiality of the British empire, it is obvious that we are witnessing a steadily increasing attitude of dominion over the colonies. Oldmixon's generation had a concrete sense of possessing America.

Even more revealing, perhaps, than the increasing English consciousness of dominion over America is the accompanying sense of condescension toward the American colonists. Back in the first generation of settlement, no clear distinction could be drawn between the character and habits of Englishmen at home and abroad, since all had been born and bred under the same environment. Not so with the third generation. We have noted that Mather and Beverley each emphasized the special character of his colonial society and concluded that it was the best on earth. Conversely, Oldmixon's argument presumed that homebred English society was superior to provincial American. Smugly satisfied with his own standards for polite society, he found (quite correctly) that the colonists had tended during their years of isolation to stray from the parental model and become eccentric, unpolished, and old-fashioned. Oldmixon's favorite target was New England society, the most pretentious example of provincial American culture. In an interesting passage he disparaged Harvard College, the very institution Cotton Mather was proudest of, on the grounds that "till they throw off that wretched Affectation which we commonly call *Cant.* . . , we cannot see what great use their Academy will ever be to them. . . ." He goes on to say that the greatest storehouse of cant was seventeenth-century New England's chief cultural monument—Mather's *Magnalia*—which "rather resembles School Boys Exercises Forty Years ago, and *Romish* Legends, than the Collections of an Historian bred up in a Protestant Academy."[57] To argue the justness of Oldmixon's charge

56. *Ibid.*, 164. Curiously, when Oldmixon revised his history for a second edition in 1741, the proportion of space devoted to each colony became more unbalanced than ever. The section on New England was doubled, thanks to his use of Daniel Neal's *History of New England* (1720), while his feeble accounts of the middle colonies were left unchanged.

57. Oldmixon, *British Empire in America*, I, 108-9.

is beside the point. Oldmixon, Mather, and Beverley corroborate each other, for each man was expressing the social distance between Englishmen at home and in America, which was the product of a century of colonization.

There is, of course, no novelty to the conclusion that a century of colonization produced a difference in outlook between Virginians and New Englanders, or between home Englishmen and colonials. We may, however, conclude something more than that. It seems evident from our inspection of seventeenth-century historical writing that the transatlantic difference in outlook was steadily widening, while the regional colonial difference was not. Beverley thought of himself as a Virginian first and an Englishman second. Cotton Mather thought of himself as a New Englander first and an Englishman second. It would be anachronistic to suppose that they thought of themselves as Americans, for there was as yet no community of interests to make colonials conscious of their collective American identity. The establishment of a local tradition, however, was certainly a first step toward the eventual formulation of a national tradition. That Beverley and Mather expressed divergent local interests and achieved strikingly different historical styles is hardly open to question. Surely it is more significant that both Virginian and New Englander worked within a firmly established native American historical framework, in contrast to Oldmixon's imperial view.

INDEX